Donna Bain Butler
Developing International EFL/ESL Scholarly Writers

Studies in Second and Foreign Language Eduction

Editors
Anna Uhl Chamot, Wai Meng Chan

Volume 7

Donna Bain Butler

Developing International EFL/ESL Scholarly Writers

—

ISBN 978-1-61451-378-0
e-ISBN (PDF) 978-1-61451-269-1
e-ISBN (EPUB) 978-1-978-1-5015-0085-5

Library of Congress Cataloging-in-Publication Data
A CIP catalog record for this book has been applied for at the Library of Congress.

Bibliographic information published by the Deutsche Nationalbibliothek
The Deutsche Nationalbibliothek lists this publication in the Deutsche Nationalbibliografie;
detailed bibliographic data are available on the Internet at http://dnb.dnb.de.

© 2015 Walter de Gruyter GmbH, Berlin/Boston/Munich
Typesetting: PTP-Berlin, Protago T$_E$X-Production GmbH, www.ptp-berlin.de
Printing and binding: CPI books GmbH, Leck
♾ Printed on acid-free paper
Printed in Germany

www.degruyter.com

MIX
Papier aus verantwor-
tungsvollen Quellen
FSC® C003147

For international graduate students and scholars

Foreword

This book contributes to some significant shifts in the way we theorize and teach academic writing for multilingual students. Donna Bain Butler has combined her research expertise and teaching experience effectively to show how both can fruitfully inform each other to develop more empowering pedagogies for multilingual students.

Butler's focus on strategies helps resolve some unhealthy divisions in teaching academic writing. A focus on the forms and conventions of academic discourses and writing is still a pragmatic way to handle the needs of multilingual students for many teachers and scholars. Among its many limitations is the fact that it leads to a normative orientation, ignoring the discourses and values students bring from their own communities. Alternatively, a focus on cognitive process has been important for others, who are on the quest for universal strategies skilled writers adopt for effective composing. However, this approach ignores differences in content and writing objectives that can motivate authors to adopt diverse writing strategies. In treating strategies as the key focus, Butler is part of a growing movement of scholars who are committed to learning the practices writers themselves adopt in order to negotiate their communicative objectives, ideologies, and knowledge claims in shaping their texts. While process and form are important, they are both accommodated under the strategies adopted to meet the objectives and backgrounds of the authors. This approach values the goals and interests of the authors, guarding against the pedagogical objectives and agendas of teachers gaining more importance. It also affirms the agency of authors, respecting their capacity to draw from their own knowledge, codes, and conventions to shape their texts.

However, there is more work to be done in discovering these strategies and classifying them. The challenge is that strategies can be very individual and idiosyncratic, relating to the learning styles, values, and contexts of each author. To continue this exploration, it is important for teachers to combine research with instruction. As we introduce the dominant writing conventions and norms to students, we have to also learn how they appropriate them for their own purposes. Butler offers the resources and tools to conduct this teaching/research activity productively. She demonstrates how teachers can learn from their students as they continue to teach them.

Butler's approach enhances the reflectivity of not only teachers, but of students. In examining their writing objectives, processes, and strategies, students are increasing their reflective awareness. Such reflective awareness helps multilingual students in developing their agency and autonomy. It is through such awareness that students will develop their capacity to identify the strategies that are most appropriate for their writing goals and interests. Through a pedagogy designed to develop the awareness of students about their preferred strategies, Butler is gradually moving students to the center stage of writing and positioning teachers as facilitators of such strategy development and awareness raising.

Though Butler's work falls within the respectable field of learner strategy development, it will inform the work of other scholars who are undertaking similar explorations from the point of view of discourse strategies and interactional strategies in fields such as sociolinguistics and conversational analysis. These efforts will help us understand more about the strategic competence that we all need in the context of globalization and diversity when we cannot predict which norms and conventions will be relevant in a given communicative situation. Strategic competence is rightly gaining more importance in multilingual and multicultural communication. Butler's work helps us understand the nature of this competence better.

Suresh Canagarajah
Edwin Erle Sparks Professor
Director, Migration Studies Project
Departments of Applied Linguistics & English
Pennsylvania State University, U.S.A.

Preface

International graduate students face an academic writers' dilemma when they choose to study in English-medium universities and professional schools. They are assumed to be able to use English to report and discuss disciplinary research. However, international students bring different cultural norms and literacy practices when writing academic English papers. There is a gap between what is expected and what is possible without explicit attention to developing EFL/ESL academic writer needs. This gap does not pertain just to grammar or documentation. It opens the door for new knowledge, advanced academic literacy, and an advocacy/participatory approach to scholarly writing instruction at the tertiary level. This gap is particularly relevant in U.S. law school context where EFL/ESL graduate students may implicitly learn how to avoid dealing with issues of power and difference in academic English writing. In this context, charges of plagiarism may be a threat or regular occurrence and empirical research beyond the scope of professional or pedagogical practice. Hence the importance of reading this book and advocating for academic writing instruction for international graduate students based on empirical research and the strategically self-regulated writing program provided here.

This book contributes to the literature on developing international students' written language and strategy use in second language (L2) English for Specific and Academic Purposes with the aim of helping learners study, conduct research, and work in L2 English. It is an empirically validated source book for organizing strategy-based writing instruction at the professional level. It makes transparent what international graduate students need to know and do when writing disciplinary research papers beyond documenting a variety of sources. It helps L2 academic writers at all levels address challenges such as articulating a research problem, supporting a thesis, avoiding plagiarism, and integrating quotations and other source material. It explores the kind of improvement EFL/ESL scholarly writers may need to make for clearer expression of meaning, original thinking and inner voice.

The mixed methods (quantitative and qualitative) research in this book discloses how EFL/ESL graduate student writers may improve language use, composition, and writing knowledge by connecting learning with teaching and assessment (pedagogy): quantitatively in terms of more facts, and qualitatively from the dimension of depth and sophistication. Competence-based strategies instruction promotes new knowledge, skills and behaviors. Students become better equipped to perform in their discipline and transform to a higher level of development through their research and writing. The underlying idea is that knowledge of scholarship skills and strategies combine as input to advance academic literacy, critical thinking, and clear communication as output, defining proficiency in any language and competency in any discipline or occupation.

The learner development perspective in this book is an alternative to developmental editing of doctoral dissertations, masters theses, and professional papers as well as to superficial grammar correction by native-speaker editors. It is concerned with language use and learning. Just as this research is embedded in different levels of validity from a mixed methods research perspective, there are different levels of skills and strategies embedded in scholarly writing processes that can be used effectively and efficiently for systematic writing instruction and competent production. Explicit attention to EFL/ESL research writers' needs at various stages of academic writing helps students develop intellectually and pragmatically. It is necessary because L2 academic writer development lags behind language learning.

This research was intended to inform my teaching practice by giving multilingual writers in law school the skills and knowledge they need (cognitively and socioculturally) to publish and enhance the quality of their work with tools for learning and assessment. The research has implications for international EFL/ESL students in undergraduate programs and EFL/ESL graduate students in other disciplines. It facilitates a competence-based, learner-centered classroom so that multilingual writers can create and refine their academic English writing meaningfully and authentically with informed feedback, without simplifying ideas or communication.

My research may improve your teaching practice too by deepening knowledge and understanding of international graduate student writers and the dynamic interplay between advanced literacy strategies and language skills. It may strengthen your existing competence for teaching native and non-native academic English writers at the graduate level. It can do for you what it does for international graduate students – add to your existing repertoire of strategies and skills for learning and communicating. It is a "must read" for native-speakers working in international education in English-medium institutions that rank internationalization as a high priority, including professional schools hosting visiting scholars and government agencies managing international exchange programs.

Some readers may find some parts of this book more beneficial than others. Expert researchers, for example, may find the methodology chapter long whereas novice researchers may appreciate the detail to understand and replicate the research. Practitioners, on the other hand, may prefer to skip over the technical parts altogether and concentrate on the pedagogical applications of the research findings. Similarly, disciplinary faculty and staff can learn from the beginning and ending chapters, trusting that the book reflects sound research design, documentation, and validation. Lastly, L2 graduate students and professional writers may want to examine the tools for strategically self-regulating their own processes for scholarly writing explained herein and included in the Appendix. For all, an Index with key definitions is provided after the References section.

Acknowledgments

I am grateful to those who have been formative in helping me develop this project. I thank Anna Chamot, co-editor of this book series, whose feedback helped me know how to begin. In terms of learning and development, I am indebted to Patricia Alexander at the University of Maryland College Park. As a mentor, scholar, and fully engaged teacher, Pat has helped deepen my experience of learner-centered research over time and how to present it. With respect to the Forward, I am grateful to Suresh Canagarajah for expert review and straightforward comment. His observation of "truthiness" in U.S. society extends to teaching lawyers in U.S. law schools unaware of evidence-based instruction and learner-centered methodologies inclusive of cultural and linguistic diversity.

I give thanks also to my PhD mentor and friend, Betty Lou Leaver, Provost at the U.S. Defense Language Institute. Her work developing professional-level language proficiency has influenced me greatly. Betty connected me with Gerd Brendel, Chief of the Institute's Test Review and Education Division at the Foreign Language Center, for manuscript review from a high stakes learning and assessment perspective. The close reading, in-depth understanding, and feedback encouraged me to revise my academic writing for clarity. From a U.S. legal writing perspective, I am grateful to Jennifer M. Davis, Director of Graduate Programs Skills at the University of New Hampshire School of Law. Jennifer's peer review for professional development purposes showed collaboration across disciplines to benefit all students crossing cultural, linguistic, and disciplinary borders.

Last but not least, I give heartfelt thanks to Jeb Butler, my husband, and close friends for their continuous support and feedback: Manju Sah since our time together as young graduate students, Anna Syrquin since our preparation in a U.S. professional school program, Yalun (Helen) Zhou and Michael Wei since our shared experience as international students in a first class U.S. research institution, and Rebecca Oxford for being our PhD advisor.

Contents

Part I   Combining Research with Instruction

Part II Learner-User Research

Part III   Learner-User Perspectives

Appendix

Part I: **Combining Research with Instruction**

1 Making a Difference in the Academic Writing of International Graduate Students

1.1 Why this topic matters

It is quietly understood that international graduate students with contrasting academic and cultural backgrounds may not engage authentically, legitimately, or appropriately in academic English writing. They may not have (a) prior knowledge or experience with second language disciplinary discourse, (b) textual routines associated with genres and the writing processes, or (c) advanced literacy strategies and language skills. Faulty problem-solving may occur with contrasting ideas about academic English writing and writer versus reader responsibility, for example, or the role language plays in the academic writing process and domain learning situation. "No descriptive research has studied the whole range of students' techniques for writing from sources" (Howard, Serviss & Rodrigue, 2010, p. 178); however, this research offers perspectives on written language use by EFL/ESL graduate student writers learning to use strategies and skills for accomplishing important goals in scholarly (academic) writing. The research has implications for shifting pedagogical priorities and revising assessment objectives (Canagarajah, 2005a) for international student writers producing academic research papers in a context-reduced, native-speaker, professional setting.

The book focuses on developing EFL/ESL scholarly writers and what international graduate students may do to develop their academic writing. Learning is emphasized, with teachers and professors facilitating the learning process. The research informs second language writing and teaching practice, relevant for anybody working with international students at an advanced level. It provides in-depth knowledge of what informed, graduate-level language users do for success in writing research papers for law school – useful for disciplinary writing practitioners, scholars, and curriculum developers in foreign and second language education interested in the role and development of student writer competences and other forms of educational knowledge. The book targets international EFL/ESL graduate student writers and scholars, ESP/EAP practitioners, and legal writing specialists who may "feel at a loss of where to start in helping students with the language difficulties they encounter" when writing from disciplinary sources (Davis, J., personal communication, November 3, 2013). As Cook (2012) argues, "language teaching should be based on the successful second language (L2) user, not on the idealised native speaker" (p. 1).

The EFL/ESL graduate writer research in this book narrows the gap in foreign and second language education because it uses research to inform pedagogy for non-native English students (NNES) crossing academic cultures of learning. It has significance for graduate school areas in which NNES students learn to write professional-level research papers and journal articles, with implications for all students developing skills and integrating knowledge in academic domains requiring high levels of literacy and "academic communicative competence" (Swales, 1990, p. 9). Understanding how non-native English graduate students are grounded in language and literacy contributes to an empowering curriculum and writing pedagogy that is "process-oriented, autonomous, and experiential" (Canagarajah, 2006, p. 15).

The term "literacy" is often used by researchers in place of "writing" (Schultz, 2006). Researchers in both English composition and second language studies "have come to recognize the complexity and multidisciplinary nature of second-language writing research and teaching" (Matsuda, 2006, p. 23). Professional school programs in the U.S., however, may still assume a "difference- as-deficit" (Canagarajah, 2002) position for non-native English writers in relation to native English writers. Writing, as learner output, plays a part in second language acquisition (Ellis, 2005) by incorporating more and better attributes of language performance (Byrnes, 2002). Learner output in writing obliges learner attention not only to grammar, but also to development of discourse skills and professional voice (Skehan, 1998; Swain, 1995).

An important goal of this book is to align professional development with knowledge of written language use and advanced literacy (Braine, 2002) for international students writing research papers for subject-matter courses and independent study. Advancing literacy in U.S. graduate education means transforming text to construct new knowledge through selecting, connecting and organizing key information from source text with appropriate attribution, as well as plain language techniques for clear and accurate communication.

Academic writing in U.S. higher education is a problem-solving activity used by professors to develop content knowledge, with knowledge seen as a by-product in students' term papers, research projects, theses, and dissertations (Krashen, 2011). Over time, graduate students may implicitly learn to produce knowledge through their research, and undergraduate students may explicitly learn how to analyze knowledge and take a position in relation to their research through U.S. college writing programs. This kind of academic writing is a tool for learning and assessment in U.S. law schools, for example, but not generally part of the educational curriculum in other countries such as China and Russia. At the very least, writing research papers in international legal education context means that students must be able to (a) analyze, synthesize and evaluate legal research in English, and (b) describe, compare/contrast, and/or critically examine legal content. From a pedagogical perspective, analytical reasoning and critical thinking in L2 legal English require students to integrate knowledge of law and language use when writing from primary and secondary source texts.

Systematically developing EFL/ESL academic writers in law school is necessary because U.S. legal English differs from ordinary English "not just in vocabulary, but also in morphology (structures of words), syntax (structure of sentences and parts of sentences), semantics (meaning of words, phrases, and sentences), and other linguistic features" (Wydick, 2005b, p. 10). As students acquire domain knowledge through legal research in English, they develop language awareness in relation to their legal research topics, with possibilities for analytical reasoning and presentation in academic writing. Like native English legal writers, L2 legal writers need to express clear meaning, critical thinking, and effective communication in a paper that does not reproduce the poor legal style they read that may be cluttered, wordy, indirect, and full of unnecessary technical words or phrases. This obscure writing style, known as "legalese," is not to be emulated. Re-producing text or templates for legal writing is neither transformative nor growth-oriented for non-native English writers aiming to demonstrate a high degree of skill required for their graduate degree or career. Communication in writing is especially needed by international graduate students and legal scholars preparing to work internationally with English as their professional *lingua franca* (common language). However, U.S. law school policies and practices may maintain English dominance by ignoring EFL and ESL student writer needs.

The problem setting the stage for this research relates directly to pedagogy: the relation between teaching and learning. The researcher wanted to know how L2 legal research writers develop knowledge of written language use through explicit strategies instruction to show competence or expertise in scholarly (academic) writing. As Hinkel (2006) observed, "achieving proficiency in writing requires explicit pedagogy in grammar and lexis and is important because one's linguistic repertoire and writing skills often determine one's social, economic, and political choices" (p. 124). Hence the importance of this research for international graduate students.

Knowledge, understanding, and skills integration in L2 academic writing translates into social, cultural, and economic "capital" (Bourdieu, 2001) for foreign-trained graduate student writers in many English-medium universities and professional schools, opening the possibility to publish articles in English and present at international (academic and business) conferences. Explicit strategies instruction (Oxford, 2011) puts emphasis on learning contrastive approaches to academic and disciplinary writing, filling gaps in knowledge and experience, building on EFL/ESL students' backgrounds, developing academic language and disciplinary discourse, and providing both social and cognitive tools necessary for "bilingual literacy" (Pray & Jiménez, 2009a, 2009b). With respect to advancing literacy, academic and disciplinary writing are intertwined from a learner/user perspective. Both may be seen as transactional tools for communicating. Strategies support students' ability to be aware of their first academic/legal language to develop understandings of their second academic/legal language (Pray & Jiménez, 2009b).

Explicit pedagogical approaches are also part of the solution to complex problems associated with linguistic plagiarism in academic legal writing. Pecorari (2008) defines plagiarism as "fundamentally a specific kind of language in use, a linguistic phenomenon" (p. 1). Her literacy research on international graduate student writers found that language skills "are deeply implicated in plagiarism" (Pecorari, 2008, p. 7). Through linguistic analysis comparing international graduate student writing with written sources, Pecorari (2008) shows how some plagiarism can be regarded as a "failure of pedagogy" rather than a deliberate attempt to transgress. Like mine, her research points to a gap among (a) institutions' expectations of foreign-trained graduate students, (b) their performance, and (c) institutional awareness, asserting that pedagogical solutions need to be implemented at all levels. Reducing threats and charges of plagiarism for international graduate student writers in U.S. law schools may be one possible outcome of learning from this applied linguistics research.

1.2 Learner-centered research and pedagogy

This research is learner-centered, meaning that the author explores her EFL/ESL graduate students' changing needs, processes, and practices as academic writers rather than their writing products. The focus is on the learner as language user. The research contributes to professional development and professionalization in international education with development of materials that meet international EFL/ESL graduate students' developing needs as academic English writers. As an ESP/EAP course designer and teacher, the researcher explores her international students' levels of composing from legal source text and the research-based strategies they find most useful for writing a scholarly paper. Strategies are known to be under learners' conscious control, and students use them to compensate for gaps in writing knowledge, language, and composition skills. Strategies guide students' written language use and learning, while research and writing expand and deepen student learning in a content area like law.

Research on L2 writers' strategic behavior suggests three dynamic interplays: (a) L2 writers implement a wide range of general and specific strategic actions when they learn to write and express themselves in L2 writing; (b) the L2 writer's strategic behavior is dependent on both learner-internal and learner-external variables given the socio-cognitive dimensions of composing; and (c) the writer's strategic behavior is mediated by the instruction received and can be modified through strategy instruction (Manchón, Roca de Larios, & Murphy, 2007). Explicit strategies instruction was the case for the EFL/ESL graduate student writers participating in this research. Strategic knowledge is reflective knowledge, considered important for all learners at high levels (Anderson, Lorin & Krathwohl, 2001). It is especially important for language users connecting factual knowledge of L2 writing with procedural knowledge of discipline-specific skills and techniques.

Besides being descriptive and learner-user centered, this research is classroom-based with the intention of improving international graduate student writing quickly, within one academic semester. The research took place within the context of an academic legal writing intervention. "All knowledge, especially but not exclusively linguistic knowledge, is the result of learners' interaction with their social context, and acquisition is both social and cognitive" (Sanz, 2005, p. 4).

Findings revealed that student writer participants underwent a strategic shift from learning to communicating as they wrote their research papers during one academic semester (14 weeks). Research instruments disclosed how language was both a cognitive tool for learning law and a sociocultural tool for communicating ideas about law for the two groups of culturally and linguistically diverse student writer participants. One research group of student writers was acculturated, having undergone EAP classroom instruction the previous semester. These students had crossed over from being EFL language learners to ESL language users. The other research group of students was unacculturated and had not experienced this change. They were undergoing EAP instruction while writing research papers for various law school courses during the time of data collection. What is interesting is that all student participants came to see the data collection instruments as interactive tools for learning that helped them engage consciously in their research and writing processes. Strategies and goals for knowledge construction and transformation contributed to original writing and critical thinking in L2 English. The interactive tools also stimulated awareness of writing strategies that student participants were using efficiently and effectively. They acted as a tool kit that can be adapted by teachers and modified for international EFL/ESL academic writers in other disciplines – in traditional (face to face) or online classroom teaching. The tool kit provided students with "tangible strategies that address the complexities and anxieties they experience" as high-level multilingual writers and critical thinkers rather than a set of rules that ignores their background knowledge and life experiences (Kamler & Thomson, 2008, p. 512).

It is important to point out that this research adopts a *sociocognitive literacy development* perspective that views (a) international EFL/ESL student literacy as culturally based, involving higher intellectual skills, and (b) ESL academic writing as situated language use within the context of intercultural literacy. It follows a tradition of L2 (EFL and ESL) writing strategy research that sees strategies "from the perspective of the actions carried out by L2 writers to respond to the demands encountered in the discourse community where they write and learn to write" (Manchón et al., 2007, pp. 231–232). It provides "empirical evidence of the interplay between the social and cognitive dimensions involved in the development of the L2 writer's strategic competence" (Manchón et al., 2007, p. 234). It is useful to teachers because it links teaching to student learning and self-efficacy or control in L2 academic writing and how it can be developed (Bandura, 1997). It is useful to EFL/ESL academic writers because it helps them develop and believe in their own competencies. Exploring student writers' strategic competence, a component of communicative competence (Canale & Swain, 1980) in the Hymesian tradition of contextualized communicative competence, was a research goal. Findings support strategic competence as a key factor for EFL/ESL academic writer development – especially for students having difficulty (a) critically engaging in L2 English writing from multilingual sources (discourse synthesis), and/or (b) expressing thoughts clearly in L2 English writing, even with good analytical skills.

Meaningful communication and development of learners' communicative competence, central to integrated and multiskill instructional models (Hinkel, 2006), are central to EFL/ESL scholarly writer development. Canale's (1983) proposition that strategic competence is knowledge of skills and strategies that either enhance or repair communication applies to international EFL/ESL scholarly writers. Celce-Murcia and Olshtain (2005) suggest that "strategic competence (Canale & Swain, 1980; Celce-Murcia, Dörnyei, & Thurrell, 1995) refers to how well language users can deploy the knowledge and resources at their disposal in order to communicate their intended meanings" (p. 731). Leaver and Shekhtman (2002) suggest a need for engaging communicative competence components along the L2 learning-producing continuum, especially strategic competence for students at the novice to advanced high levels who may "need to change from mostly compensatory to mostly metacognitive" as they strive for "near-native" proficiency in writing (p. 10). Metacognitive knowledge comprises knowledge about the writing task, strategic knowledge, and self-knowledge (Anderson, Lorin & Krathwohl, 2001). They all contribute to developing proficiency or competence in L2 writing. Alexander (2006) supports learners' need for strategic engagement along the novice-expert continuum for effective learning and continued academic growth.

Her (1997, 2003) Model of Domain Learning links knowledge, motivation, and strategies across three stages of increasing expertise inherent in the writing process. The important point here is that EFL/ESL scholarly writers develop along more than one learning continuum, and learners develop a number of competences. This research therefore utilizes a framework of learning strategies for developing strategic competence, a term used in the L2 writing literature as "the ability to use a variety of communicative strategies" (Hyland, 2003, p. 32) which may include linguistic, sociolinguistic, and discourse strategies – all relevant and interesting for developing international EFL/ESL scholarly writers.

The academic legal writing intervention was classroom context for this research. It was formative for learners because the instruments used to collect data helped the EFL/ESL student participants regulate or control their scholarly writing output. These instruments were research-based so patterns might be identified and performance enhanced. They took the form of self-assessments that develop learner-user agency. They consisted of (a) strategies questionnaires for guiding learners' processes of writing a research paper to produce clear, readable text, and (b) checklists of goals for improving product quality at different stages of recursive research and writing: that is, pre-writing, drafting, and revising. From a pedagogical perspective, these were practical tools that acted as learning rubrics for self-regulating and self-assessing academic writing at different stages of development. Being formative, they contribute to what Pennington (2010) calls a "proactive writing pedagogy" for developing EFL/ESL writers that is "*progressive* and *scaffolded* in the sense of writing from sources being developed in stages with teacher and other assistance at each stage" (p. 152). These research-based, formative tools disclosed the dynamic, changing nature of learner-internal and learner-external variables that influence strategic competence for developing EFL/ESL scholarly writers aiming for professional (or higher) writing proficiency.

1.3 How this book is organized

The book consists of four parts. The first part reports what the research literature tells us. The second part reports the quantitative data analysis. The third part reports the qualitative data analysis. The fourth part explains how we can learn from the research to benefit all student writers. These four parts consist of ten chapters with empirically validated pedagogical tools that can be adapted for self-regulated writing and teaching in the appendices, a list of references, key definitions, and a subject index.

After the Introduction in Chapter 1, Chapter 2 begins with a review of research trends and topics describing international student writer challenges in a university program. It summarizes what we know about EFL/ESL academic writer challenges and differences. It also describes the U.S. professional school setting of the international graduate student writers participating in this research. Chapter 3 provides background research for the multistage self-report instrument used to describe what developing international EFL/ESL scholarly writers say they know and can do. Chapter 4 addresses the representativeness and variability of the research population. It provides methodological details for mixed methods (quantitative and qualitative) research within the classroom context of an academic writing intervention for EFL/ESL scholarly writers preparing papers for a graduate law degree. Chapter 5 describes all the evidence-based tools used to collect data from research participants that enhanced their performance. Chapter 6 presents results of the quantitative data analysis with quantitative findings identifying student participants' use of literacy strategies and language skills across three stages of writing: pre-writing, drafting, and revising. Chapter 7 presents results of the qualitative data analysis with student perspectives of their written language use across the three stages of writing. Chapter 8 discusses the major, synthesized, research findings showing interrelations for strategic competence that acted as catalyst for EFL/ESL scholarly writer development. The ninth chapter deals with pedagogical strategies connecting learning with teaching for writing teachers and content professors. It points to the interaction between prior knowledge and learning, the strategic learner and the student-centered classroom, and academic writer engagement, assessment, and pedagogy. The chapter ends with suggestions for how the research-based pedagogical tools can be used and what every educator can do. The book closes with a coda chapter that highlights important themes linking empirical research, learner-centered pedagogy, and transformation in higher education.

2 What We Know About Academic Writer Challenges and Differences

2.1 Empirical research and institutional knowledge

Knowing about EFL/ESL student writer challenges can inform existing pedagogy in U.S. and international higher education contexts. Extensive empirical research has shown clear differences between first (L1) language and L2 writing (Silva, 1993) defined by Silva as "purposeful and contextualized communicative interaction, which involves both the construction and transmission of knowledge" (1990, p. 18). "Cognitive, linguistic, social, cultural, educational, and affective factors...distinguish L2 writers, writing processes, and texts" (Ferris & Hedgcock, 2014, p. 24). However, even after 40+ years of empirical research, L2 academic writers in U.S. law school programs may be perceived as remedial or their specialized instruction given second class status even though more, not less, knowledge is required to teach them.

Hinkel (2006; 2011b) underscores the need for systematic, intensive, and extensive pedagogical approaches that take "into account the cultural, rhetorical, and linguistic differences between L1 and L2 writers" (p. 123). She makes the point that "even advanced and trained L2 writers continue to have a severely limited lexical and syntactic repertoire that enables them to produce only simple text restricted to the most common language features encountered predominantly in conversational discourse" (Hinkel, 2006, p. 123). Although written language proficiency is distinct from oral language proficiency, observed breakdowns may occur at any point at which the L2 writer (or speaker) is unable to accomplish a language task in a manner that satisfies the performance expectations of a university professor or disciplinary writing teacher. Merely socializing international student writers about native speaker cultural context for (academic or disciplinary) writing is not enough and can actually mislead learners if the core issue of writing proficiency is not understood by disciplinary writing teachers and professors assessing student learning with student writing. Merely socializing students about academic or disciplinary writing through lecture, for example, is not teaching if it does not contribute to student learning: that is, positive change in L2 writer behavior. The core issue of L2 writer development, therefore, is as relevant for foreign trained (EFL) students in U.S. professional school programs as it is for domestically trained (ESL) students not getting the metalinguistic support they need to develop as professionals in a society defined by cultural, linguistic, and racial diversity.

Overview and synthesis of L2 writing research in recent years shows that academic writing challenges constituted "by far the most important trend in L2 writing research" in 2012 (Silva, Lin & Thomas, 2012). They were also a significant trend in 2013 (Silva, Thomas, Park & Zhang, 2013) and in 2011 (Silva, Pelaez-Morales, McMartin-Miller & Lin, 2011). Challenges that ESL/EFL academic writers are known to face include the following: writing and publishing in English, reading to write and academic writing processes, plagiarism and textual borrowing, writing strategies, corrective feedback, the textual and linguistic demands of writing, reading and writing differences, curriculum, and support for students learning to write in their disciplines (Silva et al., 2013; 2012; 2011).

This research trend is not surprising given previous research targeting the L2 graduate experience in the last twenty-five years showing "the disparity between students' high level of disciplinarity and their lower degree of familiarity with language, writing, and sometimes cultural issues, and the difficulty of getting focused help with overcoming these obstacles (Leki, Cumming & Silva, 2008, p. 42). According to Hu (2009, p. 630), "as the number of international graduate students has risen rapidly and their academic problems have become more pronounced, researchers have noticed the need to study advanced levels of disciplinary literacy, particularly in graduate schools (Huxur, Mansfield, Nnazor, Schuetze & Segawa, 1996; Prior, 1991; Swales, 1990)." Concerns in U.S. higher education, however, remain focused on "beginning and intermediate levels of learning rather than advanced literacies" (Byrnes, 2005, p. 291). U.S. educators in professional school programs may depend on their own personal experience with foreign language learning rather than second language learning, not knowing the difference between the two or the impact on learners. Insufficient attention has been given to empirical research in U.S. law school context where practice makes practice and individual teacher beliefs may inform pedagogy more than evidence-based perspectives linking learning with teaching and assessment.

Low level institutional knowledge and lack of empirical research at the professional level explain in part why the responsibility for plagiarism in U.S. law schools can rest with foreign-trained student writers rather than with the universities and professional school programs hosting them and claiming knowledge of them on their university websites. International students may know what they want when they apply to a U.S. professional school program but not what they need. They may rely on (a) host institution staff whose expertise is moving students quickly through the system without challenging existing power structures, or (b) faculty who have no interest in knowing how L2 academic English writers may be similar or different from L1 English academic writers culturally, rhetorically, or linguistically for competence-based instruction and assessment.

Professional development and interdisciplinary collaboration are cost-effective means for upgrading institutional knowledge and international program content. Another avenue assumes an interdisciplinary approach where writing specialists work with graduate student writers as in a law school writing center, for example. An applied linguistics ESP/EAP approach works well in a professional school program that reflects principles and practices associated with developing (a) student growth and creativity (transformation), and (b) problem-solving skills (transaction) in writing, as in the EAP classroom context for this study. Such an approach contrasts with the outdated professional school transmission model that aims at "passing the canon" from one generation to the next through professor-oriented instruction, giving only the appearance of educating students who are culturally and linguistically diverse even at higher levels of proficiency.

2.2 Challenges of international graduate students in U.S. law schools

Master's and dual-degree programs for international students in English-medium universities and U.S. law schools are increasing rapidly. There is a need to prepare all graduate student writers for success. According to one report by the Institute of International Education (2013), Master's programs in English rose in continental Europe by 38 percent in 2013. Similarly, international student enrollment has been increasing steadily in the U.S. each year. However, the needs of international graduate students in U.S. law schools and Master of Laws (LL.M.) programs have often been overlooked (Wojcik & Edelman, 1997). "Law schools tend to thinly-staff the graduate programs in terms of both faculty and administrative support, so that most of the tuition dollars paid by international students in the LL.M. programs are supported by costs already incurred in connection with [native-speaker English] J.D. programs" (Silver, 2006, p. 155). Further, many, if not most, LL.M. programs "impose some sort of writing requirement on students" in the form of a thesis, an independent research project, or a paper in a seminar (Silver, 2006, p. 162) even when the length of the program is short (2–3 semesters). Evidence of scholarship may be required without attention to developing international EFL/ESL writer needs.

Expert legal writing specialists agree that there is a need for international law students to develop oral and written communication skills (Wojcik & Edelman, 1997); legal writing teachers "currently give students more feedback than other professors in the law school setting" (Sperling & Shapcott, 2012, p. 83). Like law professors though, they may not have a teaching/learning background other than their own shared experience as native English users. Legal writing curricula may not develop with law school graduates at the staff level. Learner-centeredness is not characteristic of U.S. legal education generally, and teaching lawyers may not know how to give meaningful feedback to EFL/ESL graduate writers without professional development informed by empirical research. Teacher corrections of EFL/ESL student writing may be limited to the concrete: for example, grammar in writing or pronunciation in speaking. Empirical research may be as invisible as accurate measures for student learning in U.S. law school context. The relation between learning and teaching remains unclear for many L2 legal writing practitioners. Similarly, law professors may focus more on the law than on the legal learner. Plagiarism may be a threat to all, however, with native-speaker emphasis placed on documenting a variety of legal sources rather than overcoming academic writer challenges like avoiding plagiarism, integrating sources into draft text, and clearer expression of original thinking.

In addition to skills related to written language use and culture in disciplinary legal context, there are other obstacles faced by international students in U.S. law school programs (Wojcik & Edelman, 1997). These include preparing for class, following class conversations, taking notes in class, unfamiliarity with common American legal documents, and lack of experience with the primary and secondary legal research sources available in English (Wojcik & Edelman, 1997). U.S. legal writing specialists involved in global legal education contend that such challenges are reasons to create support programs and specialized courses for international graduate student writers offering "1) consistent, systematic, individual attention and 2) instruction specifically tailored to the special purposes of legal writing" (Wojcik & Edelman, 1997, p. 130).

Multilingual legal education is an emerging field of interdisciplinary research and teaching practice. The study of law is no longer restricted to national boundaries. EFL/ESL legal professionals worldwide need to communicate in English. International graduate students in a law school program, therefore, need to learn to write effectively for professional practice. Knowledgeable, systematic writing instruction tailored to the needs of L2 academic writers – not just to their writing products – is part of ethical teaching practice at the professional level.

Second language acquisition researcher, Vivian Cook, identifies how L2 users differ from L1 users in important ways: (a) L2 users have different ways of thinking; (b) they use language in different ways; (c) they have an increased awareness of language itself; (d) they have a slightly different knowledge of their first language; and (e) they have greater effectiveness in their first language (Cook, 2011; 2012). With respect to learners' use of language, Cook says that "students studying through the medium of a second language may be able to do things they cannot do in the first language – write essays and reports for example" (Cook, 2012, p. 5).

Knowledgeable, systematic writing instruction, aimed at advancing the literacy of international graduate students culturally and linguistically, speeds up and enhances effectiveness in L2 academic writing. In addition, learning how to write as a scholar using L2 academic English advances writing proficiency because it is the writer who develops, not just the writing product. Based on Anderson (1996), L2 legal writers have a double need: (a) to understand language with its production rules as rhetorical knowledge, and (b) to understand language chunks in disciplinary context as substantive knowledge.

2.3 Concerns of EFL/ESL academic legal writers in this research

Self-assessments revealed two main areas of concern for the six (N = 6) graduate students writing academic papers for this research: language and composition (N = 6), and writing knowledge (N = 4). Issues pertaining to language and composition included grammar, punctuation, clear meaning, style, register, organization, stages of writing, social-cultural appropriateness, references and citations to scholarly works. Issues pertaining to writing knowledge included genre, academic culture, assessment criteria, U.S. law school conventions, writing from sources, language use and the basic linguistic system. When reconciled with the syntheses of L2 writing research trends (Silva et al., 2011–2012), student participant concerns fall into three overlapping categories: (1) plagiarism and textual borrowing, (2) the textual and linguistic demands of academic writing, and (3) support for graduate students learning to write in their discipline.

Participants were not only acculturating to U.S. academic culture but transitioning to a more professionalized, more demanding legal-academic culture and to a far more rigorous level of expectation regarding their performance in academic legal English composition. They were making the transition from writing academic compositions or abstracts in undergraduate-level English as a foreign language in their home countries to composing a graduate-level legal research paper or publishable article in English as a second language in the U.S. This is a great leap for international students enrolled in legal writing programs in U.S. law schools. This transition is also potentially relevant for EFL/ESL graduate student writers who cross writing and research traditions in the Humanities and Fine Arts, the Social Sciences, the Physical Sciences and Engineering, and the Biological and Life Sciences.

2.4 International legal studies context

All graduate student participants in this research were receiving specialized writing instruction in a mid-Atlantic university at the time of data collection. Like international students in other U.S. Master of Laws (LL.M.) programs, participants were studying international law and interested in global legal issues. They wanted to advance their understandings of law for professional practice and scholarship and improve their written English for both.

To be admitted, LL.M. students had to have completed a law degree at a U.S. law school accredited by the American Bar Association (ABA) or at a foreign law school with equivalent standards. There are no ABA standards for international students in U.S. LL.M. programs but, like international students generally, participants had to provide proof of competency in English in terms of TOEFL. "Although these students must take the Test of English as a Foreign Language (TOEFL) exam as a condition of admission to various programs in law school, a high score on that exam does not necessarily guarantee that the student will have sufficient practice in listening, speaking, and writing English to succeed in law school classes" (Wojcik & Edelman, 1997, p. 129). "The gravest error that universities make is to assume that a certain TOEFL...score, say 550, is equated with the ability to comprehend text in a particular academic area, even though the TOEFL is used by almost all English-speaking college and university faculties to judge students' preparation for studies" (Gunderson, D'Silva, & Odo, 2014, p. 49). Problems like plagiarism arise in U.S. law school context when academic deans, faculty, and staff assume academic writing proficiency when international students demonstrate good social English orally, have met the university requirement for TOEFL, or have been socialized to U.S. legal writing culture. Teaching professors may feel compromised, however, when a seemingly low proficiency student enters their class with the expectation of passing the requirement of an academic research paper when the student has never written one in English.

To graduate, LL.M. student participants had to complete (a) 24 credit hours in two or three semesters, (b) a two-part course that introduces foreign-trained lawyers to the U.S. legal system and to U.S. legal writing, and (c) two research papers demonstrating a "high degree of skill in legal scholarship and writing" according to the university website. Students with a TOEFL score below 580 (237 CBT and 93 IBT) were required to take an English for lawyers (ESP) course, taught in conjunction with the U.S. legal writing course sharing the same content base. The two skills courses mirror each other with mutually coordinated written assignments. The difference between them is that the U.S. legal writing course focuses on U.S. legal reasoning whereas the ESP course focuses on legal English use. The purpose of the ESP course is to develop LL.M. students' technical legal reading and writing skills so they can understand and communicate complex or difficult legal material rather than just general material. In addition to these required skills courses, international student participants could opt to take an academic legal writing (EAP) course if planning to write one or more research papers during the semester. This one-credit EAP skills course was designed for academic legal writers crossing cultures of learning and traditions of scholarship at the graduate (master's and doctoral) level.

Like the ESP course, the EAP course was designed specifically for international graduate student writers originating from different legal traditions and cultures of scholarship. The purpose is to (1) support LL.M. students throughout recursive processes of researching and writing one or more papers from multilingual sources until publication in English, if desired; and (2) develop students' academic language skills and literacy strategies in legal context so they can (a) thrive (versus survive) in their LL.M. program, (b) contribute to their legal field in L2 academic English, and (c) avoid plagiarism, if a concern.

Upon entering law school at orientation, international students receive severe warning against plagiarism, presented as academic dishonesty. The rules are clear and the penalty is harsh. Law school emphasis on plagiarism is generally ethics-based without attention to the fact that academic legal English and discourse are linguistics-based. Academic writing instruction and research in this book, therefore, explicitly addresses (a) skills for legal language processing, and (b) strategies and goals for legal reading and writing (literacy) typically embedded in generic academic writing requiring higher-order thinking, analysis, synthesis, and evaluation of research – required of all graduate students in U.S. higher education. The challenge for the author as researcher was to explore what works best in L2 writing instruction when it is tailored to individual students' disciplinary research and writing needs, interests, and levels of competence (proficiency). The challenge for the author as teacher was to engage authentically with her L2 graduate students' higher, as well as lower, concerns: that is, language, composition, and limited knowledge of research and writing. The researcher-teacher roles overlapped.

Student research participants were highly motivated, and some write very well in their first and second academic languages. All had elected to take the academic legal writing (EAP) course, and all gave permission to the researcher-teacher to investigate their perspectives as L2 academic writers. Through research, the teacher wanted to gain insight into her students' development as writers, and consider information regarding their strengths and difficulties to adapt (academic and disciplinary) L2 writing instruction accordingly.

Segev-Miller (2004) had conducted similar research during classroom training on her Israeli college students' first language (L1) writing from sources, as did Zhang (2013) on EAP students' discourse synthesis writing. Both found that explicit instruction had a positive effect on students' writing. In the Segev-Miller (2004) study, explicit instruction improved post instruction discourse synthesis processes and products. Linguistic transforming proved very difficult for her students as "copying, paraphrasing, and summarizing reflected different 'depths of textual processing" (Campbell in Segev-Miller, 2004, p. 25). Segev-Miller's (2004) student participants found it very difficult to get away from the language of their texts, as did international students taking the academic legal writing (EAP) course in previous semesters.

Classroom-based research was therefore necessary for two reasons: (1) needs analysis is fundamental to (specific versus general) ESP/EAP language instruction, and (2) university/law school administrators kept asking the L2 legal writing teacher to edit international student papers assumed to be grammar deficient. So the teacher-researcher had to find another way of working with international student writers in a U.S. professional school environment that placed a premium on native-speaker English grammar and legal content transmission through lecture, without considering effective techniques or strategies to guide student learning or their academic English writing. Text work is an integral part of the academic experience for international LL.M. students in the U.S., even without prior knowledge of, or experience with, graduate-level research and writing in L2 academic English. Therefore, a number of questions generated by the Segev-Miller (2004) study were interesting and relevant to this researcher. First, do student participants think that explicit strategies instruction improves academic legal discourse synthesis processes and products? Second, do student participants use the same or similar criteria to assess the quality of their writing products as in the Segev-Miller (2004) study: for example, inventing a macroproposition or thesis, organizing information previously selected in an appropriate rhetorical structure, and linguistically transforming the information? Third, does linguistic transforming such as paraphrasing and summarizing prove difficult and involve different depths of textual processing related to writing purpose for student participants? Fourth, are there differences between student participant self-assessments of their writing products at various stages of the scholarly writing process and the teacher assessments? Such questions generated by the Segev-Miller (2004) study informed the research questions and design of the study presented in this book, going beyond action research to assist students improving and refining their L2 academic writing.

2.5 Academic legal writing instructional context

This research considers the situation of international graduate student writers who cross (a) systems of law and legal education, (b) academic and legal languages, and (c) sociocultural, rhetorical, and linguistic conventions of scholarship in legal research and writing. The potential mismatch between prior writing experience and L2 academic legal writing conventions is particularly important in the writing of seminar papers, observed Feak, Reinhart, and Sinsheimer (2000). Legal academic writing in U.S. law school context is considered a form of scholarly writing that is intentional, reasoned, and oriented to problem-solving. According to Bhatia (1993), legal genres include (a) academic legal writing as in law journals, (b) juridical legal writing as in court judgments, and (c) legislative legal writing as in laws, regulations, contracts, and treaties. Writing for law practice in the U.S. has been referred to as instrumental legal writing. Discourse synthesis is common to both instrumental and academic legal writing, but practices for referencing and citing source text may be different. Conventionalization is the key characteristic of genres, according to Bhatia (2002).

In addition to instrumental and academic legal writing, Goddard (2010) points to another variety used by lawyers to communicate with clients requiring a more "reader-friendly" style of written communication than that used with law professionals. Whatever the kind of legal writing, research skills and written language skills form a vital part of professional education and training for L1 English graduate students in U.S. law schools. In contrast to other cultures where some steps in reasoning may be assumed, steps in reasoning must be made explicit in U.S. legal writing culture, especially in writing for law practice (Ramsfield, 1997). Directness and explicitness are two characteristics of U.S. legal prose style that may contrast with stylistic conventions in other academic cultures (Oates & Enquist, 2009).

For international graduate student participants enrolled in the academic legal writing course, strategies awareness helped disclose differences in culture and practices in written language use. Cross-cultural academic awareness and the concept of strategies (conceptual knowledge) was introduced to student participants through a *Preliminary Writing Strategies Questionnaire* (adapted with permission from Mu and Carrington, 2007). The teacher-researcher used this survey as a pre-writing intervention tool to make explicit contrasting ideas about culture and academic English writing before students began work on their legal research papers for the semester. This 100 item survey is research-based and highly effective for creating common ground in a culturally and linguistically diverse graduate classroom setting. The *Preliminary Writing Strategies Questionnaire* has since been revised and published as a separate, independent study.[1] Global issues in writing are revealed when teachers use the 50 item *Academic English Writing Questionnaire* (Appendix A) for student reflection and classroom discussion. Cultural contrasts emerge, allowing the teacher to discern the influence of academic culture and background learning, providing opportunities to address expectations of the target (academic and disciplinary) culture. By probing student responses, teachers can very quickly understand who their students are as international academic writers and what skills students may bring with them from their home countries: for example, referencing authority assumed to be common knowledge in a culture or discipline.

This kind of research-based pedagogy discloses the impact of culture on international students' formation of writing knowledge, basis for intellectual growth and professional development in a graduate field of study like law. Transitioning to a more professional program with a more rigorous level of expectation regarding performance in written language use and composition necessitates comprehensible input for learners within the context of academic culture, besides strategies for problem-solving in academic or legal writing that help develop language and academic proficiency (Krashen, 2011). According to Oates and Enquist (2009), "Most ESL law students report that their foreign language classes concentrated only on vocabulary and sentence grammar; they stopped short of addressing the larger cultural issues that affect the overall approach to writing" (p. 283). This sociocultural gap is addressed by the Academic English Writing Questionnaire.

Student participants were further prepared for strategies research with two practice questionnaires not needed for classroom use: one explored legal skills and the other explored legal language use. The purpose of these preparatory materials was to bridge the genres of instrumental legal writing (another course) with academic legal writing (this course). The former was a 48-item strategies questionnaire specific to legal memo writing designed by the teacher-researcher. The latter was a 100-item questionnaire specific to learning legal English and academic legal writing based on Oxford (1990). Both were strategies questionnaires taken at the end of class that raised consciousness for student participants as they shared their preferred strategies and discussed new ones that could help them draft original, authentic text and avoid plagiarism. These in-class questionnaires assumed a process approach to writing, as do the research instruments designed for this research. Explicit strategies instruction occurs when students ask questions or

---

1 First published in "When the culture of learning plays a role in academic writing" by Donna Bain Butler, Yalun Zhou and Michael Wei in the special issue on "academic English across cultures" of *ESP Across Cultures* vol. 10 (2013), co-edited by Marina Bondi and Christopher Williams.

pose problems during the semester. The academic legal writing classroom is thus dialogic and interactive (Vygotsky, 1978). It is not teacher-centered, transmission oriented, or genre dependent.

In the academic writing intervention for this research, the role of the EAP teacher is to guide learners through processes of researching and writing one or more graduate-level academic research papers until completion. The intention is to develop students' existing competencies with expert level strategies and skills for generating, drafting, and refining text without focusing on surface-level (grammar) corrections until the end (Hyland, 2003; Raimes, 1992). The approach to teaching is never prescriptive but descriptive with research-based, interrelating strategies for (a) discourse synthesis; (b) knowledge-telling and linguistic transforming; and (c) plain language use for clear meaning (versus legalese or obscure language use). In addition to cognitive and metacognitive strategies for L2 legal academic writing, social strategies are very important for student participants to communicate effectively and professionally with their law school professors at various times during the semester about their legal research.

Student participants' understanding of their own strategies came from taking the in-class questionnaires and keeping a reflective journal with open-ended questions. Students were asked to describe: (a) their major law school writing task for the semester, (b) the kinds of knowledge they thought they would need to perform their task, (c) what made them anxious about writing a legal research paper, (d) their process for choosing a suitable research topic and any related difficulties, (e) how research writing purpose might relate to claim/thesis/argument and any related difficulties, and (f) their reflections on the scholarly writing text they were using as a process model. Students' journals were dialogic, with the writing teacher responding to students' reflections and questions individually and collectively. Overall, student responses to the prompts for reflection and items on the questionnaires guided consciousness-raising discussions of writing strategies in the classroom, facilitating contrasting approaches to students' prior academic writing habits and legal education experiences.

In sum, the academic legal writing classroom not only raised individual student awareness of evidence-based legal reading and writing (literacy) strategies and language skills, but also dealt with their beliefs about writing and their self-confidence as L2 legal writers. A teacher-made questionnaire based on Casanave (2004) asks students how they characterize "improvement in their scholarly (critical) writing" and what they believe about graduate-level research writing from sources, explicit instruction, and feedback. This questionnaire, useful for classroom purposes, is included in Appendix B. "Unless learners alter some of their old beliefs about learning [and writing], they will not be able to take advantage of the strategies they acquire in strategy training" (Oxford, 1990, p. 201). Like L2 learning, L2 writing requires "active self-direction" on the part of the learners to reach professional levels of communicative competence (Oxford, 1990, p. 201). Agency, culture, identity, language and the law merge when EFL/ESL graduate student writers learn to construct and communicate knowledge from their legal research through explicit (strategies and skills) instruction.

2.6 Variability in EFL/ESL graduate student writer sampling

The descriptive research in this book focuses on the six students ($N = 6$) enrolled in the academic legal writing intervention during two different academic semesters. Purposeful sampling determined two levels of graduate student writers: (a) three were entering the LL.M. program (fall semester), and (b) three were exiting the LL.M. program (spring semester). The three fall participants considered themselves novices, acquiring language of the law (that is, legal English) at the same time as they were acquiring knowledge of basic concepts in American legal culture with English as the medium of instruction. The fall participants were from Cameroon, Palestine, and Ukraine. The three spring participants, in contrast, had some L2 academic writing experience, having completed an academic legal writing intervention the previous semester. Having successfully completed one academic semester, they were somewhat acculturated into the LL.M. program. These participants were from Italy, Moldava, and the United States. Students in both groups differed in terms of research experience and writing proficiency (competence, expertise). Competencies stressed in the intervention included use and understanding of scholarly legal English writing and cognitive academic language proficiency (CALP) in international EFL/ESL legal education context. CALP refers to skills in (formal) academic language learning contrasted with (informal) social language learning: that is, listening, speaking, reading, and writing about content-area material with English used as a tool for learning (Cummins, 1981, 2000, 2001, 2003).

   Student participants in the acculturated (post-intervention) group were more linguistically diverse than student participants in the unacculturated (intervention) group. All considered themselves language learners, however, in that they all wanted to improve their understanding and use of academic English for scholarship purposes. At one end of the language use continuum was a U.S. trained lawyer who has been residing in the U.S. since the age of five. English is her first academic language. At the other end of the continuum was a doctoral student from Italy who entered the LL.M. program with only a modicum of spoken English. She was finishing her doctoral dissertation in Italy at the time of data collection and had advanced knowledge of her legal research topic. The third spring participant was a polyglot with three academic languages who, prior to entering law school in her home country, had planned on becoming an interpreter. English is her third academic language. Overall, languages identified by the graduate student participants before data collection are as follows:

- native Mbo; foreign English, French: *Cameroon*
- native Italian; foreign English: *Italy*
- native Arabic; foreign English, French: *Palestine*
- native Romanian; foreign English, French, Russian: *Republic of Moldava*
- native Ukrainian; foreign Russian, Polish, English: *Ukraine*
- native Urdu, English; foreign Spanish, Arabic: *United States (U.S.)*

It is important to point out that the native Urdu research participant, already familiar with U.S. legal English reading and writing because of her prior U.S. law school experience, was diffident. Only when she was a graduate student in U.S. law school, for example, did she discover that a present perfect tense existed in English. Explicit (conscious) language instruction, and knowledge of the present perfect tense in English grammar, had not been part of her formative years or her pre-law U.S. educational experience. This discovery in professional school made her doubt her language use abilities, even with a non-native English editor of her law review project. In contrast to this ESL student participant, the EFL polyglot in her group was highly confident in her English language use.

All five international EFL student participants had had conscious learning of English grammar before entering U.S. professional school. However, they had not been exposed to (a) formal writing or explicit language instruction at advanced levels; (b) concepts like "legalese" and "plain language" that characterize style in academic and disciplinary writing at the professional level; (c) techniques and strategies for achieving clarity in academic and disciplinary writing; or (d) process routines for academic and professional writing that put the onus for communication on the writer, not on the reader as in many academic cultures.

All six research participants were highly motivated to learn more about how to use language for composing, editing, and publishing a scholarly paper or article. All were engaged in processes of writing a research paper for various LL.M. degree courses taught by different law school professors at the time of data collection. Through (meta) linguistic awareness and writing strategies instruction, all had been learning to tailor their language to their audience and purpose for communicating—a hallmark of distinguished language use, necessary for advancing professional proficiency in writing. "Integration of language, meaning, and social context is essential for really effective Distinguished language use," according to Ehrman (2002), as is a "maximization of sophisticated choices" (p. 245).

3 Determining What International Student Writers Know and Can Do

3.1 Self-report instrument describing strategic competence

A set of questionnaires was designed to collect data from the six research participants that maximized sophisticated choices for engaging in multilingual academic legal research and scholarly writing. The concept of "strategic competence" was operationally defined as appropriate use of learner internal and learner external literacy strategies and language skills to show communicative competence and domain learning in scholarly legal writing. *The Strategic Competence Questionnaire* (SCQ) developed for this study consists of four instruments corresponding to different stages in the writing process (pre-writing, drafting, and revising). Taken at different times, they show how students' understanding develops. The SCQ developed from the research literature over time but began as a comprehensive (46 item) post-intervention questionnaire of factors affecting professional proficiency in scholarly legal writing. Originally, it included individual learner background and proficiency factors, in addition to literacy strategies and language skills premised on a writing survey by Jasser, Khanj and Leaver (2005). Leaver (2005) explains that the researchers' goal was "to identify the critical factors that must be present for students to reach a Level 4 [advanced professional proficiency] equivalent in writing in English" (p. 19). Their survey was re-tooled from a speaking survey for native Arabic speaker students who had acquired English to the near-native level, and it was re-tooled again by the researcher for this study.

The SCQ consists primarily of quantitative items for multilingual graduate student writers in (ESL/EFL) scholarly U.S. legal writing context. Except for the Ph.D. student from Italy, all participants in this study had acquired spoken English close to professional or near-native speaking proficiency, and all expected to be using L2 English in their legal careers. Many jobs and internships that prepare foreign-trained lawyers for work in global corporations and international institutions presume a need to write in English at the level of professional proficiency or higher: that is, functionally native proficiency. To meet this need for professional proficiency in L2 legal writing, the researcher condensed, contextualized, and quantified the proficiency definitions and selected items from the Jasser, Khanj and Leaver (2005) writing survey to create the different sections of the SCQ.

Two important demographic questions were retained as contributing factors from the Jasser, Khanj and Leaver (2005) survey instrument: (1) formal instruction at higher ranges, and (2) professional use of languages. In addition, their checklist of factors for developing advanced professional proficiency was adapted for the SCQ: that is, refined use of grammar; increased acquaintance with a range of writing styles; how written texts are organized; and building endurance in writing. Their questions about the importance of direct (explicit) instruction for achieving advanced professional proficiency in writing in English were also retained for the SCQ (section 3.b). The reason for this inclusion is that opting to take an advanced L2 academic writing course is a strategy in itself for learner development and enhanced L2 English production at the graduate level where time and money are significant factors. It would be impossible to separate the learner from the context of writing or explicit strategies instruction in this longitudinal (14 week) study.

The sections in the SCQ investigate the (a) use of writing strategies, (b) CALP skills, (c) levels of writing purpose, (d) languages used for writing, (e) proficiency, and (f) writing strategies instruction as factors developing competency in scholarly legal writing. These derive from sources other than Jasser, Khanj and Leaver (2005). For example, (a) problems in writing knowledge areas originate with Hyland (2003) and Grabe and Kaplan (1996); (b) non-linear writing process skills originate with Grabe and Kaplan (1996); (c) the names of the SCQ stages originate with the Fajans and Falk (2005) scholarly writing teaching model; (d) the idea of a legal writing process extends from Ray and Ramsfield (2005); and knowledge-transforming strategies, based on Bereiter and Scardamalia (1987), extends from Segev-Miller's (2004) strategies for intertextual processing or transforming.

Section 3.b of the SCQ derived from proficiency level descriptions characterizing written language use developed by the Interagency Language Roundtable (ILR), an organization of U.S. federal agencies. The researcher chose this particular scale for three reasons. It was advanced, meant for professionals, and the researcher had experience using it from an oral proficiency testing (OPT) point of view. Practical OPT experience with a U.S. government agency gave me credibility as an L2 teacher in the professional school environment, and I wanted to know more about professional proficiency for writing. Statements on the SCQ (3.b) describing accuracy refer to typical stages in the development of competence in U.S. agency formal training programs. Emerging competence may parallel these characterizations. The ILR scale consists of descriptions of five levels of language proficiency, ranging from no proficiency (level 0) to functionally native proficiency (level 5). They are similar to the ACTFL scale for Presentational Writing (Written Production) more widely used in the academic world http://www.actfl.org/sites/default/files/pdfs/Can-Do_Statements.pdf. The "plus level" descriptions, being supplementary to the "base level" descriptions, were not used in the SCQ because learners' writing abilities were not being tested, just described with Can Do Statements. These SCQ statements were contextualized to help research participants understand what legal writing proficiency is and to self-identify their abilities across levels of proficiency. With this tool, the researcher-teacher could understand what participants believed they could do across levels of writing proficiency (a) in relation to each other, and (b) to the academic legal writing intervention. As with the other SCQ checklists, SCQ 3.b helped learners become engaged in their own learning, set personal goals for improving their language use and proficiency (competence), and increase their motivation.

In sum, the SCQ synthesizes questions about writing proficiency, language and literacy strategies, and levels of writing purpose from the L1 English research literature with CALP and related skills from the L2 English research literature that may or may not transfer appropriately when writing from sources. With respect to transfer, Cummins (2000) advances the theory that there is a common underlying proficiency (CUP) between languages. In the CUP model of bilingualism, skills, ideas and concepts students learn are thought to transfer across languages, and experience with one language can promote the development of the proficiency underlying both languages, given adequate motivation and exposure. In other words, there may be "interdependence of academic skills and knowledge across languages (or what Riches and Genesee, 2006, describe as a reservoir of knowledge, skills, and abilities that underlie academic performance in both languages)" (Cummins, 2009, p. 383). From a grammatical perspective, "SLA [second language acquisition] researchers still generally agree that learners transfer at least some of the features of their L1 into their L2" (Ellis, 2006, p. 89).

A key underlying idea for the SCQ is that an L1 skill for writing from sources, such as summarizing, could also be an L2 cognitive strategy when a student writer consciously employs it to achieve a specific purpose in scholarly writing (for example, knowledge transforming to produce text work that deepens learning when writing from sources). Dole, Nokes, and Drits (2008) define cognitive strategies as learners' mental procedures to accomplish a cognitive goal, including how information is processed, organized, stored and retrieved from the memory system.

For the categories grouping items in the SCQ, quantitative questions developed from the L1 writing, L2 writing, and L2 learning strategies research literature that closely approximate exact measures of the strategic competence and communicative competence variables of interest. The rationale was to select and adapt categories (and items) from existing research that could affect L2 legal writers' strategic competence at the level of professional (ILR Level 3) proficiency or higher. Both L1 and L2 sources provided ideas relevant to academic legal writing at professional levels of writing proficiency in the following key categories:

(a) strategies for stages in the recursive writing process (pre-writing, drafting, revising);
(b) strategies for language learning and language use functions (that is, metacognitive, cognitive, affective, and sociocultural-interactive strategies);
(c) skills for language use and strategies for language re-use when writing from sources that develop deep CALP (summary, paraphrase, synthesis); and
(d) strategies for transforming knowledge when writing from sources that develop composing competence (proficiency): conceptually, rhetorically, and linguistically.

3.1.1 Stages for writing

The term "competence" in the research literature is equated with "proficiency" and "expertise" and the terms have been used interchangeably. So the SCQ also considers expert use of strategies for stages in the recursive writing process and used the Fox (1989) *Inventory of Writing Strategies* as a model. Her questionnaire identifies strategies used by experts (professors) when writing a paper. It is organized into three sections: (1) Pre-Writing Strategies, (2) While-Writing Strategies, and (3) Revising Strategies/Before Submission/After Writing. To validate the questionnaire, the strategies were elicited directly from professors and teaching assistants. Then when the checklist was developed, Fox used "a members check" (Lincoln & Guba, 1985) or informant feedback with the same group to validate it. After that, she used it with other disciplinary groups, adding and revising some of the strategies for clarity. Students taking this questionnaire were told to compare their writing strategies with those used by the professors, who are considered experts. Students were also told that there is no one way to write, but if they find that they are checking "never" most of the time, they may consider trying some of the other strategies to improve their writing—and possibly make the writing process easier.

Fox's (1989) writing survey has been useful from both a research and a pedagogical perspective. First, international students coming from EFL environments are not as familiar with writing strategies, process writing, or process-oriented pedagogies as ESL students or native English speakers in the North American educational milieu (Hedgcock, 2005). Second, research within the fields of English for Specific Purposes (ESP) and English for Academic Purposes (EAP) suggests that international student writers in a U.S. graduate setting may not treat writing as a process that includes rewriting for a target audience or composing in the revision stage (Myles, 2002). Strategies for composing in the SCQ, therefore, are most numerous in the revision stage.

3.1.2 Strategies for language learning and language use

The integration of (a) strategies for stages of writing, with (b) strategies for language learning and language use originates from an earlier survey instrument, based on Oxford's (1990) *Students' Strategy Inventory for Language Learning* (SSILL). The teacher-researcher added advanced writing to Oxford's inventory, being influenced by Fox's (1989) inventory. The survey gathered information about how foreign-trained lawyers use English and go about learning legal English and analytical legal writing in L2 English, examining the frequency of students' use of language learning strategies and their utilization of these strategies in a specific legal memo (instrumental) writing task. The classification of metacognitive, cognitive, affective, and sociocultural-interactive strategies from that survey instrument is relevant to discussion of L2 legal writers' key strategies in this research study, extending from O'Malley and Chamot (1990) who classified learning strategies into metacognitive, cognitive, and socio-affective strategies.

The L2 learning strategies literature reveals that central kinds of knowledge like the (a) metacognitive knowledge of planning, organizing, and evaluating (Chamot & O'Malley, 1994); and (b) conditional knowledge of strategies (Newell & Simon, 1972; Oxford, 2011) can be fostered for professional performance in an L2 English research paper or scholarly article. The L2 learning strategies context helps clarify the construct of strategic competence for scholarly L2 legal writers in its social, cultural, affective, and cognitive dimensions (Leaver & Shekhtman, 2002). For example, in contrast to compensation strategies "vital at lower proficiency levels," developing knowledge of how to paraphrase is relevant at higher proficiency levels (Ehrman, 2006, p. 251).

3.1.3 Skills for language use and strategies for language re-use

The inclusion of cognitive skills for language use (that is, summary, paraphrase, synthesis) when writing from legal sources comes from professional teaching experience and using college level texts that focus on writing from sources. Research inquiry into methods of source use like summary, paraphrase, patchwriting, and copying (Howard, Serviss & Rodrigue, 2010) further supports inclusion into the SCQ. Graduate level CALP necessitates paraphrasing, quoting, summarizing, synthesizing to write research from primary and secondary legal sources. Collier's (1995) research, for example, has shown that teachers must address all of the components of cognitive, language, and academic development equally to develop "deep" academic proficiency in a second language. Because "research on what aspects of literacy transfer from a learner's first language is conflicting" (Hyland,

2003, p. 35), the SCQ developed for this study includes items that address both L1 issues of literacy and L2 issues of language use explicitly, for each stage of writing.

Similarly, the inclusion of strategies for language re-use when writing from legal sources has roots in empirical research. Hu's (2001) study explored the writing processes and challenges of fifteen (N = 15) Mainland Chinese graduate students as they wrote disciplinary assignments and research proposals during their first two years at a major research university. The researcher challenged the traditional notion of plagiarism, arguing that language re-use can be reconceptualized as a textual strategy in the development of ESL students learning and using disciplinary language and content (Hu, 2001). Recent research indicates that patchwriting may occur "as an intermediate stage between copying and summarizing" and that "inexpert critical readers patchwrite when they attempt to paraphrase or summarize (Moore Howard, Serviss, & Rodrigue, 2010). "Textual plagiarism and source use should be the focus of explicit instruction," according to Pecorari (2008, p. 143). Language re-use with citation is therefore viewed as a strategy associated with L2 disciplinary literacy and legal content in the SCQ. Literacy practices of students must conform to the expected literacy practices of the disciplinary community even though these students' writing practices may have been valued and purposeful in other cultural contexts (Grabe & Kaplan, 1996).

Proper citation is required in most U.S. legal writing situations, and scholarly L2 legal writers need to learn how to compose with citation to avoid different types of plagiarism – all considered a form of theft of intellectual property in U.S. legal context (Contento, 2009). Types of plagiarism include (1) using ideas without attribution, (2) using exact words without quotation, (3) quoting without attribution, (4) paraphrasing without attribution, and (5) summarizing without attribution. From a disciplinary perspective based on Ramsfield (1997), legal writers must show (a) what authority is predominant, (b) how the sources of authority are linked, (c) what weight to give each in coming to a conclusion, and (d) provide comment with critical thinking. These are acts of literacy that combine with cognitive academic language skills like paraphrase and summary. They require depth and complexity of understanding, as well as interaction with L2 legal text and with others across cultures of (law and language) learning.

3.1.4 Strategies for knowledge-transforming

Writing from sources, or discourse synthesis, requires students to select, organize, and connect content from source texts as they compose their own texts (Segev-Miller, 2004). Transforming strategies relevant for discourse synthesis in the SCQ derive from Segev-Miller's (2004) research study, "Writing from Sources: The Effect of Explicit Instruction on College Students' Processes and Products." Transforming strategies are important because academically valued writing is assumed to require composing skills which transform information or transform the language itself (Grabe & Kaplan, 1996).

Drawing from discourse synthesis research, Segev-Miller defines (a) *process quality* in terms of the strategies relevant to the performance of the task (a literature review in her study), and (b) *product quality* in terms of the selection, organization, and connection of relevant information from source text (2004). Her subjects (N = 24) attributed improvement in their post-instruction processes to the effect of explicit instruction in three major categories: (a) knowledge of transforming and relevant cognitive and metacognitive strategies; (b) motivation and self-efficacy; and (c) self-reassessment as learners. The subjects assessed their post-instruction products to be of higher quality than their pre-instruction products with regard to three criteria: (1) inventing a macroproposition when synthesizing, (2) organizing an appropriate rhetorical structure; and (3) linguistically transforming the information. These and other knowledge-transforming strategies for developing composing competence (conceptually, rhetorically, and linguistically) have been included in the SCQ using different terminology (pre-writing, drafting, and revising).

In sum, the SCQ is a research-based instrument employed within the disciplinary, social-cultural context of an L2 academic legal writing intervention with the potential to disclose the changing nature of variables that influence student writers' strategic competence in academic English writing. It is a multistage instrument designed to collect data at different stages of writing (pre-writing, drafting, and revising) that recalls Pritchard and Honeycutt (2006) who suggest that writers use procedural strategies for going through the writing process to generate text and other strategies to develop schemata. Strategies (a) help writers understand the social, cultural, and disciplinary context for writing; (b) tap general background knowledge and reading ability; (c) sharpen cognitive processes for problem-solving; (d) create emotional dispositions and scholarly attitudes for problem-solving, (e) develop macro-level understandings about organization, conventions, cohesion, topic, genre, and audience; and develop micro-level skills such as sentence construction (Pritchard & Honeycutt, 2006, p. 285).

Part II: **Learner-User Research**

4 Research Population Representativeness and Research Methods

4.1 International students as L2 users in advanced academic settings

Cook (2011) emphasizes that "L2 users are no more standardized than monolinguals" (p. 2). Multilingual students in more advanced academic settings – like the international legal studies context for participants in this research – belong to diverse cultural, linguistic, and academic groups. They do not have homogeneous backgrounds for academic English writing. International students may be part of multilingual communities, for example, where several languages are spoken. One research participant belonging to this particular group is Anyo, from Cameroon. He uses two academic languages, English and French, and transfer from French into English may be visible in his writing. He, like the author, originates from a country with two official languages where both French and English are taught and used for professional legal purposes. Similarly, Tory from Republic of Moldava is a student participant who uses three academic languages: English, French, and Russian. The difference between the two student participants is program acculturation and academic literacy in English. Whether a student operates in more than one academic language is a crucial consideration for (academic and disciplinary) L2 writing teachers because, as Cook (2011, p. 3) observes, students "are not learning a language in isolation but are learning it with a mind that already knows another language. This influences their knowledge and use of both languages." These students were selected as participants because multilinguals such as these often seek out and need some level of professional L2 instruction and support.

Short-term and long-term visitors constitute other groups of international students in more advanced academic settings. Some are learners of English as a foreign language (EFL) as in many Asian and Russian educational contexts where students learn in language classrooms in their home countries. EFL students are generally not L2 users before coming to the U.S. to study, however, because they lack experience using L2 English academically and professionally. Ferra, the doctoral student participant from Italy, belongs to this EFL group of international students.

In contrast, there are many international LL.M. students who have good oral skills because of media, geographical proximity to the U.S. and time spent in the host country, but their L2 English writing may contain (patterned) error or mistakes. Writing style, fluency and accuracy may be of concern to international students in this group. Graduate LL.M. students from Latin America, Spain, and France, moreover, may have some experience with L1 academic legal writing, basis for comparison with L2 academic legal writing. There are also many LL.M students from the Middle East, Russia, and some Asian countries who have no academic research writing experience during any of their four years studying law for an undergraduate degree. Sam, from Palestine, and Liv, from Ukraine, are student participants belonging to this group.

Research participants are thus representative of different groups of EFL and ESL student writers who combine to form a large graduate student population currently using, or wanting to use, English for professional purposes outside of the language classroom. In the situated instructional context for this research, foreign lawyers practicing outside of their home jurisdictions may have U.S. clients and are therefore highly motivated to study abroad in English. Foreign-educated and licensed lawyers are also being hired in increasing numbers by U.S. law firms for their foreign and domestic offices (Silver, 2001). Graduate LL.M. students as well as visiting scholars may also want to publish their research to effect change, nationally or internationally. Increasingly, international lawyers and international LL.M. students are L2 users in a global age that necessitates the use of L2 English as an academic and professional *lingua franca*, an international means of communication among native speakers of other languages (Cook, 2011). Examples include the sixth (ESL) research participant. As previously noted, she is an experienced academic legal research writer – an LL.M. student with a Juris Doctor (JD) degree from a U.S. law school. She contrasts with the EFL student participants who are novice academic legal writers. Her research name is Gee, a native speaker of two languages (Urdu and English) and a foreign language learner in two languages (Spanish and Arabic). Gee contrasts with the EFL student participants in this research because she is a literate user of only one academic language (English) but like them, she wanted to learn and develop as a writer for professional purposes. She was not confident in her legal English writing abilities.

It should be noted that there are other domestic L2 user groups not represented here in this research. They form cultural heritage groups and are heritage language speakers across all languages. Examples are ESL students in the United States who may speak Spanish at home but who may not be literate in Spanish. According to 2006 census data, 44.3 million people in the U.S. were Hispanic or Latin American by origin. When students culturally identify with their heritage language, they are called "heritage language learners" in the U.S. and "community language learners" in the UK (Cook, 2011). It should be noted that international and domestic JD students who are L2 academic writers did not have access to the academic legal writing instructional context for this research. Only one sec-tion of the EAP course is offered each semester, and it is always full.

Empirical research – and research-based pedagogy – should be implemented across all departments in U.S. law schools to understand more about these L2 users as complex student populations. This is because international graduate stu-dents are underrepresented quantitatively and misunderstood qualitatively when studying with highly confident L1 native English speakers. A second imperative is that L1 legal writing specialists get the professional development they need to be effective with L2 users since professional employment for law students depends on skills and academic transcripts. Because (international and domestic) law stu-dents in the U.S. must engage in academic writing for law school and learn to write for law practice, furthermore, native English teachers must also find ways to sup-port their multilingual students' cultural identities without perceiving them as remedial or deficient for not writing like English natives, especially if students are to feel successful. Graduate students from high-context cultural orientations, as in Asia, may also have to be accommodated when shifting to low-context teaching cultures in the U.S. and Canada. So, besides L2 writer knowledge, L2 writing con-text is important from a teaching-learning perspective: that is, knowing what L2 graduate student writers need to do to make the scholarly writer shift, culturally and linguistically. The research described in this book discloses that knowledge.

4.1.1 Implications for teaching

Going beyond the native speaker standard is an imperative in L2 user educational contexts. Cook (2012, 2011) identifies four implications for language teaching based on empirical research: (1) the status of the native speaker, (2) the role of the first language, (3) the goals of language teaching, and (4) the role of the non-native speaker. He points out that "if the purpose of language teaching is to create successful L2 users then [*sic*] everything changes . . . ; what counts [for students] is the ability to use the second language purposefully for their own reasons" (Cook, 2011, p. 3). The rationale for communicative language teaching, he says, "needs to be couched in terms of the abilities of L2 users, not of native speakers. . . . Lan-guage teaching should relate to the L2 user, using L2 user role models and L2 language and uses" (Cook, 2011, p. 4).

> But education is also about changing the student themselves.... [B]ecoming an L2 user is a transforming experience where the person's thinking, awareness of language etc are changed....And of course a vital decision for most language teaching is which kind of L2 user the students are aiming to become, which will influence many aspects of the curriculum

and the teaching methodology. ... The responsibility of language teachers is to help our students make this transformation in their lives. (Cook, 2011, p. 4)

Hence this book and the research participants in it – EFL/ESL students representative of many L2 users in advanced academic settings. Conscious attention to grammar, vocabulary, syntax, and style in L2 writer performance supports subconscious language acquisition from extensive reading in an academic domain of high literacy like law. However, without professional attention to L2 written language use and strategies for L2 discourse construction that includes analysis and synthesis in disciplinary and academic writing context, L2 users may feel threatened by, or be subject to, linguistic charges of plagiarism affecting their wellbeing or professional career. International EFL/ESL students are particularly at risk in the narrow, U.S. legal academic context that regards plagiarism as a form of theft of intellectual property (Contento, 2009). If professionals in higher education contexts were to recognize that there are forms of language re- use unrelated to academic dishonesty but related to L2 writer development, international students might be more forthcoming about the issues and challenges they face as L2 English users. A sociocognitive literacy perspective helps reveal understandings and knowledge that L2 users bring to their composing processes (Schultz, 2006, p. 365). Strategies instruction, couched in a process approach to research and writing, helps L2 graduate students learn to write better.

4.2 Research-based writing intervention

Much of the research on L2 writing has been dependent on L1 research (Myles, 2002). Of particular importance has been the Hayes and Flower (1980) model of skilled writing informing this L2 research. Hayes and Flower (1980) considered three factors relevant to writers: (1) learner external factors influencing the writing task; (2) learner internal mental operations and cognitive processes of planning, revising, and editing, and (3) writers' knowledge about the topic, audience, and plans for accomplishing the task. Planning and revising – high-level processes for L2 (academic and disciplinary) writers – are very important because they relate to metacognitive knowledge and metacognition in L2 student writing activity.

The academic legal writing intervention instructional context for this research was highly influenced by the Hayes and Flower (1980) research. International students at the graduate level need to employ sophisticated approaches for writing from L1 and L2 source text. Based on Graham's (2006, p. 188) highlights of effective writing instruction stimulated by Hayes' (1996, 2004) modification of the original L1 model, the L2 academic legal writing intervention was designed to raise students' levels of sophistication with a focus on research and writing for authentic law school assignments. Key elements may be shared in the classroom like research problem and purpose for writing through short oral presentations in L2 English followed by lengthier question and answer (Q&A) sessions in L2 English. International students benefit (a) conceptually from peer interaction and teacher feedback in L2 English, (b) linguistically from speaking about their research interests in L2 English and processing the information as L2 users, and (c) culturally from a translingual approach that does not necessarily separate languages in the drafting stage or from other learning processes and types of knowledge. In other words, L2 research writers may draft with more than one language by referencing original source text. From a linguistic accuracy (literacy) perspective, translation should probably be avoided but L2 writers may do it anyway, for various reasons. Summary, paraphrase, and synthesis, followed by critical comment in L2 English after long, multilingual quotations, may be more expedient.

As the semester progresses, students are able to use L2 English to discuss their research topics in speaking and writing, and some may come to think in English. Originality, ownership, and scholarship in L2 English are emphasized, along with a process approach to scholarly writing that encourages planning (30%), drafting and translating with citation (30%), and revising (30%) in L2 English. Editing may be accomplished with corrective feedback at different stages of writing; it is not necessarily left until the end as it may be for native English writers. Writing instruction is intrinsically motivational because students work on perceived areas of weakness within the context of their individual needs, wants, and interests. It is extrinsically motivational also because each learner has the opportunity to earn a first class grade regardless of writing proficiency or academic L1. The main difference among L2 student writers generally is that some have to revise more than others, so planning for the revision process becomes important. The worksheet in Appendix C shows how the students in this research-based writing intervention planned, how the teacher graded, and how strategic behavior may be facilitated through goal setting in the form of checklists for self-assessing writing quality in stages.

In addition to Hayes and Flower (1980), fundamental insights relevant to conceptual changes and sophistication in composing processes for the writing intervention came from Bereiter and Scardamalia (1987). These L1 researchers suggested that differences in ability may be due to different writing processes. They highlighted the (a) difference between skilled and less skilled writers; (b) variable processing demands of writing; (c) importance of strategic planning and processing; (d) need for planning that moves beyond content generalization; and (e) need to foster self-regulating, evaluating abilities and self-reflection. Foundational concepts from their L1 research that help international graduate students move beyond content generalization in writing are (a) knowledge telling, and (b) knowledge transforming. The two concepts are made explicit in the *Academic English Writing Questionnaire* previously mentioned, and subsequently treated in the academic legal writing intervention as strategies for converting text-based information to knowledge in a research paper or journal article. Based Bereiter and Scardamalia (1987), knowledge telling has been defined as a less-skilled process approach to writing that is more concerned with generating content than planning and revising (Hyland, 2003). Knowledge transforming, on the other hand, suggests a more-skilled process approach to writing that includes problem-solving, analysis, reflection, and goal-setting "to actively rework thoughts to change both...text and ideas" (Hyland, 2003, p. 12).

From a teaching-learning standpoint, Bereiter and Scardamalia's (1987) depiction of writing as a goal oriented-activity implies writer agency, self-regulated learning, "strategic actions and thus learning strategies as part of the act of writing and the development of writing abilities (Grabe, 2006, vii–viii). Strategy instruction "is effective in improving students' writing performance," can be generalized "to new tasks and situations," and can "be integrated with other forms of instruction to create a more effective writing program" (Graham, 2006. pp. 204–205). In the academic legal writing intervention associated with this research, process strategies and product goals take the form of questionnaires and checklists to show how research writing is a dynamic, reflective, and continuous process.

In recent years, research on L2 writing development has been "rapidly superseding research on first language (L1) writing in university...contexts in which L2 students' needs for effective instruction is obvious and readily measurable; where there is a greater urgency to 'try to get it right'" (Grabe, 2006, vii). Impetus for this book comes from bridging cultures of learning and disciplines of practice with different values, goals, and research perspectives. However, the academic culture of the host institution may have no sense of urgency at all for international students as learners because their speech and writing production habits ("habits of mind") may not be recognized as relevant to learning. International students, as border crossers, necessarily experience a transcultural intersection when they choose graduate school in an English-medium university or study in a dual-degree program. In the context of this research, international students cross two learning cultures: (1) U.S. legal education, with its own (low-context) cultural discourse; and (2) L2 education which intersects and interacts with a variety of cultures and discourses specific to the L2 English users. Bourdieu's idea of culture as (social, economic, and political) capital is meaningful to international students and visiting scholars wanting to practice as professionals in the global community where English is the first language in NATO, U.N., IMF, OPEC, the European Free Trade

Association, and the World Bank. "As the use of English becomes increasingly worldwide, more concerns are voiced that it carries 'the baggage' of one culture" (Jandt, 2007, p. 138). The importance of the sociocultural in L2 educational research and writing pedagogy cannot be overstated at the professional level.

Empirical studies on the writing abilities of L2 users in advanced academic settings have been carried out from two main research perspectives: (1) a qualitative, social perspective; and (2) a quantitative, cognitive perspective (Polio, 2012). The sociocultural perspective previously mentioned is very important and has been emphasized in recent years. The cognitive remains important from an L2 user standpoint, however, because written language use is a cognitive activity that can be used to support general language learning (Polio, 2012). Conversely, language proficiency (competence) "includes the ability to write in the L2 in a fundamental way" (Myles, 2002, p. 1). Effective teaching practice, therefore, takes into account both strategy development and language skills development when working with this population (Myles, 2002). From both a (social) qualitative and a (cognitive) quantitative (mixed) approach, this research discloses L2 students' perspectives on written language use and their preferred use of strategies for L2 discourse construction (analysis and synthesis) in disciplinary context.

From a second language acquisition perspective, L2 writing research can be classified in two ways: by the (1) focus of the study, and (2) research method (Polio, 2012). Examples of focus are (a) texts produced by the L2 writers; (b) L2 writers' [strategic] processes, attitudes, and motivations; and (c) the L2 writing context which may include writers' academic and professional needs (Polio, 2012). Examples of method include text analysis, process [strategies] analysis, and content (genre) analysis (Polio, 2012). "Despite the positive impact of strategy instruction on students' writing, it is not as widely used in classrooms as other writing methods, such as the [L1] process approach to writing" (Graham, 2006, p. 205). This may be one reason why there has been little research on L2 strategic processes and process strategies to date.

Techniques for collecting data from both the (focus and method) perspectives include the survey and the interview. Both were used in this L2 research that views writing strategies within the wider context of "process writing" (Manchón et al., 2007, p. 229). Specifically, quantitative surveys were used across three stages of writing, followed by a qualitative interview probing student responses to items on the survey. The instruments revealed students' perceptions of the mental actions they engage in while composing and their situated (contextualized) experiences with (a) literacy strategies, (b) language skills, and (c) goals for writing. Strategies related to students' writing processes and goals related to students' writing product at different stages of learning and development. The end result is "a unique source book for organizing strategy-based writing instruction" (Brendel, G., personal communication, January 20, 2014). By using a variety of methods and techniques, the researcher was able to triangulate the data. The prolonged (14 week) data collection also allowed for a more representative sample (Polio, 2012). "Research findings...validate the conceptual soundness and methodological appropriateness for generalizing the findings beyond the limited number of 6 participants in the study" (Brendel, G., personal communication, January 20, 2014).

4.3 Overview of procedures

Research procedures involved three parts in three stages corresponding to the writing process: pre-writing, drafting, and revising. "The process approach generally divides writing into three steps: '(a) prewriting, with its planning, researching, analyzing, and organizing functions; (b) writing preliminary drafts ...; and (c) editing, revising, and polishing the drafts'" (Spanbauer, 2007, p. 24). This professional view of the writing process combines the editing and the revising stages, placing greater emphasis on editing which influences content. Also, the pre-writing stage carries considerable weight substantively and cognitively, especially for academic research writers. Overall, emphasis is placed on cognitive (analytic and linguistic) skills and knowledge in a process approach to writing in stages which are "recursive, interactive and potentially simultaneous" (Hyland, 2006, pp. 316–317). All three stages involve language use (and re-use) for the L2 academic writer, which is why the researcher collected data from participants at different times during their writing process.

Three complementary sets of instruments were used to collect data at each stage of writing (pre-writing, drafting, and revising): (1) a questionnaire (survey), (2) a checklist, and (3) an interview. In the first part, student participants were asked to complete the *Strategic Competence Questionnaire* at each stage of writing. This survey instrument was tailored to students' specific academic (legal) writing situation for pre-writing, drafting, and revising. It asked them about *writing strategies, scholarly writing instruction*, and *legal writing proficiency.* In the second part, students were asked to self-check their own work product at each of these stages in writing using the *Student's Quality Assessment Tool*. This is a checklist of goals designed for students to raise their level of performance at each stage of writing. The checklist was presented to students as an educational tool to self-check and improve their substantive (pre-writing) outline, their preliminary draft, and their best revised draft. In the third part, participants were asked to meet with the researcher for an interview so she could probe students' responses to the strategies questionnaire.

4.3.1 Instructions to students participating in the research

Informed consent was part of the research procedure. It was very important for the six student participants to understand their role in the research. Student participants were told why they were chosen and what they had to do. They read and signed a *Students' Consent Form* that gave the project title, summarized why the research was being done, and what students would be asked to do. The form assured them that only the researcher would know their names and that they could withdraw from the research at any time and *change or edit* any of their responses on the questionnaire or in the interview, which none of them did. Students were told that there were no known risks for participating in the educational research.

From a benefits perspective, students were also told that may understand more about their own writing and development so they could rewrite and edit their scholarly (research) writing for publication, something that Gee (from the U.S.) was already doing but having difficulty with when she took the academic legal writing course. In addition, students were told that they may discover new writing strategies that they did not use before and that a summary of the whole-group results would be available to them if they were interested.

4.4 Research questions

As previously mentioned, part of the study's pedagogical purpose was to develop a research-based instrument for guiding learners' processes of writing a graduate-level research paper or scholarly article in an instructional setting. The *Strategic Competence Questionnaire* (SCQ) was designed for this purpose. The SCQ facilitated reflection for student writer participants and description of writing process quality in terms of strategies relevant to the performance of the writing task. In addition to strategies, other dynamic factors (changing variables) were explored that influenced strategic competence for the student participants learning and developing as L2 graduate writers.

Four research questions helped disclose these variables, and two research instruments in addition to the SCQ were subsequently developed: that is, (1) an open-ended interview, and (2) student/teacher assessments of writing product quality in the form of matching checklists. Mixed methods research, therefore, included both statistical (quantitative) and interpretative (qualitative) analyses of variables affecting strategic competence for students operating at professional (or higher) writing proficiency in a research paper where there is no manipulation of the variables. The research questions, with their respective data collection instruments, follow.

Research question 1

For each stage of the scholarly L2 legal writing process, what are the learners' reported use of writing strategies and cognitive academic language proficiency (CALP) skills?

This question is addressed by specific categories on the *Strategic Competence Questionnaire* (SCQ) identifying literacy strategies and language skills for each stage of scholarly legal writing – variables related to strategic competence and professional level writing proficiency. The SCQ yielded primarily quantitative data.

Research question 2

For each stage of the scholarly L2 legal writing process, which writing strategies and CALP skills do the learners think are the most useful and why?

This question is addressed by the *Interview Protocol* (IP) with quantitative SCQ items to stimulate recall. The IP probed the helpfulness of strategies used from the SCQ self-reports to yield qualitative data.

Research question 3

For each stage of the scholarly L2 legal writing process, what are the learners' and teacher quality ratings of the learners' scholarly L2 writing product?

This question explores product quality and is addressed by the *Student's Quality Assessment Tool* (SQAT) and the *Teacher's Quality Assessment Tool* (TQAT). These related instruments include specific items and genre categories from the scholarly legal writing literature relevant to strategic competence and professional level writing proficiency.

Research question 4

For each stage of the scholarly L2 legal writing process, what interrelationships can be seen among (a) learners' writing strategies and cognitive academic language proficiency (CALP) skills, and (b) learners' and teacher quality ratings of the learners' scholarly L2 writing product?

This question explores the interrelation between process quality and product quality. Discussion of the interrelation takes place after (quantitative and qualitative) data analyses of all the variables relating to strategic competence and professional proficiency, based on all the instruments, have been made.

4.5 Mixed methods research design

A mixed methods, concurrent triangulation, multi-stage design was used to explore the changing variables that influence strategic competence for research participants. This is a type of mixed (quantitative and qualitative) design in which different but complementary data were collected at the same time on the same research topic: strategic competence for scholarly legal writers. Creswell (2003) points out the many strengths of this model useful for the research: (a) two types of data can be collected simultaneously during a single data collection phase or stage; (b) different perspectives can be gained from the two types of data; and (c) perspectives emerge from the different stages within the study. The mixed methods design was efficient because both types of data were collected during the same stage of the research at roughly the same time. It was convenient because each type of data was collected and analyzed separately and independently, using techniques traditionally associated with each data type (Creswell & Plano Clark, 2007).

The design also allowed triangulation because quantitative and qualitative methods were implemented during the same time frame and with equal weight in stages corresponding to the writing process (that is, pre-writing, drafting, and revising). The reason for collecting both quantitative (numeric) and qualitative (written and spoken text) data was to bring together the strengths of both forms of research to cross-validate or triangulate the results. The qualitative data enriched and deepened understanding of variables affecting strategic competence as they related to student participants' processes of scholarly L2 legal writing. Integration of the approaches occurred in data collection with both quantitative and qualitative data collected at each stage. Then the findings from each stage of data collection were merged into an interpretation for each stage of research and finally into one overall interpretation.

4.5.1 Worldview

The primary worldview underlying this design is *pragmatism* with questionnaire, interview, and measurements of writing quality for research procedures. The pragmatist worldview orients educational research toward teaching practice, "what works" and solutions to problems deriving from the work of Peirce, James, Mead, and Dewey (Cherryholmes, 1992; Creswell, 2003; Creswell & Plano Clark, 2007; Oxford, 2011). What has been shown to work in this study, through the data collection instruments, are strategies that help L2 legal writers know about (declarative knowledge) and produce (procedural knowledge) scholarly writing in U.S. legal academic context to make the graduate student shift from writer-centered to reader-centered writing in L2 academic English. Making this shift is necessary because of the fundamental socio-cultural expectation of U.S. legal readers that the writer is responsible for successful communication, not the reader as in many other academic cultures. The writer, therefore, has to make his/her critical thinking visible to the reader. The law professor (or reader) in U.S. legal education context wants to know what the law student (or writer) is thinking. Two common features of prose style that may contrast with writing style in other academic cultures are directness and explicitness (Oates & Enquist, 2009). These are features of plain English writing style that can be learned or refined in one semester so L2 academic writers (a) write clear sentences that can be understood the first time they are read, and (b) make a complex topic easy for the legal reader to immediately comprehend (Oates & Enquist, 2009).

Because it is a challenge for international graduate students to show analytical thinking in L2 academic English writing when the writer comes from a culture with different assumptions about readers and purposes for writing, this mixed design claims knowledge through an *advocacy/ participatory approach* in the tradition of Brazilian lawyer and language teacher, Paulo Freire (1921-1997). A most important and influential writer on the theory and practice of critical education in the twentieth century, Freire remains extremely influential today. He advocated collaboration, empowerment, and voice for participants (Creswell, 2003). Emancipatory education for Freire was not simply transmitting knowledge, as in a U.S. law school lecture or PowerPoint presentation, and knowing was not simply accumulating facts or information or "what he called 'banking'. Rather, knowing is constructing oneself as a subject in the world, one who is able both to rewrite what one reads and to act in the world to radically alter it" (Apple, Ganddin & Hypolito, 2001, p. 130). Freire's idea of knowing pertains not only to the graduate student writers participating in this study but also to visiting scholars who cross languages and cultures when researching, writing, and working for change in their home countries using L2 academic English. Freire's idea of knowing pertains to transformation (personal growth) in education where the goal of the learner is to develop ability to accomplish tasks through a learner-centered syllabus and self-assessment (Leaver & Shekhtman, 2002). An outcome is self-regulation (control) in L2 writing. Key features of the Freirean approach for adult literacy are dialogue and problem-solving, both of which were part of this design.

4.5.2 How the design operates

Figure 4.1 below shows how the design operates. In Figure 4.1, the purpose of Stage 1 (pre-writing) is "researching to learn"; Stage 2 (drafting) is "writing to learn"; and Stage 3 (revising) is "writing to communicate."

Stages 1, 2, and 3 writing
All participants in this study self-report on the following: pre-writing (stage 1), drafting (stage 2), revising (stage 3.a), professional writing proficiency and formal instruction (stage 3.b). The section 3.b self-report at the end of data collection performs two functions. First, it signals the end of the intervention for graduate student writers participating in this study. Second, it explores writing strategies instruction as a variable that relates to strategic competence when it affects development of an efficient writing process and an effective writing product at advanced levels ranging from professional level writing proficiency to functionally native writing proficiency (Leaver, 2005).

Fig. 4.1. Triangulated, multi-stage design.

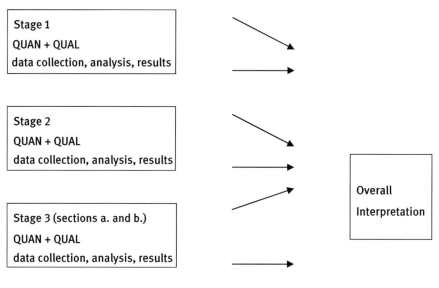

Stage 1
QUAN + QUAL
data collection, analysis, results

Stage 2
QUAN + QUAL
data collection, analysis, results

Stage 3 (sections a. and b.)
QUAN + QUAL
data collection, analysis, results

Overall
Interpretation

QUAN = quantitative
QUAL = qualitative

Stage 4 publishing

It should be noted that Stage 4 data collection was planned but did not occur in this study. It would have occurred if a student's legal research paper had been recommended for publication by the content law professor for whom the paper was written or if the student had had enough time to rewrite, revise, or summarize the research for publication before the start of the next semester. If this were to have occurred for all or most of the student participants, the study would have extended into the next semester.

4.6 Validity

Reporting on validity serves the purpose of checking the quality of the data and the results. In addition to triangulation, a number of strategies were used to determine validity for the research instruments and for the qualitative findings. Quality checks for the qualitative findings are given here, under this heading. Validity and reliability for each research instrument are given later, under Instrumentation.

First, *member checking* was used in which the researcher took preliminary findings back to student participants to check the quality of data and the rhetorical structure for presenting the data in writing so research results would be clear and meaningful. After preliminary analyses, the researcher asked student participants to reflect whether findings for the first three research questions accurately described participants' processes of scholarly legal writing and whether the researcher's interpretation of participants' language output and writing product at each stage of writing was accurate and comprehensive.

Second, the researcher *presented disconfirming evidence*: that is, a perspective from a teaching colleague contrary to the one established in recent research on multilingual writers. Reporting disconfirming evidence "confirms the accuracy of the data analysis, because in real life, we expect the evidence for themes to diverge and include more than just positive information" (Creswell & Plano Clark, 2007, p. 135). The teacher's point of view proved enriching because in education, there may a divergence between research and pedagogical perspectives. So it is important to note that in this study, writing strategies for the questionnaire were chosen from a research perspective, with implications for teaching. In other words, teaching practice did not determine which strategies would be included in the questionnaire. This makes the SCQ research-based.

Third, the researcher *asked others to examine the data* such as "peers who are familiar with qualitative research as well as the content area of the specific research" (Creswell & Plano Clark, 2007, p. 134). Oxford (2011) calls this strategy "peer debriefing." A Chinese researcher-teacher peer, concerned with teaching and learning to near-native levels of language proficiency, was asked to examine 15%–20% of the qualitative data.

Fourth, the researcher *spent prolonged time in the field*. While preparing for data collection, analyzing the data after it had been collected, and writing up the research after analyzing the data, the researcher-teacher engaged with international LL.M. students for two more writing interventions. She used the same research instruments as reflective tools for student writers and descriptive (not prescriptive) tools for the L2 writing teacher, confirming their effectiveness for teaching practice – systematically bridging gaps between second and foreign language writing production.

Fifth, the investigator engaged in *thinking theoretically* with macro and micro perspectives throughout the processes of analysis and presenting the results. She engaged in *theory development* by moving with deliberation between a micro perspective of the data and a macro conceptual/theoretical understanding when re-visiting the research through revising and rewriting. Theory development is related to *theoretical validity* (Oxford, 2011).

Sixth, the investigator considered *predictive validity*: that is, validity of a measurement tool that is established by demonstrating the ability of the measure to predict the results of an analysis of the same data made with another or measurement tool (Mosby, 2009). Research results confirm that the research tools developed for this study predict enhanced student performance in a scholarly legal paper or research article. Specifically, the questionnaire exploring strategic competence predicts communicative competence and high communicative precision in a legal research paper measured by the study's (formative) assessment tools. The study's quality assessment tools predict planning competence (stage 1 writing), genre competence (stage 2 writing), and communication competence (stage 3 writing) for the academic legal writer.

Finally, predictive validity relates to *content validity* in this study because processes of research and writing for participants were associated with legal content learning as well as with legal analysis development and communication in writing: that is, communicating legal thinking and original conclusions to a law school educated reader in L2 academic English. Student participants showed competency in their academic legal writing with respect to content knowledge and problem-solving. This competency was supported by law professors' summative assessments of participants' legal research papers. A major benefit of the writing intervention for student participants was that they got objective, systematic feedback at each stage of writing (pre-writing, drafting, and revising) which helped them develop as thinkers and as writers. "Empirical validations of self-regulated writing programs at the professional academic level are very rare" (Brendel, G., personal communication, January 20, 2014).

5 Performance Enhancing Measures

5.1 How self-report was used to collect data from student participants

Self-report is a type of verbal report for collecting data from student participants. Two types of verbal report were used as sources of data in this study: (1) the written questionnaire, and (2) the oral interview. Data obtained from the written questionnaire were uniformly organized for student participants. They lent themselves to (quantitative) statistical analysis and to (qualitative) uniform description of participants' academic writing processes, allowing for comparison. Data obtained from oral interview, used in conjunction with probes about student participant responses to the written questionnaire, provided clarification and elaboration, "allowing the researcher and learners to pursue topics of interest which may not have been foreseen when the questions were originally drawn up" (Cohen & Scott, 1996, p. 91). The written questionnaire and the oral interview dovetailed in the study so that "the researcher and the learner could generate a description of the most important aspects of the learner's strategy use" at each stage of writing. (Cohen & Scott, 1996, p. 92).

There are limitations as well as advantages to self-report. First, the small *sample size* constitutes a limitation because six (N = 6) is a small number for quantitative analysis in mixed methods research and does not allow for generalizations for the field. Quantitative analysis in this study facilitated a composite profile of student participants' language use after explicit writing strategies instruction, with implications for what worked in the academic legal writing intervention. Second, any type of *self-report* is subject to the limitations of the individual reporting even if, as in this study, (a) the complexity of the research writing task is broken down into stages; and (b) the questionnaire is filled out immediately after each stage of writing so that respondents do not have to rely solely on information stored in memory to respond to the questionnaire items. Self-report in this study works because each of the graduate student participants gained enough self-awareness and language awareness from the writing intervention to be able to engage critically and metalinguistically. Third, the use of an *actual-task questionnaire* constitutes a limitation in the sense that the writing task was not standardized. Participants wrote research papers for different law school professors, as graduate students typically do, so research results cannot be compared to other studies (Oxford, 2008; Chamot, 2004). Only the questionnaire was standardized so that every respondent got the same set of questions in the same order at roughly the same time during the writing process (pre-writing, drafting, and revising).

Even with these limitations, self-report measures may still be "the most viable" means for obtaining empirical evidence as to strategy use, according to Cohen and Scott (1996, p. 95). This is because self-report allows for detailed description of what learners do for increased understanding of language learning and language use (Cohen & Scott, 1996) – useful for pedagogical purposes. Research suggests that self-report and protocol analysis can be advantageous in a well-planned research design by (a) revealing in detail information attended to while performing tasks, (b) eliciting information about conscious processing associated with the writing process, and (c) acting as a measure for predicting behavior (Cohen & Scott, 1996). Self-report provides mentalistic data regarding cognitive processing that contrasts with naturalistic observation used by psychologists and other social scientists that involves observing subjects in their natural environment (Cherry, 2010). While classroom observation may produce "indications or clues as to the strategies learners use," self-report is the method that provides instances of actual strategy use (Cohen & Scott, 1996, p. 95).

5.2 Instrumentation validity and reliability

Four research tools designed to enhance student performance were used to collect the data from the student participants. The research instruments included the SCQ questionnaire, the interview, and student/teacher measurements of writing quality in the form of checklists. The SCQ was developed from the research literature to explore strategic competence as a component of communicative competence for the academic legal writers in this study. Its development is described in Chapter 3. The interview and the quality assessment checklists were used as triangulation measures, and their development is described below. Together, the four instruments collected quantitative and qualitative data for each stage of academic legal writing at multiple time points. All are named and described, with sample items listed. Information about validity and reliability is also given for each instrument:
1. Strategic Competence Questionnaire (SCQ), a primarily quantitative instrument;
2. Interview Protocol (IP), a qualitative instrument used with the SCQ to stimulate recall;
3. Student's Quality Assessment Tool (SQAT), a quantitative instrument; and
4. Teacher's Quality Assessment Tool (TQAT), a quantitative instrument.

5.2.1 Description of the Strategic Competence Questionnaire (SCQ)

This survey instrument is a structured, task-oriented, 38-item questionnaire, also known as *actual-task strategy assessment* (Oxford, 2011). The questionnaire presents a range of strategic choices for analytical and persuasive (expository) writing from legal sources within general normative (naive-English speaker) constraints of university students writing research papers for law school courses. The SCQ was implemented in three separate stages (pre-writing, drafting, revising) to collect data from each participant during actual processes of writing a legal research paper. The fourth (publishing) stage was not implemented in this study due to the time constraints of the winter semester which was very short. Interested graduate students are likely to have more time to submit to law journals after the spring semester, in the summer months.

The SCQ investigates the use of writing strategies, CALP skills, levels of writing purpose, languages used for writing, and writing strategies instruction as factors or variables affecting strategic competence. In the SCQ, these are nominal categories that interrelate or shift partnerships, developing learner competency (proficiency) across stages in the genre of scholarly (academic) legal writing. The categories and the rationale for item selection are given below.

Rationale for item selection

After a thorough review of the L1 and L2 writing research literature, the researcher used the two previously mentioned questionnaires as basis for her written questionnaire: (a) the Jasser, Khanj, Leaver (2001) 25-item learner/user questionnaire for acquiring advanced professional proficiency in L2 English writing, and (b) Fox's (1989) 47-item Inventory of Writing Strategies which identifies strategies used by L1 experts in the recursive writing process. The rationale was to create a self-report instrument that could advance literacy and language use with expert strategies for professional level writing proficiency in an academic paper or journal article. With permission, the researcher used relevant items from the base questionnaires and synthesized them with items from two more in-class questionnaires (previously described). Items selection was filtered through the researcher's teaching experience with both L1 and L2 English writers in her academic legal writing classes, most of whom were international students.

The process of synthesis included removing any redundant or poorly-written items and adding five categories of items from both the empirical research and pedagogical literature: (a) legal reading strategies for writing from expert legal sources (Oates, 1997; Bain Butler, 2004); (b) language re-use as an L2 writing strategy from Hu (2001), (c) 14 transforming (discourse synthesis) strategies based on

Segev-Miller (2004); (d) 4 iterative language processing skills based on Spatt (1999), and (e) 18 grammar strategies based on Oates and Enquist (2005). In sum, the researcher selected items relating to strategic competence and professional (or higher) writing proficiency useful for teaching graduate student writers learning about scholarly legal writing, not just as a genre but as a translingual/transcultural way of working with text when writing from sources.

Competence-related constructs

Competence-related constructs underlying the SCQ include the following: (a) the writing process as stages for development in scholarly legal writing, (b) legal domain and writing knowledge necessary for scholarly legal writing, (c) multiple language use for scholarly legal writing, (d) L1 academic writing proficiency, (e) L1 academic legal culture, (f) research writer interest, (g) purpose and levels for composing an L2 English research paper, (h) writing strategies for knowledge telling and knowledge transforming, (i) discrete language abilities that define professional (and higher) level writing proficiency, (j) learner response to writing strategies instruction, and (k) learner response to different kinds of feedback for scholarly legal writing. An interactive, developmental view helps to understand scholarly legal writing as a dynamic or changing construct in relation to students' learning and development in social-cultural, disciplinary context.

From a mixed methods standpoint, the SCQ is a numerical questionnaire with two open-ended questions at the end of each stage of the questionnaire (prewriting, drafting, and revising) to get an accurate understanding of what respondents wanted to say about variables affecting their strategic and communicative competence (Nunan, 1992). The content of the SCQ is summarized in Table 5.1 and explained narratively, stage by stage, before the table.

Stage 1. *Pre-Writing* in the SCQ

At this stage, the SCQ contains nine items organized into six sections: *Reading to Write Strategies* with three sub-types: conceptual, rhetorical, linguistic; *Reading to Learn* (CALP) skills that may be used strategically when preparing to write from L1 or L2 legal sources: paraphrase, summary, synthesis, and analysis; *Developing Proficiency* through other legal writing activities; *Language, Composition, and Knowledge* areas of concern before scholarly research writing; *Use of Language* other than English for pre-writing; and two open-ended questions that ask about developing as a legal writer, linguistically and culturally: that is, how writing strategies help develop linguistic proficiency, and how this pre-writing stage may be different from participant's L1 academic, linguistic, and cultural experience. In sum, the SCQ (stage 1) asks student participants to identify statements that best describe them while they were preparing to write the first draft of their major legal research paper at the time of the study.

Some examples of items are: (*item 1*) I used these legal reading strategies to find a topic, thesis, or claim for my major analytical research paper; (*item 3*) I used these cognitive academic language skills to prepare to write the first draft of my major analytical research paper; and (*item 4*) I used these legal writing activities to develop my ability to write an analytical research paper.

Stage 2. *Drafting* in the SCQ

At this stage, the SCQ contains six items organized into five sections: *Drafting Strategies*; *Writing to Learn* CALP skills that may be used strategically to draft from L1 or L2 legal sources; *Purpose and Levels of Composing* for this stage: that is, knowledge-telling (simply stating knowledge) and/or knowledge transforming (deepening level of understanding to include analysis, synthesis, evaluation of research); *Use of Language* other than English for drafting; and *Developing as a Legal Writer*, linguistically and culturally. In sum, the SCQ (stage 2) asks student participants to identify statements that best describe them while drafting their major analytical legal research paper at the time of the study.

Examples of items are: (*item 1*) I used these strategies for getting words and concepts down effectively on paper while drafting my major analytical paper; (*item 2*) I used these cognitive academic language skills for effectively drafting my major analytical paper; (*item 3*) I used these broad levels of writing purpose for effectively drafting my major analytical paper.

Stage 3. *Revising* in the SCQ

Section 3.a. To end the process of writing the scholarly research paper, the first section of the SCQ for stage 3 contains 12 items organized into eight sections: *Revising Strategies*; *Editing Strategies*; *Grammar Strategies*; *Writing to Communicate* CALP skills that may be used strategically to write analytically from L1 or L2 legal sources; *Purpose and Levels of Composing* (as in stage 2); *Knowledge Transforming* strategies that deepen "level of understanding to include analysis, synthesis, evaluation of research"; *Use of Language* other than English for revising; and *Developing as a Legal Writer*. In sum, the SCQ (3.a) asks student participants to identify statements that best describe them while they were revising their major analytical legal research paper at the time of the study.

Section 3.b. The second section of the SCQ for stage 3 contains five items organized into two sections that signal the end of the scholarly writing intervention and data collection for the participants in the study. The sections contain (a) a checklist defining abilities for three levels of professional proficiency in writing, and (b) some closed-ended questions about writing strategies instruction as a tool or learner support for developing an efficient writing process and an effective writing product. In sum, student participants were asked to identify everything they "can do now in legal (expository) writing" after revising their major analytical legal research paper at the time of the study.

Examples of quantitative checklist items defining abilities are: (*item 1* for *General Professional Proficiency*) I can write without the kind of errors that may interfere with reader comprehension; (*item 1* for *Advanced Professional Proficiency*) I can use English to write accurately in both formal and informal styles pertinent to my professional school needs; (*item 1* for *Functionally Native Proficiency*) I can write and edit both formal and informal professional correspondence. Examples of quantitative closed-ended questions about writing strategies instruction as a tool or learner support are: (*item 2*) Check how important direct (explicit) writing strategies instruction was for you to develop an efficient writing process (all stages); and (*item 4*) Check how important direct (explicit) writing feedback was for you as a second language (L2) legal writer to complete your research paper (all that apply). To conclude, SCQ 3.b informs interpretation of the data at each stage and overall, with items that describe how student participants had been developing as scholarly legal writers throughout interactive processes of scholarly legal writing.

Stage 4. *Publishing* in the SCQ

At this stage, not implemented in this study, the SCQ contains six items organized into five sections: *Publishing Strategies*; *Writing to Communicate* CALP skills; (3) *Purpose and Levels of Composing*; *Use of Language* other than English in this stage; and *Developing as a Legal Writer* in this stage. The SCQ (stage 4) asks student participants to identify statements that best describe them while preparing to publish their research paper in English. Examples of items are: (*item 1*) I asked myself if I could make the revisions my professor suggested; (*item 2*) I used these cognitive academic language skills for preparing to publish my major analytical paper (*item 4*) I used a language other than English in this (publishing) stage for rewriting my paper.

Table 5.1. SCQ description (x38 questions total).

Pre-Writing (x9 questions)	Drafting (x6 questions)	Revising (x12 quest.) Proficiency and Instruction (x5 quest.)	Rewriting to publish (x6 quest.)
Stage 1	Stage 2	Stage 3 (sections a. b.)	Stage 4 (tentative)
Reading to write strategies	Drafting strategies	Revising strategies Editing strategies Grammar strategies	Publishing strategies
Reading to learn:	Writing to learn:	Writing to communicate:	Writing to communicate:
CALP skills used	CALP skills used	CALP skills used	CALP skills used
Developing proficiency Areas of concern: (a) language/ composition (b) knowledge	Levels of composing	Levels of composing Knowledge transforming	Levels of composing
Languages used	Languages used	Languages used	Languages used
Developing competency	Developing competency	Developing competency 3.b Checklist defining abilities; Value of strategies instruction	Developing competency

Summary of stages for writing in the SCQ
In sum, the four stages of writing in the SCQ examined: (a) writing strategies, (b) CALP skills that may be used strategically for analytical or persuasive writing from L1 or L2 legal sources, (c) levels of composing and writing purpose, and (d) languages used by participants for writing and developing competency at the different stages of the (recursive) research writing process: the Pre-writing "researching to learn" stage; the Drafting "writing to learn" stage; the Revising "writing to communicate" stage; and the Publishing "rewriting to publish" stage, if that were to have occurred at the time of the study.

Related to these four stages in the writing process, SCQ section 3.b examined (a) learner abilities and levels of proficiency in expository legal writing, and (b) strategies instruction as a tool or support for learner development at each stage and level of legal writing. SCQ 4 has been described as "tentative" in the table to show that all student participants had the opportunity to rewrite and submit their paper for publication in a law school journal in the (very short) winter semester but did not take advantage of this opportunity at the time of the study.

Triangulation

Triangulation was used as a major form of instrument validation. For triangulation, results from certain instruments were compared with results from other instruments in specific ways. This means that for the questionnaire, results from each stage of the SCQ were compared with results from the qualitative interview (IP) and then merged into an interpretation for each stage in the research writing *process*. These research results were then compared with results from the SQAT and TQAT that evaluate participants' writing *product* and then merged into one overall interpretation that addresses the study's research purpose of disclosing the dynamic or changing nature of factors that influence strategic competence at the level of professional writing proficiency for the scholarly L2 legal writers in the study.

Field test

The original, comprehensive, post-instruction version of the questionnaire was revised after being field tested before data collection. Six L2 graduate student writers and three teaching colleagues were purposively selected. One former student and one teaching colleague had professional experience working with international lawyers who were using English as the legal *lingua franca*. Two former students and two teaching colleagues were from the same professional school program where the study took place. One graduate student writer was a native Spanish-speaker who performed a "thinkaloud interview" (Sudnam, Bradburn & Schwartz, 1996), and one peer reviewer was a Ph.D. candidate in applied linguistics at the time of the study. Their experience and feedback ranged from (a) novice to expert, (b) native to non-native English, and (c) generic to genre specific literacy in academic writing.

The twofold purpose of the field test was to (a) determine the length of time respondents needed to complete the questionnaire, and (b) ensure all respondents would be answering the same question (reliability). Field test results initially showed a range of time, from 45 minutes to three hours (that is, for one novice student writer with the lowest proficiency who had to use a dictionary to look up some unfamiliar words). Average response time was 1.38 hours ($N = 4$). The questionnaire was subsequently revised so it could be administered in stages to reduce average response time. To ensure reliability, respondents (N = 6) were asked to identify questions with which they had difficulty responding on the questionnaire. Feedback from respondents was generally positive, but the field test determined that some changes had to be made.

Changes based on the field test included the following to ensure that everyone would be answering the same question. First, professional terms were either omitted or defined. Second, definitions were used on the questionnaire for each stage of writing. Third, more examples of concepts or terms were included. Fourth, the mixture of response scales was reduced so that there were more closed-ended checklist items and fewer open-ended items.

Additional changes were made as well. Upon recommendation from expert reviewers, the length and scope of the questionnaire were further reduced to address the issue of respondent fatigue. This means that student participants could now fill out the SCQ in three stages corresponding to the writing process (prewriting, drafting, and revising). Additionally, the questionnaire was modified so that incoming, first-semester students learning about scholarly legal writing for the first time could be included in the study. Questions pertaining to conceptual and rhetorical transformation strategies were therefore omitted in the SCQ to accommodate these un-acculturated student participants who had not been exposed to writing L2 legal research papers and who had not completed the academic legal writing course. Recalling positive research findings in the Segev-Miller (2004) study, the questionnaire was revised to disclose how student participants could linguistically transform information to avoid (a) relying on the language of the source text, or (b) plagiarizing in their academic writing. The end result was a revised instrument that had a narrowed focus on factors for strategic competence and that could be implemented in stages for real-time measurement in temporal sequence for students learning how to write as scholars for the first time. See Appendix D for the SCQ (4 stages).

Validity of the SCQ

The process for validating the SCQ was similar to the process Fox (1989) undertook to validate her Inventory of Writing Strategies. She elicited strategies directly from teachers and graduate student teaching assistants who were considered expert writers to create a checklist. Then she used a 'members check' with the same group to validate it (Lincoln & Guba, 1985; 1989). After that, she used it with other disciplinary groups, adding and revising some of the strategies for clarity. In contrast to Fox's reliance on L1 expert strategies for validating her inventory, however, the strategies for this study originated with the L1 and L2 writing research, filtered through L2 writer feedback in the academic legal writing course (approximately 5 years).

After the checklist for the SCQ was developed from these different sources, the researcher used expert review of criteria from member checks that included the following: (a) two former academic legal writing students; (b) one legal English teacher who was an expert writer herself; (c) one qualified legal English specialist (J.D./M.A. TESOL); (d) three different L2 expository writers at the level of professional (or higher) writing proficiency; and (d) one language learning strategies expert to validate it. With Dr. Rebecca Oxford's expert feedback, the SCQ quantitative checklist of strategies for each stage of scholarly legal writing was revised for accuracy, clarity, and concision.

In sum, every quantitative item in the SCQ was validated by (a) adequate representation of relevant types of strategies based on primary sources (content validity); (b) expert-judgment on this theoretical construct (construct validity); and (c) a "think-aloud interview" (Sudnam, Bradburn & Schwartz, 1996) with one other field test participant: that is, a graduate student writer who worked professionally with legal English writers in an international, not-for-profit organization who was able to give immediate, reflective feedback on each SCQ item (response validity).

For the open-ended questions on the SCQ, validity was similarly established through expert member-checking and triangulating the data. No disconfirming evidence was reported, although the researcher's teaching peer did challenge the notion of annotating in a language other than English for stage 1, pre-writing. Because this strategy came from recent L2 writing Ph.D. dissertation research, it could not be omitted. Support for this strategy also came from the field test where a Korean student writer reported that she annotated in her first academic language because annotation with Korean characters is more efficient procedurally than annotating in English, as each character represents a concept rather than a word. In sum, there was some tension between effectiveness and efficiency associated with the strategies L2 writers might use, felt not only by the teaching peer in this validity check but also by student participants in their reports later in the study. Table 5.2 on page 58 presents the validity checks summary.

Reliability of the SCQ

Reliability of the SCQ was determined by ensuring consistency of responses for items measuring the same specific construct within categories of the instrument: that is, the actual use (or non-use) of strategies and CALP skills having to do with summary, paraphrase, and synthesis for each stage of writing (pre-writing, drafting, and revising). See Table 5.3 on page 58 for the reliability checks summary.

Table 5.2. Validity checks summary: SCQ quantitative data.

Content validity	Consulted with target group members and two groups of experts (legal writing/legal English teachers and a strategies expert) for relevance, coverage, representativeness, and exactness of wording.
Construct validity	Compared with theory and up-to-date empirical research literature.
Response validity	Used a "think-aloud interview" (Sudnam, Bradburn & Schwartz, 1996) with one field test participant who worked professionally with 2 legal English writers in an international organization.

Table 5.3. Reliability checks summary: SCQ quantitative data.

Test-re-test method	No. The same instrument was not given twice to the same group of people.
Adaptation of equivalent (parallel or alternate) form method	Yes, an adaptation of this reliability tool was used. Equivalent forms of the SCQ instrument were created to measure (conscious use of) writing strategies and (conscious/unconscious use of) CALP skills for each stage of scholarly writing performance. In addition, certain strategies and CALP skills having to do with summary, paraphrase, and synthesis were repeated for each stage of scholarly writing.
Internal consistency method	Cronbach's alpha, for example, was not used to measure internal consistency because it is usually used for scores that fall along a continuum like those on a Likert scale. Student participants in this study were not asked to make performance judgments, and the item formats intentionally were of three kinds.
Scorer agreement	Parallel forms of (a) formative assessments by the writing teacher-researcher, and (b) self-assessments by the student participants provided information about the students' progress, developing knowledge, understanding, skills and strategies for each stage of writing (pre-writing, drafting, revising). In addition, summative assessments were given by the content law professors who assigned grades to the student participants' legal research papers.

5.2.2 Description of the Interview Protocol (IP)

Concurrent with each stage of SCQ data collection, semi-structured interviews were conducted to probe students' responses to the closed and open-ended questions about the strategies they actually used and found to be most helpful for each stage of writing. These interviews were conducted and recorded at the end of data collection and writing intervention, after the SCQ had been completed for each student participant. The purpose of the interviews was triangulation and exploration of student perceptions, meanings, and interpretations of strategic competence variables that might relate to proficiency, competence, or expertise in scholarly legal writing *in situ* at the research site.

The Interview Protocol consisted of two questions after student participants filled out the SCQ for each stage of writing (SCQ 1, 2, and 3.a) and for ending the data collection phase for the writing intervention (SCQ 3.b). The IP data analysis process entailed the researcher listening to each recorded interview for at least 90 minutes, taking detailed notes and re-winding multiple times to comprehend learners' understanding of the strategies and skills identified most helpful for each stage of student writing.

Each stage of writing, Question 1

The first IP question asked participants to identify which strategies helped most for writing at each stage (pre-writing, drafting, and revising). SCQ sections 1, 2, and 3.a were on hand to stimulate recall and to collect quantitative data: that is, participants pointed to the most helpful strategies they actually used AND found most helpful on the SCQ, and the researcher circled each one. The researcher gave participants as much time as they needed to identify the most helpful strategies they used for writing at each stage.

Each stage of writing, Question 2

The second IP question asked participants to tell the researcher more about each strategy found most helpful for effective writing at each stage (pre-writing, drafting, and revising). The researcher probed student participants' responses to the first IP question to collect the richest possible qualitative data. Participants elaborated on each most helpful selection from the SCQ (sections 1, 2, and 3.a). Because this second IP question was guided by initial responses of the interviewees, the IP instrument is considered to be "semi-structured" (Nunan, 1992).

Ending the research/intervention, Question 1

At the end of the interview, participants were asked to review the SCQ section (3.b) on proficiency and instruction. The first IP question asked participants to review and elaborate on their perceptions of writing strategies instruction in the tape-recorded interview.

Ending the research/intervention, Question 2

The second IP question asked participants to review their proficiency checklists to elaborate how they had been building proficiency (competence, expertise) in legal writing since taking the academic legal writing course – instructional context for this study. As before, student participants pointed to specific items on the SCQ (section 3.b), and the researcher marked each one that interviewees focused on, asking questions when needed to maximize comprehension.

The reason for collecting both quantitative data and qualitative (that is, written and spoken text) data from the IP was to bring together both forms of research and to cross-validate and triangulate the results, as noted earlier. In addition to triangulation, the purpose of the IP qualitative data was to enrich and deepen the researcher-teacher's understanding of the student participants' experience with writing strategies, strategies instruction, stages of development and learning, and L2 writer performance in the genre of scholarly legal writing.

How the IP was developed

The IP was developed as a valid measure for triangulation to answer *Research Question 2*: For each stage of the scholarly L2 legal writing process, which writing strategies and CALP skills do the learners think are the most useful and why?

As mentioned above, this two-part question was addressed by participant-selected items on the SCQ and the researcher's IP probes dealing with writing strategies, CALP skills, and formal instruction – the latter considered a "critical factor" for advancing professional proficiency in writing.

Because first-semester LL.M. students who were uninitiated into American academic legal culture and writing (process) habit were included in this study, the SCQ was limited to strategies actually used with IP questions that followed, asking about specific strategies found most helpful for effective legal writing at different stages of research writing. Use of the IP with the SCQ in this way helped address two sets of issues related to L2 writers: (a) self-report issues of respondent fatigue and memory lapse, and (b) the possibility that the novice legal research writers in the study would not be able to think about or distinguish between strategies and skills used, or effectiveness, when responding to a self-report questionnaire.

As mentioned earlier, none of the first-semester LL.M. student participants in this study had been exposed to (a) formal academic writing or ESL instruction at advanced levels; (b) concepts like "legalese" and plain English that characterize style in legal writing at the level of professional proficiency; (c) techniques and strategies for achieving accuracy, brevity, and conciseness in research writing from primary and secondary legal sources to avoid plagiarism; or (d) process writing that puts the onus for communication on the writer, not on the reader as in some other academic cultures. The IP can be found in Appendix E.

Validity and reliability of the IP

The IP is considered valid because the content for the semi-structured, tape-recorded interview was selected purposefully by each student participant who identified specific writing strategies on the SCQ that were most helpful among those actually used in each stage of writing a scholarly legal research paper.

Reliability of interview data is inter-coder, with (a) a peer-reviewer participating in the coding and interpretation of a randomly selected 10–15% of the IP data, and (b) the researcher comparing her IP codings and interpretation with the peer-reviewer's IP codings and interpretation. See Table 5.4 on page 62 for verification strategies ensuring reliability and validity of the IP.

According to Morse, Barrett, Mayan, Olson, and Spiers (2002), all of these verification strategies incrementally and interactively contribute to and build reliability and validity in the study, thus ensuring rigor. "The rigor of qualitative inquiry should thus be beyond question, beyond challenge, and provide pragmatic scientific evidence that must be integrated into our developing knowledge base" (Morse et al., 2002).

5.2.3 Description of the task-based Student's Quality Assessment Tool (SQAT)

The SQAT is one of two sets of performance indicators to show where improvement is needed at each stage of writing. It is a structured, formative assessment instrument. From a student's perspective, the SQAT facilitates self-assessment for self-regulating scholarly legal writing in stages.

Stage 1 in the writing process in the SQAT

This STUDENT'S QUALITY ASSESSMENT TOOL (SQAT) is a pre-drafting checklist of 17 items for students. Each participant checks what has been done to date to prepare for writing the first draft in L2 English. Examples are:

____15. I have organized my legal research into a working outline.
____16. I have decided on my approach (e.g., descriptive, analytical, comparative, critical)
____17. I feel prepared to write draft #1 (that is, to synthesize and integrate my legal sources into an essay format for a "paper").

Table 5.4. Verification strategies ensuring both reliability and validity of the IP qualitative data (Morse, Barrett, Mayan, Olson, and Spiers, 2002).

Ensuring methodological coherence	Yes. The questions match the method which matches the data and the analytic procedures. The questions were revised and the method modified as the study progressed to reflect stages associated with L2 process and recursiveness in writing from linguistics-based writing research literature. Sampling plans were extended at the proposal stage to include non-acculturated student participants.
Sampling sufficiency related to SCQ categories and interview themes	Yes. Two levels of student participants, those who had exposure to a scholarly legal writing intervention at the beginning and at the ending of their LL.M. program, best represent and have knowledge of the research topic to ensure efficient and effective saturation of the SCQ categories. The sample of writers was of sufficient quantity and quality to investigate the SCQ categories, and there was enough SCQ data from the writing research literature and time spent in the field to explore the construct of strategic competence and sub-constructs. A (negative case) J.D. student participant also ensures validity by indicating aspects of the developing thematic analysis (e.g., motivation) that were initially less than obvious.
Developing a dynamic relationship among sampling, data collection, and analysis	Collecting and analyzing the quantitative data for each student participant was done concurrently with collecting and analyzing the qualitative data for each student participant at each stage. The multi-stage design provided not just triangulation but an iterative interaction between data and analysis, the essence of attaining reliability and validity (Morse et al., 2002). Further, the researcher's maco-experience writing the results and then revising them provided an iterative interaction among data, analysis, and theory in terms of association, reflection, and short-term working memory.
Thinking theoretically	Yes. Thinking theoretically required macro and micro perspectives, inching forward without making cognitive leaps, constantly checking and rechecking, and building a solid theoretical foundation.
Theory development	Yes. The researcher moved with deliberation between a micro perspective of the data and a macro conceptual/theoretical understanding when revising multiple times. In this way, theory was developed through two mechanisms: (a) as an outcome of the research writing process, in addition to being adopted as a framework to move the analysis along; and (b) as a template for comparison and further development.

Stage 2 in the writing process in the SQAT

This STUDENT'S QUALITY ASSESSMENT TOOL (SQAT) is a checklist of 17 items that guide the student from outlining to drafting the research paper or law review article. It shows the rhetorical structure of a scholarly legal paper, what the student needs to have in each part, and what parts to write first if the student has a problem in the drafting stage. Examples are: *Analytical Discussion: (This section gives your original analysis of the subject matter; may consist of both a critique of existing approaches and a proposed solution. Re-introduces thesis or focus; provides brief background summary; provides analysis with support in each paragraph, for each issue, in each sub-section.)*

Large-scale organization
___ A. I have discussed the major issues.
___ B. I have separated issues and sub-issues (with Headings and Sub-headings).
___ C. I have ordered issues logically (e.g. A-1, A-2/ B-1, B-2, B-3/ C-1, C-2).

Small-scale organization
___ 1. I have introduced and concluded on each issue.
___ 2. I have presented my argument and rebutted opposing arguments.
___ 3. I have very clear organizational paradigms (patterns) where appropriate (e.g., problem-solution, cause and effect, comparative pattern.)

Stage 3 Section a in the writing process in the SQAT

This STUDENT'S QUALITY ASSESSMENT TOOL (SQAT) is a checklist of 28 items (based on Ramsfield, 2005) that prepares the student to end the revising process and submit what is expected as finished product for law professor evaluation and course credit. Examples are:

Purpose

Is your overall purpose evident throughout the paper?   ___
Does it relate directly to a precise and explicit thesis statement or claim?   ___
Is your paper original, analytical, and creative–not just descriptive?   ___

Stage 3 Section b in the writing process in the SQAT

This STUDENT'S QUALITY ASSESSMENT TOOL (SQAT) is the student's self-report on legal writing proficiency and writing instruction. It asks students specifically how they may have improved expository writing proficiency during the course of the semester. Examples related to General Professional Proficiency (Level 3) are:

- *I can control structure, spelling, and general vocabulary to convey my message accurately, clearly, and concisely (even if my style may be obviously foreign).* _____
- *I can write without the kind of errors that may interfere with reader comprehension.* _____
- *I can generally control my punctuation in legal writing.* _____

Stage 4 in the Writing Process in the SQAT
This STUDENT'S QUALITY ASSESSMENT TOOL (SQAT) is a checklist of characteristics that make a scholarly legal paper publishable. Students are given the 10 item checklist as criteria for assessing (a) whether their scholarly second language (L2) legal writing publishable, and (b) where they may need to revise. Examples are:

My paper is	Yes	No	Somewhat
Correct in wording			
Clear			
Readable			

How the SQAT was developed
The SQAT developed primarily from U.S. legal research and writing secondary sources: that is, key authors and foundational texts for teaching American graduate students. This pedagogical literature provided the best self-guided questions and explicit evaluation criteria for student participants to be able to internalize a process approach to academic legal writing that included conscious use of literacy strategies. The researcher adapted, created, or selected key points and checklists from this literature and, with permission, filtered them through her teaching experience to create SQAT checklists for product quality that corresponded to the scholarly writing process. The reasoning behind selection was for the student writer participants to learn from the process of completing the legal research writing task in stages for self-regulation (control) in future scholarly/academic writing. See Appendix F for the checklist (4 stages).

Validity and reliability of the SQAT

For SQAT *criterion-related validity*, student self-ratings of writing quality were compared to separate teacher-researcher quality ratings at each stage. Written language output for the three stages took the form of (1) a substantive outline with a working bibliography, (2) a best draft, and (3) at least one final revision. A student/teacher comparison of quality rating would have occurred for stage 4 if student participants were to have published during the winter semester.

Both the SQAT and the TQAT quality rating scales have *construct validity* because they correlate well with the strategy use questionnaire for effective writing produced at each stage. They represent the quality standards found in the most scholarly academic legal writing sources for *content validity*: that is, they represent appropriate measures of standards for the scholarly legal writing genre in each stage of the writing process, as well as for the finished product.

Reliability for both these rating scales comes through parallel (equivalent) forms of reliability: that is, two equivalent forms of the same instrument – one for the teacher and one for the student – at each stage. Tables 5.5 and 5.6 below provide a summary of the validity and reliability checks.

Table 5.5. Validity checks summary: SQAT/TQAT quantitative data.

Content validity	Consulted with teachers, target group members, L2 writing research and legal writing texts for relevance, coverage, representativeness, and exactness of wording.
Construct validity	Compared with secondary source pedagogical literature (e.g., checklist for revising).

Table 5.6. Reliability checks summary: SQAT/TQAT quantitative data.

Equivalent (parallel or alternate) form method	Yes. Two versions of the same instrument were created; the SQAT and TQAT were assumed to measure genre literacy and product quality at each stage of scholarly writing. Both instruments were completed in the same time period.
Scorer agreement	Formative assessments at each stage of scholarly legal writing (prewriting, drafting, revising) were made by the student participants and by the teacher-researcher; summative assessments of the final product were made by the students' respective law professors.

5.2.4 Description of the task-based Teacher's Quality Assessment Tool (TQAT)

The TQAT is the second set of performance indicators to show where improvement is needed at each stage of legal writing. Like the SQAT, it is a structured assessment instrument. The TQAT facilitates (a) teacher-researcher assessment of the scholarly writing product produced at each stage, and (b) interactive and corrective feedback, depending on the student writer's need at the time.

Stage 1 in the writing process in the TQAT

The TEACHER'S QUALITY ASSESSMENT (TQAT) is the pre-drafting external control of the 17 items for the researcher-teacher. For example, "The student has..."

_____ 7. stated a point of view or opinion on the topic; knows what (s)he wants to say about the topic; or
knows how (s)he sees or thinks about the topic.

_____ 8. identified the type of research paper (s)he wants to write (e.g., an *analytical* paper that explores or fleshes out an unresolved legal topic or a *persuasive* paper that takes a stand on a legal issue and uses evidence to back-up the student's stance).

_____ 9. formulated a working thesis.

Stage 2 in the writing process in the TQAT

The TEACHER'S QUALITY ASSESSMENT TOOL (TQAT) is the drafting external control of the 17 items for the teacher-researcher. It shows the rhetorical structure of a scholarly legal research paper and what the student needs to have in each part. It is allows for corrective feedback easily, effectively, and systematically in each part. Examples pertaining to the Introduction section of a legal research paper are:

_____ 1. Student has introduced and noted why topic is important.

_____ 2. Student has briefly summarized necessary background information.

_____ 3. Student has stated thesis: an original and supportable proposition about the subject; problem + solution; "one new point, one new insight, one new way of looking at piece of law" (R. Delgado).

_____ 4. Student has conveyed organization of the paper.

Stage 3 Section a in the writing process in the TQAT

The TEACHER'S QUALITY ASSESSMENT TOOL (TQAT) is the 28 item L2 writing teacher's external control measure, based on Ramsfield (2005) that mirrors the student's version. It allows for quick and easy feedback, systematically and comprehensively. Examples are:

B. Is the structure obvious to any reader?   _____
    – Will any reader, at any point, not understand the writer?
    – Does the Introduction present a roadmap or blueprint for the paper?
    – Is each section's relationship to the thesis statement or claim clearly reflected by its order in the organization?
    – Is the paper written in layers, using headings, footnotes, or paragraph blocks so that the reader can easily identify each part's role in the whole?

Stage 3 Section b in the Writing Process in the TQAT

The TEACHER'S QUALITY ASSESSMENT TOOL (TQAT) provides feedback on language use and performance at the end of the writing intervention. Through comparison with the SQAT, and additional background information provided by students at the beginning of instruction, the teacher-researcher can discuss how a student may have improved proficiency as a writer and understand the importance of direct (explicit) writing strategies instruction for that student. This knowledge allows for revised approaches to teaching/learning strategies for academic legal writing. Examples related to instruction are:

2. *Check* how important direct (explicit) writing strategies instruction was for you to develop an *efficient writing process (all that apply).*
____ direct instruction was important at *early* stages (e.g., pre-writing–drafting)
____ direct instruction was important at *later* stages (e.g., drafting–revising)
____ direct instruction was important at *all* stages (e.g., pre-writing, drafting, revising)

Stage 4 in the writing process in the TQAT

The TEACHER'S QUALITY ASSESSMENT TOOL (TQAT) is the researcher-teacher's 10 item checklist of identifying characteristics for a publishable scholarly legal paper or law review article. It discloses strengths and weaknesses in the re-written or condensed final product. Examples are:

Assessment criteria for scholarly second language (L2) legal writing

Student's paper is	Yes	No	Somewhat
Logical in large-scale organization—major issues, sub-issues			
Logical in small-scale organization—individual issues			
Concise—according to law journal specifications			

How the TQAT was developed

As with the SQAT, the published legal research and writing literature provided the best self-guided questions and explicit evaluation criteria for student participants to be able to internalize a process approach to scholarly L2 legal writing that included conscious use of literacy strategies. As before, the researcher adapted, created, or selected key points and checklists from this literature and, with permission, filtered them through her L2 legal teaching experience to create TQAT checklists for product quality that corresponded to the scholarly writing process. The reasoning behind selection was for student writer participants to learn from the processes of completing a legal research paper with feedback in stages for self-regulation (control) in future scholarly/academic writing. See Appendix F.

Validity and reliability of the TQAT

For TQAT *criterion-related validity*, teacher ratings of writing quality were compared to student ratings of writing quality for the writing output produced at each stage: (1) a final outline, (2) a final draft, and (3) a final revision. A quality rating would have occurred for a (stage 4) revision with expert legal feedback if that stage were to have occurred and if data collection had been implemented.

Both the TQAT and the SQAT (quality rating scales) have *construct validity* because they correlate well with the strategy use questionnaire for effective writing produced at each stage. They represent the quality standards found in leading scholarly legal writing sources for *content validity*: that is, they represent appropriate measures of standards for the scholarly legal writing genre in each stage of the writing process as well as for the finished product.

Reliability for both these rating scales is achieved through parallel (equivalent) forms of reliability: that is, two equivalent forms of the same instrument – one for the teacher and one for the student – at each stage. See below for the data collection summary (Table 5.7).

5.2.5 Data collection summary

Table 5.7. Instruments used at each stage for each student writer participant.

Stage	Strategic Competence Questionnaire (SCQ) (38 questions total)	Interview Protocol (IP) (2 questions)	Student's Quality Assessment Tool (SQAT)	Teacher's Quality Assessment Tool (TQAT)
1	*Pre-writing:* re-searching to learn strategies and language skills used (9 questions)	<u>most helpful</u> strategies for effective writing	copy for teacher	copy for student
2	*Drafting:* writing to learn strategies and language skills used (6 questions)	<u>most helpful</u> strategies for effective writing	copy for teacher	copy for student
3.a	*Revising:* writing to communicate strategies and language skills used (12 questions)	<u>most helpful</u> strategies for effective writing	copy for teacher	copy for student
3.b	*Proficiency and improvement* strategies and language skills used (5 questions)	student perceptions: i) instruc-tion.stages ii) profi-ciency.levels	copy for teacher	copy for student
4	*Publishing (ten-tative)* strategies and language skills used (8 questions)	most helpful strategies for effective writing	copy for teacher	copy for student

5.3 Data collection procedures

Data collection for this study involved three parts at each stage corresponding to the writing process: pre-writing, drafting, revising. Data was collected by the multi-stage questionnaire (SCQ), two measurements of writing quality (SQAT/TQAT) at each stage, and a recorded semi-structured interview (IP). The use of stages and concurrent protocols provided a methodology that taps directly into working memory, thus giving a more accurate picture of participants' online (strategic) processing (Manchón, Murphy & de Larios, 2005).

The first part: Strategic Competence Questionnaire (SCQ)

Students completed this questionnaire for each stage of writing (pre-writing, drafting, and revising) either at home or in the law school, at times convenient to them. This questionnaire was tailored to student participants' specific legal writing situation, asking them about writing strategies, cognitive academic language proficiency (CALP) skills, explicit strategies instruction, and legal writing proficiency. Students were told that there are no right or wrong answers to this questionnaire. Time needed for filling out each stage of the questionnaire was less than 15 minutes, although more time may have been required for the revising stage which involved two sections. Total time needed for the questionnaire overall was approximately 60 minutes.

The second part: Student's Quality Assessment Tool (SQAT)

Before or after filling out the SCQ, students self-checked their own work for each stage using the SQAT, the second instrument tailored to participants' specific legal writing situation. Average time students needed to self-check their own work using the SQAT was less than 15 minutes. Total investment of students' time to use the instruments to self-check their own work overall was less than 60 minutes.

The second part: Teacher's Quality Assessment Tool (TQAT)

The researcher-teacher also checked the quality of student work produced at each stage using the parallel version of the SQAT. This instrument was called the *Teacher's Quality Assessment Tool (TQAT)*. A copy of the TQAT, that may have included comments and corrective feedback, was returned to students by email and/or individual consultation. Electronic files have been kept.

The third part: Interview Protocol (IP)
At the time students were ready to meet the researcher-teacher for interview, after submission of their legal research paper for law course credit, students were asked two questions: (1) about the SCQ for each stage of writing, and (2) for each level of self-rated writing proficiency and writing strategies instruction. The interviews were recorded on audiotape. Total time needed for the interview part of the study was approximately 45-60 minutes. Total investment of a student's time for the entire study was approximately 180 minutes or 3 hours.

Motivation
It is important to note that motivation to participate in this study was high because student writers received a major benefit at each stage: that is, knowledge and input from (a) self-reflection strategies, (b) self-assessment tools, and (c) feedback from teacher-assessment tools at each stage of writing to improve the legal writing product, affecting students' professional school grades and career success.

Timeline for the study
Timeline for the study is shown in Table 5.8 below, followed by a Master Chart with a list of tasks and components for data collection in Table 5.9.

5.4 Data analysis procedures for mixed methods, concurrent triangulation, multi-stage design

The organizational plan for explaining the analyses was specific to each research question. Both statistical and interpretative analyses (Nunan, 1992) generated answers to the research questions (Maxwell, 2005). Quantitative data analysis includes descriptive statistics for nominal data (frequencies, percentages, and modes), with descriptive analyses conducted using SPSS 12.0 software, Version 12, to show patterns for each stage of writing. Qualitative data analysis includes rich description and thematic "key word" (Nunan, 1992) text analysis of data using a modified grounded theory approach (Oxford, 2011). The next section explains the quantitative and qualitative data analysis in detail for each research question.

Table 5.8. Data collection: Timeline, stages, instruments.

Timeline	Instruments	questionnaire	interview probe	quality check	quality check	quality check
Month	Stage: number name purpose	SCQ Graduate students self-report on strategies/skills used 1. Yes 2. No 3. Don't know	IP Researcher- L2 writing teacher probes most helpful strategies through interview	SQAT Graduate students rate quality of product produced at each stage	TQAT Researcher-L2 writing teacher rates quality of product and gives feedback at each stage	Law professor rates quality of final product and may recommend publication
Nov.–Dec.	1. Pre-writing: planning and researching to learn	yes	yes	yes	yes	n/a
Nov.–Dec.	2. Drafting: writing to learn with footnotes	yes	yes	yes	yes	n/a
Dec.	3.a Revising: writing to communicate with revisions	yes	yes	yes	yes	yes
Dec.	3.b End of semester self-ratings for writing proficiency/improvement	yes	yes	yes	yes	n/a
Feb.	4. Rewriting for (international) publication	tentative for winter semester	tentative for winter semester	tentative for winter semester	tentative for winter semester	tentative for winter semester

Table 5.9. Master Chart with list of tasks and components for data collection.

Stage	What student does for the writing intervention	What student does for the research study	What researcher does with student writer participants
1	limits topic; decides on purpose; describes approach; formulates thesis; presents to class; prepares outline with bibliography; meets with L2 writing and law professors; sets deadlines (*Student Deadline Checklist*)	1. completes SCQ 2. completes SQAT 3. consults L2 writing teacher-researcher for individual consultation 4. consults *Student Deadline Checklist* with researcher-teacher for next stage	1. gives *Student Deadline Checklist* 2. gives *Student's Consent* forms x2 3. gives/emails SCQ/SQAT 4. implements SQAT 5. probes SQAT and records IP 6. applies TQAT to student's work product (e.g., best outline) 7. gives interactive + corrective feedback as requested
2	drafts (writing to learn) with footnotes	1. completes SCQ 2. completes SQAT 3. consults L2 writing teacher-researcher for individual consultation 4. consults *Student Deadline Checklist* with researcher-teacher for next stage	1. gives/emails SCQ/ SQAT 2. implements SQAT 3. probes SQAT + records IP 4. applies TQAT to student's work product (e.g., best draft) 5. gives interactive + corrective feedback as requested
3.a	revises (writing to communicate) and submits for law course credit	1. completes SCQ 2. completes SQAT 3. consults teacher-researcher for individual consultation and interview	1. gives/emails SCQ/SQAT 2. implements SQAT 3. probes SQAT + records IP 4. applies TQAT to student's work product (e.g., best revision) 5. gives interactive + corrective feedback as requested
3.b	ends the writing intervention	1. completes SCQ 2. completes SQAT 3. reports final grade with law professor's comments, if any, to the researcher	1. gives/emails SCQ/SQAT 2. implements SQAT 3. probes SQAT + records IP 4. applies TQAT to student's work product (e.g., best revision) 5. gives interactive + corrective feedback as requested
4	rewrites for publication	1. completes SCQ 2. completes SQAT 3. consults teacher-researcher for individual consultation	1. gives/emails SCQ/ SQAT 2. implements SQAT 3. probes SQAT/ records IP 4. applies TQAT to student's work product (e.g., best revision) 5. gives interactive/corrective feedback.

Research question 1

For each stage of the scholarly L2 legal writing process, what are the learners' reported use of writing strategies and cognitive academic language proficiency (CALP) skills?

This is a quantitative research question addressed by specific questions in the Strategic Competence Questionnaire (SCQ). As a quantitative instrument, the SCQ was used to find learners' reported use of literacy strategies and language (CALP) skills for each stage of the scholarly legal writing process across (a) individual learners, and (b) all learners. Additional SCQ (closed and open-ended) items for each stage provide context for overall interpretation because "human judgment is always context-dependent in surveys as in daily life" (Sudman, Bradburn, & Schwarz, 1996, p. 257). Further, "combining the answers to several questions often is an effective way to increase the validity of measurement" (Fowler, 1995, p. 77).

The basic procedures for quantitative data analysis involve descriptive statistics for the SCQ strategies and CALP skills used in each stage of scholarly legal writing. This quantitative data was interpreted in light of other SCQ quantitative and IP qualitative data that disclosed strategic competence variables that may overlap at any given stage in the recursive processes of scholarly writing. Table 5.10 below shows SCQ constructs for data analysis in each stage of writing to answer *Research Question 1*.

Descriptive numeric analyses were conducted on the items in the underlined categories to obtain frequencies, percentages, modes and ranges. Participants' use of writing strategies and language skills were identified for each stage of writing and compared, with research results presented in tables.

It should be noted that a nominal scale of measurement was purposefully selected for the SCQ categories and items. The researcher elected to measure behavior (that is, the strategies and skills actually used by learners) through *yes/no/don't know* responses to questions rather than ask students culturally distanced from U.S. notions of writing process to make judgments on frequency with a continuous *Likert* scale, for example.

Research question 2

For each stage of the scholarly L2 legal writing process, which writing strategies and CALP skills do the learners think are the most useful and why?

This is a qualitative and quantitative research question based on the SCQ. The Interview Protocol (IP) was used to explore learners' qualitative perspectives on the strategies they found most helpful for effective writing at each stage that included student perspectives on strategies instruction. Overall, the questions on

Table 5.10. SCQ quantitative data analyses, Research Question 1.

Research question #1	Pre-Writing	Drafting	Revising	Publishing (tentative)
(a) writing/literacy strategies used	Reading to write strategies	Drafting strategies	Revising strategies Editing strategies Grammar strategies	Publishing strategies
(b) CALP language skills used	Reading to learn CALP skills	Writing to learn CALP skills	Writing to communicate CALP skills	Writing to communicate CALP skills
(c) Context for interpretation	Developing proficiency; Areas of concern	Composing levels	Composing levels; Knowledge transforming	Composing levels
	Language(s) used	Language(s) used	Language(s) used	Language(s) used
	Developing as a legal writer	Developing as a legal writer	Developing as a legal writer	Developing as a legal writer

the SCQ, combined with the semi-structured interview data from the IP, yielded accurate, rich description for each learner at each stage of writing.

The basic procedures for qualitative data analysis involve many phases (Marshall & Rossman, 1999). First, the most helpful SCQ strategies for effective scholarly writing were probed orally for each learner and interpreted in light of the IP data. Second, the open-ended SCQ items were considered for each learner. See Table 5.11 below.

Table 5.11. IP qualitative data analyses, Research Question 2.

Research question #2	Pre-Writing	Drafting	Revising section 3.a	section 3.b
Perspectives on the reported use of most helpful strategies and strategies instruction:	Influence of strategies	Influence of strategies	Influence of strategies for knowledge transforming	Influence of strategies instruction
(a) the writer's process (b) the writer's product	Influence of culture/ socialization	Influence of culture/ socialization	Influence of culture/ socialization	Influence of feedback in stages

Third, key words and phrases were generated and coded from the data as they occurred. Fourth, emergent understandings were tested by looking for connections with SCQ themes. Fifth, any contradictions or alternative explanations were considered and dealt with in *member checks* and *expert checks*. Sixth, the constant comparative method set forth by Strauss and Corbin (1990) was used to constantly compare found themes with the data, making adjustments in the themes as researcher understandings became more refined through analyses. Lastly, the researcher constantly integrated her understanding of the sociocultural setting to anchor the interpretations and ensure that they are meaningful as per Oxford (2011). Open-ended SCQ responses that provided context and interpretation at each stage were especially useful.

The researcher finalized the written report after determining validity using the following two measures: (a) a *peer reviewer* was asked to interpret some of the IP data, and (b) *member checks* were requested from the three (acculturated) student participants. U.S. student participant #1 (Gee), for example, ensured the researcher that she was accurately understood and represented in the final report for research questions 2 and 3. This member check helped to clarify the rhetorical structure for the written report.

Research questions 1 and 2

In sum, the first two research questions (RQ) share the same stages, strategies, and skills measured by the SCQ quantitatively (RQ 1) and qualitatively (RQ 2). Results for these two questions, therefore, can be read together to tell the story of learners as they developed their process of writing a research paper in legal academic context. The results for *Research Question 3* focus on the learners' scholarly writing product at each stage of writing.

Research question 3

For each stage of the scholarly L2 legal writing process, what are the learners' and teacher quality ratings of the learners' scholarly L2 writing product?

This question was addressed by the Student's Quality Assessment Tool (SQAT) and the Teacher's Quality Assessment Tool (TQAT). It is a quantitative research question that uses the SQAT and TQAT as checklists to systematically compare the learners' and the teacher's quality ratings of the learners' scholarly legal writing product for each stage of writing. See Table 5.12 below.

Table 5.12. SQAT/TQAT quantitative data analyses, Research Question 3.

Research question #4	Pre.Writing x17items	Drafting x4 parts	Revising x6 parts	Publishing x10.criteria
Learners' and teacher quality ratings of the learners' scholarly legal writing product	a) checklist of what has been done to prepare for writing	a) checklist of what has been done b) in each part or section of the paper	a) checklist of what has been done b) in each part c) to see what needs to be done to demonstrate communicative competence and domain learning	checklist of genre characteristics

Descriptive, numeric analyses were conducted to see how each student rating compared to the teacher rating, by item and by category.

5.5 How the methodology relates to theory and development

The researcher moved with deliberation between (a) a micro perspective of the data describing student participants' processes of scholarly writing (RQ 1 and RQ 2) and their language output for each stage (RQ 3), and (b) a macro conceptual understanding based on three interrelating theories in education: (1) Vygotsky's (1978) dialogic model of teaching and learning in which developing writers interact with a "more competent other" at each stage of written language use (pre-writing, drafting, revising) to produce quality text; (2) Alexander's (1997, 2003) Model of Domain Learning which links knowledge, motivation, and strategies across three stages of increasing expertise to describe writer development during processes of scholarly writing; and (3) Canale and Swain's (1980) discussion of communicative competence with a focus on strategic competence for developing professional-level (or higher) writing proficiency.

By exploring participants' in-process and post-intervention understandings of their strategies, skills, self-assessments, and stages for scholarly writing, the researcher-teacher better understood how student participants used the research tools for acquisition of professional (or higher) proficiency in their legal research papers during the course of the semester (14 weeks). In addition, discerning the changing nature of factors influencing participants' strategic competence for academic writing improved practice for other student writers in the academic legal writing classroom, increasing understanding of competence for this population of student writers generally.

5.6 Summary of the methodology

It should be emphasized that, although this study used both quantitative and qualitative data analyses to answer the first three research questions, a clear distinction does not appear in the overall interpretation that focuses on interrelations (Research Question 4). The analyses and the interpretation combine both forms of data to seek convergence among the results, culminating in a description of the student participants' processes of academic legal writing and their language output (product) for each stage (pre-writing, drafting, and revising).

Table 5.13 below shows analyses across instruments for triangulation of the quantitative and qualitative data, followed by an explanation of triangulation for the study.

Table 5.13. Analyses across instruments showing triangulation for the quantitative and qualitative data.

Research Question (RQ)	Instrument 1	Instrument 2 (Triangulation)
RQ # 1: student participants' use of writing strategies and CALP skills for each stage of scholarly legal writing	SCQ categories #1 and #2 (stages 1,2,3): writing strategies and CALP skills used a) individual learners; b) across all learners	Closed QUAN and open-ended QUAL questions
RQ # 2: student participants' perspectives on influence of writing strategies and instruction for effective, self-regulated scholarly L2 legal writing	SCQ items (stages 1,2,3) Most helpful writing strategies and CALP skills: a) individual learners b) across all learners	IP (stages 1,2,3) exploring individual student participants' SCQ items used: that is, most helpful writing strategies, CALP skills, strategies instruction, and feedback
RQ # 3: student participants' and teacher quality ratings for each stage of the scholarly L2 legal writing	SQAT (stages 1,2,3) students' self-ratings of quality compared with TQAT ↑	TQAT (stages 1,2,3) teacher ratings of quality for individual student participants
Validity check		Content law professor's evaluation of students' legal research paper product
Interrelationships among (a) writing strategies and CALP skills, and (b) learners' and teacher quality ratings of learners' scholarly L2 writing product considered.	SCQ (stages 1,2,3); a) individual difference; b) stage 1 areas of concern (items #5+6)	SQAT/TQAT (stages 1,2,3) a) interpretative summary RQ #3; b) stage 3, section b proficiency, instruction, and improvement (checklist item #1 and items #2–5)
Validity check		Member Check for numeric QUAN and interpretative QUAL analyses of most helpful writing strategies and CALP skills used for each stage of participants' writing process (RQ #2 + RQ #3)

QUAN = quantitative
QUAL = qualitative

As mentioned above, the results from each stage of the SCQ were compared with results from the qualitative interview (IP) and then merged into an interpretation for each stage of writing. These research results were then compared with results from the SQAT and TQAT that evaluated student participants' writing product at each stage and then merged into an overall interpretation disclosing the dynamic, changing nature of (learner-internal and learner-external) variables influencing strategic competence for the student writer participants engaged as scholarly legal writers.

6 Variables Influencing Strategic Competence

6.1 Introduction to chapter 6, quantitative research results

This chapter begins by presenting the quantitative results from all the data collection instruments: the Strategic Competence Questionnaire, the Interview Protocol, the Student's Quality Assessment Tool and the Teacher's Quality Assessment Tool for each stage of academic legal writing. Analyses of descriptive statistics for nominal data compound for each stage of data collection (pre-writing, drafting, and revising) so that results for each research question build upon preceding ones to show interrelationships and variables influencing strategic competence at the level of professional (or higher) writing proficiency for the six students participating in the study. Quantitative results for the first three research questions are presented in turn. Qualitative results follow with a synthesis of the quantitative and qualitative results to answer the last research question.

6.2 Learners' use of strategies and skills

For each stage of the scholarly L2 legal writing process, what are the learners' reported use of writing strategies and cognitive academic language proficiency (CALP) skills?

This question is addressed by categories of items checked "yes" in the Strategic Competence Questionnaire (SCQ) having to do with: (a) literacy strategies for scholarly (academic) writing in the writing task specific to each learner, and (b) CALP language skills for scholarly (academic) writing specific to each learner.

Introduced earlier, cognitive academic language skills are formal academic language skills relevant to content domain (legal) knowledge and higher order thinking that include analyzing, paraphrasing, summarizing, and synthesizing information from primary and secondary (L2 legal) sources. These language skills are central to L2 writing performance, allowing for L2 legal language processing and control of academic English writing that avoids plagiarizing. Based on Grabe (2001) and Bereiter and Scardamalia (1987), scholarly L2 writing from sources may move the writer from knowledge telling to knowledge transforming depending on the writer's purpose, and development may involve different levels of composing at different stages. Stating knowledge in the drafting stage, for example, may be achieved with quotations or paraphrase, while transforming knowledge in the revising stage may be achieved with summary and/or synthesis.

The basic difference between (stage 2) drafting and (stage 3) revising may be "the basic [non-linear] progression from complex and lengthy, writer-centered activity to more straightforward, reader-centered activity" (Fajans & Falk, 2005, p. 11). However, revising at the level of professional proficiency and higher requires advanced techniques for presenting information to the legal reader, such as parallel structures and substantive transitions – in addition to strategies for transforming knowledge. Such techniques may need to be taught, practiced, or at least made explicit for learners to develop language awareness. Further, although paraphrase and summary may be seen as preliminary writing skills, these still may need to be taught.

In contrast to skills that are acquired or learned over time, writing strategies are actions or activities consciously chosen from language, literacy, and culture alternatives for the purpose of self-regulating writers in a specific sociocultural setting, based on Griffiths (2008) and Oxford (2011). Examples of writing strategies relating to CALP skills in this study include the following: (a) I reused self-created materials such as notes or outlines as I revised; (b) I used summary as I revised: (c) I used paraphrase as I revised; (d) I used synthesis as I revised; and (e) I revised my paper to ensure speaker to speaker (pragmatic) coherence.

Research Question 1, therefore, explores how writing strategies and CALP skills are used by student writer participants in different stages of scholarly (academic) writing: pre-writing, drafting, and revising. These strategies, skills, and stages overlap, influencing strategic competence and legal writing proficiency (competence, expertise) for student writer participants. It is important to state that a "don't know" (DK) response can be a potentially meaningful answer, not missing data, when respondents are asked for opinions or perceptions beyond their experience (Fowler, 1995). Therefore, DK responses are noted and discussed whenever relevant to the interpretation for data.

Descriptive statistics follow in the three tables below showing frequencies, percentages and modes for individual learners and across all learners for each stage of scholarly writing to answer Research Question 1. Table 6.1 below reports the academic literacy strategies for writing and the CALP skills for language processing used by participants for pre-writing (stage 1). Table 6.2 reports the same for drafting (stage 2) and Table 6.3 below reports the same for revising (stage 3), with descriptions for each.

6.2.1 Across all learners, stage 1 pre-writing

For pre-writing, the planning and "researching to learn" stage, student participants used "reading to write" literacy strategies (55.17%) more often than CALP

Table 6.1. Descriptive statistics for individual learners and across all six learners for SCQ Stage 1 Pre-writing.

Student N = 6	Pre-writing strategies for reading and researching to learn					CALP skills for language processing		
	Type 1a	Type 1b	Total	Possible strategies	%	Type 1c	Possible CALP skills	%
Gee	5	4	9	29		1	5	20
Tory	7	7	14	29		3	5	60
Ferra	12	5	17	29		2	5	40
Liv	10	6	16	29		2	5	40
Anyo	15	6	21	29		3	5	60
Sam	12	7	19	29		3	5	60
Whole group			96	174	55.17	14	30	46.6
% Difference*	in use							<9%>
Mode(s)	12	7,6				3		

*Transformation not needed for nominal data.

Note:

1 Possible strategies are all strategies listed for pre-writing (stage 1) on the SCQ: Type 1a are conceptual, rhetorical, or linguistic strategies that help find a topic, thesis, or claim; Type 1b strategies help discover what is important or true for the writer's topic, thesis, or claim.

2 Possible CALP skills are all CALP skills listed for pre-writing (stage 1) on the SCQ: Type 1c CALP skills help the writer learn by processing academic legal English source text to prepare for writing.

skills (46.6%) with a difference of 9%. Strategies in pre-writing context are defined as actions intentionally or consciously chosen by learners from among (29) alternatives in three reading to write categories (conceptual, rhetorical, and linguistic) for the purpose of preparing for research writing in L2 English from L2 legal sources. It should be noted that, by definition of the pre-writing stage, the strategies used by learners for pre-writing have more to do with the receptive language skill of reading from L2 legal sources than the productive language skill of writing from L2 legal sources. Both the strategies and CALP skills used by learners in the next stage (drafting) deal more directly with the productive language skill of writing in L2 academic legal English (Table 6.2 below).

Table 6.2. Descriptive statistics for individual learners and across all six learners for SCQ Stage 2 Drafting

Student N = 6	Drafting strategies for gettingwords and concepts on paper			CALP skills for language processing			CALP skills associated with writing purposes		
	Type 2a	Possible strategies	%	Type 2b	Possible Calp	%	Purposes	Possible levels	%
Gee	14	27		5	5		4	4	
Tory	15	27		2	5		2	4	
Ferra	17	27		2	5		2	4	
Liv	19	27		4	5		2	4	
Anyo	22	27		5	5		4	4	
Sam	21	27		5	5		2	4	
Whole group	108	162	66.67	23	30	76.67	16	25	66.67
% difference	in use					10%			
Mode(s)	n/a			5			2		

Notes:

1 Possible strategies are all strategies listed for drafting (stage 2) on the SCQ; they are Type 2a strategies that help the writer get words and concepts down effectively on paper.

2 Possible CALP skills are all CALP skills listed for drafting (stage 2) on the SCQ; they are Type 2b CALP skills that help the writer learn by processing text while drafting.

3 Purposes identify broad levels of writing purpose that vary in processing complexity (Grabe, 2001) for effective drafting by respondents on SCQ.

6.2.2 Across all learners, stage 2 drafting

For drafting, the "writing to learn" stage, student participants used CALP skills for language processing more often than writing literacy strategies with a difference of 10%. Cognitive academic language proficiency (CALP) skills in drafting context are defined as actions intentionally taken by learners for academic and legal language processing while drafting scholarly, academic, expository prose in L2 English that may be acquired, learned, or transferred from the L1: that is, paraphrase (by rephrasing source text), simple summary (by reducing source text), complex summary (by selecting and reorganizing source text), synthesis (by combining and connecting source text), and analysis (by reflecting and breaking source material down into its parts). All student writers used at least two combinations of CALP skills, and three student writers used five (mode/central tendency).

In addition to an increased use of writing strategies (66.67%) and language skills (76.67%) in this drafting stage, all student participants reported using at least two broad levels of writing purpose (66.67%). Five out of the six writers ($N = 6$) "wrote to learn, problem-solve, summarize complexly, or synthesize source text information" while drafting. The remaining writer reported a DK answer. In this case, DK is a potentially meaningful response. Broad levels of writing purpose that may vary in processing complexity are explored further in stage 3, revising. Table 6.3 below gives descriptive statistics highlighting cumulative frequencies for individual learners and across all six learners for SCQ Stage 3 Revising.

6.2.3 Across all learners, stage 3 revising

For revising, the "writing to communicate" to the law school educated reader stage, student participants used writing strategies and CALP skills with close frequency (70%). The difference in their use was less than half a percent (.49%). Along with strategies, CALP skills associated with writing purpose increased in this stage from 66.67% (drafting) to 87.50% (revising): an increase of 20.83%. In other words, five out of six student participants used CALP skills associated with four sets of basic, broad levels of writing purposes when revising: that is, they wrote (a) to state knowledge, (b) to understand, (c) to learn, and (d) to critique what others have said before them. The sixth participant, the doctoral student writing in her area of legal specialization, reported a DK answer for the other levels of composing but checked that she "wrote to critique, persuade, or interpret evidence selectively and appropriately" – a level of composing that may include an embedded hierarchy in the SCQ purpose list (above) as suggested by Grabe (2001). Even if purposes for writing cannot be seen as an increasingly complex hierarchy of composing and processing demands on performance as Grabe (2001) suggests, results across learners for stage 3 revising show that broad purposes for writing may be overlapping.

Frequencies further show that 67% of participants (that is, four out of six learners) found revising to be the stage for knowledge transforming (in contrast to knowledge-telling or stating knowledge). This means that revising strategies, editing strategies, plain English grammar strategies, and CALP skills were used together by student participants in the revising process. Four student participants reported on the SCQ (stage 3.a #6) that they deepened their "level of understanding to include analysis, synthesis, and evaluation of research" in this final stage of writing. The situation of the other two learners, Gee and Ferra, emerged through qualitative interview data and analysis presented in the qualitative results section for Research Question 2.

Table 6.3. Descriptive statistics highlighting cumulative frequencies (cf) for individual learners and across all six learners for SCQ Stage 3 Revising.

Student N = 6	Revising, editing, and plain English grammar strategies					CALP skills for language processing		CALP skills associated with writing purposes		Knowledge transforming strategies
	Type 3a	Type 3b	Type 3c	cf	Possible strategies	Type 3d	Possible CALP	Purposes	Possible levels	Type 3e (N = 6)
Gee	13	6	7	26	61	5	5	4	4	No
Tory	26	11	17	54	61	3	5	4	4	Yes
Ferra	15	10	15	40	61	2	5	1	4	DK*
Liv	20	8	9	37	61	3	5	4	4	Yes
Anyo	21	11	17	49	61	5	5	4	4	Yes
Sam	26	8	18	52	61	3	5	4	4	Yes
Total used				258	366	21	30	21	24	4 out of 6 learners
Cumulative %				70.49		70.00		87.50		66.67
Difference %	in use					<.49>				
Mode(s)	26	11,8	17	17		3		4		Yes

*Don't know (DK) response is relevant for analysis.

Note:

1 Possible strategies are all strategies listed for revising (stage 3) on the SCQ: Type 3a strategies help the writer decide what should be changed, deleted, added, or retained; Type 3b strategies help the writer edit for conventions rather than for content; and Type 3c plain English writing strategies help the writer express legal ideas in English clearly and accurately.

2 Possible CALP skills are all CALP skills listed for revising (stage 3) on the SCQ: Type 3d CALP skills help the writer learn by processing text while revising.

3 Purposes identify broad levels of writing purpose that vary in complexity (Grabe, 2001) for effective revising by respondents on the SCQ.

4 Type 3e strategies are for knowledge transforming, making revising the most effective stage (Yes, No, DK) for deepening level of understanding to include analysis, synthesis, and evaluation of legal research.

6.2.4 Across stages, individual learners

The idea of using an index to present quantitative results from the SCQ comes from Marshall (2005), *Composing Inquiry: Projects and Methods for Investigation and Writing*. The researcher gave "1" when the student checked "Yes" for using a strategy or CALP skill and "0" when the student checked "No" or "DK" for each item on the SCQ (as she did for coding the SPSS data), then developed a scale based on the total scores of individuals. For example, out of ten questions, a participant who answered "Yes" to six and "No" or "DK" to four would get a total score of "6" on the Strategies-and-Skills-Used Index (SSUI).

Table 6.4 below gives SSUI frequencies and percentages for individual learners and across all six learners for all three stages of scholarly legal writing: Prewriting, Drafting, and Revising.

Across all stages of scholarly legal writing, cumulative frequencies show that learners' reported use of strategies and skills ranged in number from 60 to 104 (out of a possible 132). Gee, the most experienced and acculturated academic English writer, scored the lowest on the Strategies-and-Skills-Used Index (45.46%). She had been living and studying in the U.S. since the age of five. Further, she was writing an atypical paper, that took the form of a proposal, for a one credit law school independent study.

At the other end of the continuum were Anyo and Sam who scored the highest (78.79% and 78.03% respectively). Both these student participants were in their first semester, and like the other unacculturated student participant (Liv), they were learning about (a) legal English, (b) instrumental legal writing (e.g., legal memos), and (c) scholarly legal writing (e.g., research papers) for the first time. In contrast to Liv, however, Anyo and Sam were male and they originated from countries culturally distanced from the U.S.: that is, Cameroon and Palestine respectfully.

The middle block of students consisted of Tory (68.18%), Ferra (61.61%), and Liv (61.36%). These three participants were female, had experience writing research papers for law school, and originated from Europe or the former USSR. All student participants, other than Gee, were writing typical analytical research papers for three credit law school courses. Figure 6.1 below illustrates the blocks of learners.

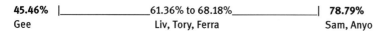

45.46% |_____61.36% to 68.18%_____| **78.79%**
Gee   Liv, Tory, Ferra   Sam, Anyo

Fig. 6.1. Blocks of learners relative to *Strategies-and-Skills-Used*.

Table 6.4. *Strategies-and-Skills-Used Index*: Frequencies and percentages for individual learners and across all six learners for all three stages of scholarly legal writing: Pre-writing, Drafting, and Revising.

Student (N = 6)	Stage 1 strategies/skills			Stage 2 strategies/skills			Stage 3 strategies/skills			All stages	Total	
	cf	Possible#	% use	cf	Possible#	% use	cf	Possible#	% use	cf	Possible#	% use
1 Gee	10	34	29.4	19	32	59.38	31	66	47	60	132	45.46
2 Tory	17	34	50	17	32	53.13	57	66	86	90	132	68.18
3 Ferra	19	34	56	19	32	59.38	42	66	64	80	132	61.61
4 Liv	18	34	53	23	32	72	40	66	61	81	132	61.36
5 Anyo	23	34	68	27	32	84.38	54	66	82	104	132	78.79
6 Sam	22	34	65	26	32	81.25	55	66	83	103	132	78.03
Cumulative "Yes"	109	204		131	192		279	396		518	792	

Individual results for each stage of scholarly writing showed that both Anyo and Sam used high percentages (% use) of legal writing strategies and CALP skills for stage 2 drafting and stage 3 revising. Their scores ranged from 81.25% (Sam) to 84.25% (Anyo). However, Sam, Ferra, and Tory's % use increased for each stage in contrast to Anyo, Liv, and Gee who showed highest % use for stage 2 drafting, the "writing to learn" stage. See Figure 6.2 below.

Pre-writing → Drafting → Revising | _____ | Drafting ← Revising
Sam, Ferra, Tory's % use   Anyo, Liv, Gee's highest % use
increased across stages   was for drafting, stage 2

Fig. 6.2. Blocks of stages relative to *Strategies-and-Skills-Used.*

For purposes of triangulation and clarification, the next table shows a comparison of cumulative frequencies and percentages from the *Strategies-and-Skills-Used Index* with those from the SCQ checklist defining abilities related to legal writing proficiency (SCQ3.b). From this SCQ checklist, an Abilities Index (AI) was derived in the same way as the SSUI was derived. In other words, Table 6.5 compares learners' self-reported use of writing strategies and CALP skills with learners' self-reported abilities defining proficiency, competence or expertise in legal writing using the two indices of cumulative frequency, based on the SCQ. Table 6.5 below shows the comparison.

Table 6.5. Comparison of *Strategies-and-Skills-Used Index (SSUI)* and *Ability Index (AI)* across stages.

Student blocks x3	*SSUI* describing strategies and skills	Maximum possible strategies and skills	% strategies and skills	*AI* describing proficiency	Maximum possible abilities	% abilities	% difference between SSUI and AI
Gee	60	132	**45.46**	16	29	**55.17**	9.17
Tory	90	132	**68.18**	27	29	**93.10**	24.92
Ferra	80	132	**61.61**	22	29	**75.86**	14.25
Liv	81	132	**61.36**	12	29	**41.38**	<19.98>
Anyo	104	132	**78.79**	27	29	**93.10**	14.31
Sam	103	132	**78.03**	21	29	**72.41**	<5.62>

Gee, who scored the lowest on the SSUI, similarly reported a low score on the AI. Anyo, who scored highest on the SSUI along with Tory, similarly reported a high score on the AI. Ferra's (14.25%) percentage of difference between the SSUI and the AI indices is close to Anyo's (14.31%). Tory's use of strategies and skills was third highest among the student participants, and she self-reported a high score (93.10%) on the AI, the same score as Anyo.

Two student participants had lower AI scores for proficiency than SSUI scores for strategies and skills, however. Calculations for Sam showed a <5.62%>difference, and calculations for Liv showed a <19.98%> difference. Qualitative analyses of these participants' SCQ and Interview Protocol data for most helpful strategies and skills explore these writer differences in the next chapter.

6.2.5 Summary of results for research question 1

Frequency and percentages of academic literacy strategies for scholarly legal writing and cognitive academic language skills for academic legal language processing used by the six participants in this study have been described and compared for each stage of writing. Two clear patterns emerged from the analyses of the quantitative SCQ data.

First, three sets or blocks of learners emerged relative to the Strategies-and-Skills-Used Index. One included the U.S. law school-educated participant, the second included those participants educated in Europe and the former USSR, and the last included those educated in Africa and the Middle East. These blocks initially suggest that cultural distance and background knowledge might influence frequencies of writing strategies and CALP skills. Culture and background knowledge in a discipline are social-cultural, learner-external variables.

Second, two blocks of stages emerged relative to the Strategies-and-Skills-Used Index. Gee, Liv, and Anyo used more writing strategies and CALP skills for stage 2 drafting than for the other stages of scholarly legal writing in contrast to Tory, Ferra, and Sam who increased their use of writing strategies and CALP skills with each stage of writing. Increased use of strategies and skills for stage 2 drafting (the learner centered stage) and for revising (the reader-centered stage) suggests that both learner internal (cognitive) and learner external (social-cultural) variables influence frequencies of writing strategies and CALP skills in the final stages of writing.

Cumulative percentages across all six participants show a progressive increase in the use of CALP skills for the three stages of scholarly legal writing. The highest use of CALP skills was found for stage 3 revising, the "writing to communicate" stage. In contrast, the highest use of writing strategies was found for stage 2 drafting, the "writing to learn" stage. This contrast highlights (a) conscious use of writing strategies for legal writer development while drafting, and (b) conscious or unconscious use of CALP skills for legal writer communication while revising. In other words, writing strategies seem to be associated more with writers' (internal) cognitive development, and CALP skills seem to be associated more with writers' (external) social-cultural development from a disciplinary literacy point of view. This is an important finding insofar as writing strategies helped student participants learn, and CALP skills helped them write from multilingual sources. See Table 6.6 below.

Table 6.6. Cumulative percentage (c %) of writing strategies and CALP skills used by all six learners for all three stages of scholarly legal writing: Pre-writing, Drafting, and Revising.

3 (recursive) stages	descriptive statistics	c % writing strategies	c % CALP skills	% difference
Stage 1 Pre-writing	based on Table 6.1	55.17	46.67	8.50
Stage 2 Drafting	based on Table 6.2	76.67	66.67	10.00
Stage 3 Revising	based on Table 6.3	70.49	70.00	.49

For stage 1 pre-writing, the planning and "researching to learn" stage, student participants used 8.5% more pre-writing literacy strategies than CALP skills. Similarly, student participants used 10% more writing strategies than CALP skills for stage 2 drafting, the "writing to learn" stage. Stabilization in use occurs after the first two learner-centered stages of writing, however. The cumulative percent difference between writing strategies and CALP skills was close to equal <.49%> for stage 3 revising, the "writing to communicate" to the law school educated reader stage. In addition, analyses for stage 3 revising showed an increase of 20.83% in CALP skills associated with levels of writing purpose, from 66.67% in the drafting stage to 87.50% in the revising stage.

This percentage increase suggests that CALP skills play an important role in academic legal composition. Stage 3 revising was found to be the stage for knowledge transforming by four of the six student participants. Qualitative data analyses in the next chapter further explores participants' transformation processes in scholarly legal writing through close, systematic examination of their most helpful strategies for each stage of writing.

6.3 Learners' most helpful strategies

For each stage of the scholarly L2 legal writing process, which writing strategies and CALP skills do the learners think are the most useful and why?

This question was addressed by the Interview Protocol (IP), using the SCQ as a quantitative measure to stimulate recall for the strategies used. The qualitative interview probed the helpfulness of strategies used from SCQ self-reports exploring student perceptions, meanings, and interpretations. Both quantitative and qualitative data merge when learners in the recorded interviews isolate certain "yes" responses on the SCQ to answer Research Question 2. Quantitative results are presented in this chapter, and qualitative results are presented in the next chapter that explores why these are the most helpful strategies and CALP skills at each stage.

Participants' most helpful writing strategies and CALP skills for effective scholarly L2 legal writing are summarized quantitatively in Table 6.7 below.

6.3.1 Overall results for stage 1, pre-writing

Results for (stage 1) pre-writing showed that, overall, participants found Type 1a and Type 1b "reading to write" strategies most helpful for preparing to write a scholarly legal research paper (11 mentions each in the interview). Type 1a are conceptual strategies defined in the SCQ as legal reading strategies to find a topic, thesis, or claim for students' major analytical research paper. They deal more with legal content (conceptual development) than with organizational structure (rhetorical development) or with language (linguistic development). Like Type 1b, they are labeled on the SCQ as "reading to write strategies" and are defined on the SCQ as writing strategies for combining reading, note-taking, and thinking to discover what is important or true for the learner about his or her legal research topic, thesis, or claim.

6.3.2 Overall results for stage 2, drafting

Results for (stage 2) drafting found that, overall, participants found Type 2a drafting strategies (37 mentions) more helpful than Type 2b CALP skills (2 mentions) for starting to write a scholarly legal research paper – even though frequencies for Research Question 1 showed that learners used 10% more CALP skills than strategies at this stage. The findings for Research Questions 1 and 2 do not conflict because IP question #1 focused on student participants' most helpful strategies, not most

Table 6.7. *Most helpful strategies and skills for each stage of scholarly legal writing:* Frequency of responses to the IP questions for individual learners and across all six learners.

Student N = 6 Stage	Gee	Tory	Ferra	Liv	Anyo	Sam	Students cf	Stages cf	% total by stage
Pre-writing stage 1									
Type 1a "reading to write"									
conceptual strategies	2	5	2	–	1	1	11	34	32.35%
rhetorical strategies	1	–	–	–	2	–	3	34	8.82%
linguistic strategies	–	–	–	–	4	1	5	34	14.71%
Type 1b strategies	1	1	2	–	5	2	11	34	32.35%
Type 1c CALP skills	–	–	1	–	2	1	4	34	11.77%
cumulative frequency(cf) most helpful, stage 1	4	6	5	–	14	5	**34**	n/a	100%
Drafting stage 2									
Type 2a drafting strategies	2	6	11	6	12	–	37	39	94.87%
Type 2b CALP skills	–	–	1	–	1	–	2	39	5.13%
cumulative frequency(cf) most helpful, stage 2	2	6	12	6	13	–	**39**	n/a	100%
Revising stage 3									
Type 3a revising strategies	2	11	10	4	8	1	37	104	35.57%
Type 3b editing strategies	1	7	–	1	6	–	15	104	14.42%
Type 3c plain English writing strategies	1	11	8	5	7	–	32	104	30.76%
Type 3d CALP skills	–	–	1	1	2	–	4	104	3.84%
Type 3e knowledge transforming strategies	–	2	4	5	6	–	17	104	16.33%
cumulative frequency(cf) most helpful, stage 3	4	31	23	16	29	1	**104**	n/a	100%
Total most helpful, overall	10	43	40	22	56	6	**177**	n/a	n/a

helpful CALP skills; it was assumed in the writing intervention that participants would be using CALP skills. Type 2a drafting strategies help the writer get words and concepts down effectively on paper. They contrast with Type 2b CALP skills which help the writer learn by processing legal text for writing.

6.3.3 Overall results for stage 3, revising

Results for (stage 3) revising found that, overall, participants found Type 3a strategies for revising (37 mentions) and Type 3c plain English grammar strategies (32 mentions) more helpful than Type 3b editing strategies (15 mentions) in the final stage of writing a scholarly legal research paper. Type 3a revising strategies help the writer decide what should be changed, deleted, added, or retained. Type 3c plain English grammar strategies help the legal writer express complex ideas in plain English, clearly and accurately. In sum, results for stage 3 revising found that deeper-level writing strategies, rather than surface-level editing strategies, were most helpful.

6.3.4 Overall results for all 3 stages combined (pre-writing, drafting, and revising)

Results across all six learners showed that reports of their most helpful strategies increased across the three stages of scholarly legal writing. Categories of strategies for drafting (Type 2a) and revising (Type 3a) relating more to content than to form were found most helpful overall, highlighting academic writing as a problem-solving activity that develops content knowledge.

Plain English grammar strategies for clear, effective academic legal writing were found by participants to be the second most helpful category across all six learners. These strategies contrast with editing strategies for correct grammar; they were explained in the SCQ as strategies for L2 legal writing that may contrast stylistically with learners' L1 preference for more complication in syntax, or more length and sophistication in vocabulary (for example, nominalization).

Third, results across all six learners found the (Type 3e) knowledge-transforming strategies most helpful. These are explained in the SCQ as primarily linguistic strategies that help "deepen" the writer's "thinking in English while revising" and help "transform text information while revising, giving [students] authorship" of their analytical legal writing.

Last, (Type 3b) editing strategies for "polishing and checking for conventions in stage 3 of the writing process" were found most helpful across learners.

What follows is a composite profile from each student participant's report of most helpful strategies across all the three stages (pre-writing, drafting, and revising). The composite profile is based on Table 6.7 (above).

6.3.5 Composite profile of learners' most helpful strategies

For stage 1 Pre-writing, participants reported the following legal reading strategies most helpful to find a topic, thesis, or claim for their papers: (a) reading for a purpose; (b) summarizing from the reading; (c) annotating with critical comment; (d) drawing conclusions from the reading relevant to the working thesis or claim; and (e) talking back to the text by problem posing while reading. These are deeper-level strategies related to content that help develop legal thinking, generating ideas for a legal research paper. Noting key legal terms for re-use in writing, as well as noting key English phrases for reading comprehension, and paraphrasing in English for both reading comprehension and for language reuse in writing were also most helpful strategies at this stage. For reading, note-taking, and thinking, (a) using texts or quotes from experts to stimulate thoughts and ideas; (b) exchanging ideas with others about one's research project; (c) reading others for modeling of style and organization; (d) making a preliminary outline; and (e) finding a quiet place to concentrate on legal writing were most helpful pre-writing strategies.

For stage 2 Drafting, participants reported paraphrasing and summarizing information from persuasive legal sources most helpful strategies to actually begin writing. Re-reading legal texts that serve as rhetorical models, and reordering information from legal source texts to use in a draft were also reported most helpful strategies for drafting. Conferencing with a content law professor, writing teacher, and peers to refine and clarify ideas were also found most helpful at the drafting stage.

For stage 3 Revising, participants reported reading critically and reflecting on one's own written drafts most helpful for deciding what should be changed, deleted, or retained. Other most helpful revising strategies were asking oneself: (a) if key words and phrases are repeated for cohesion and emphasis; (b) if the purpose and message are clear; and (c) if headings, subheadings, and logical connectors are used effectively. Strategies to solicit feedback were also found "most helpful" for revising: that is, (a) getting feedback from the writing instructor to assess how effectively the message is being communicated and to build or re-construct the analysis when necessary; and (b) getting expert legal opinion of the analysis from the law professor when available. Revising was also found to be a most helpful stage for knowledge-transforming: that is, deepening understanding to include analysis, synthesis, and evaluation of the research.

For polishing and checking for writing conventions, participants found the following editing strategies most helpful: (a) asking oneself whether the paper is an example of good legal writing; (b) proofreading for sentence structure (syntax); (c) proofreading for proper word choice (diction); (d) proofreading for punctuation; (e) proofreading for spelling (Microsoft "Tools"); and (f) proofreading for citation. In other words, proofreading "with a purpose in mind" was reported to be a most helpful strategy in the final stage of scholarly legal writing.

For clear, accurate expression of ideas, participants reported the following plain English grammar strategies most helpful: (a) making one point per sentence using simple and complex sentences; (b) avoiding long, multi-clause sentences; (c) avoiding nominalizations (the practice of changing short verbs to longer nouns); and (d) keeping subjects and verbs, and verbs and objects, undivided – without interrupting phrases. Other most helpful plain English grammar strategies reported by participants were: (a) using familiar words instead of flowery or ornate words; (b) using consistent wording and phrasing without changing words simply for variety; (c) using consistent parallel word signals such as "first" and "second"; and (d) using accurate and adequate punctuation as "road signs" to communicate effectively to the law school educated reader.

6.3.6 Summary of quantitative results for research question 2

Quantitative analyses for nominal data showed that for (stage 1) pre-writing, conceptual strategies for writing authentic text were most helpful; for (stage 2) drafting, writing strategies were more helpful than CALP skills; and for (stage 3) revising, deeper-level writing strategies – in contrast to surface-level editing strategies – were most helpful across learners. In particular, Type 2a strategies for drafting and Type 3a strategies for revising that relate more to content than to form were most helpful, followed by Type 3c plain English grammar strategies that help the student writer express legal ideas clearly and accurately in L2 academic English. Type 3e knowledge-transforming strategies were reported to be the next most helpful category across learners, followed by the Type 3b surface-level editing strategies. A summary of qualitative results for Research Question 2 can be found in the next chapter.

6.4 Learners' and teacher's quality ratings

For each stage of the scholarly L2 legal writing process, what are the learners' and teacher quality ratings of the learners' scholarly L2 writing product?

This question is addressed by the Student's Quality Assessment Tool (SQAT) and the Teacher's Quality Assessment Tool (TQAT). It is primarily a quantitative research question that uses the SQAT/TQAT as a pair of systematic checklists to give quality ratings – by category and by item – of learners' academic legal writing product at each stage of scholarly writing (pre-writing, drafting, and revising).

The SQAT is a checklist used by participants for self-assessment of quality at each stage of scholarly writing. The SQAT (a) helps learners know what may be expected at each stage of writing in broad terms of genre, and (b) helps them prepare their best work at each stage for individual consultations with the teacher-researcher to receive conceptual, rhetorical, and/or linguistic feedback to improve quality.

The TQAT is a checklist used by the teacher-researcher for assessment of quality at each stage of student writing. The TQAT helps prepare the teacher for individual consultations with students at (or near) the end of each stage of writing. The TQAT facilitates objective assessment of each student participant's scholarly legal writing product at key stages to improve quality by giving interactive and corrective feedback in three areas: conceptually, rhetorically, and linguistically. The difference in results between the two measures (SQAT and the TQAT checklist items) were discussed in individual consultations with student participants. These teacher-student feedback sessions were not tape-recorded because their purpose was instructional. Notes were taken, however.

Table 6.8 on page 98 shows the SQAT/TQAT categories for each of the three stages in the scholarly legal writing genre within the context of American English academic culture.

Table 6.9on page 99 shows cumulative frequencies of items checked by participants to improve writing quality at each stage of writing.

The difference between the student participants' SQAT and the teacher's TQAT cumulative frequencies of checked items to improve writing quality culminates in the Quality Assessment Index (QAI) for each participant.

6.4.1 Overall results across all 3 stages (pre-writing, drafting, and revising)

Cumulative frequencies of "yes" responses (checked items on the quality assessment tools) show that the difference between the learners' evaluations on the SQAT and the teacher's evaluations on the TQAT ranged in number from 15 to 27. The greatest overall difference between the SQAT and the TQAT was for drafting – the writer-centered "writing to learn" stage. The smallest difference between the SQAT and the TQAT was for revising – the reader-centered "writing to communicate stage." Student participants ($N = 6$) generally overestimated the quality of their writing, especially in the writer-centered "learning" stages.

Sam, one of the two least experienced and least acculturated academic legal writers, scored the lowest on the QAI (1.61%). His checked items to improve quality

Table 6.8. SQAT/TQAT categories for each stage in the genre of scholarly legal writing.

Stage 1 pre-writing (learner-centered) planning categories	Stage 2 drafting (writer-centered) genre categories	Stage 3 revising (reader-centered) communication categories
Researching to learn outline/draft 17 items total	Writing to learn draft(s) 17 items total	Writing to communicate draft(s)
	1. Introduction to research paper: 4 items	28 items total 1. Audience: 2 items
	2. Background: 4 items	2. Purpose: 6 items
	3. Analytical Discussion: Large-scale organization/ 3 items Small-scale organization/ 3 items	3. Content: 6 items 4. Organization: 2 main/3sub parts/5 items
	4. Conclusion: 3 items	5. Clarity: 5 parts/5 items
		6. Mechanics: 4 items

at each stage of writing were a close match to the writing teacher's checked items. Gee, an experienced legal writer but one unfamiliar with what her law professor wanted her to do (that is, write a proposal rather than a typical analytical research paper), also scored low on the QAI (8.07%). Both participants did not seem to be self-regulated writers in the early stages of writing.

At the other end of the scale was Tory, who scored the highest on the QAI (32.26%). Tory was one of the most confident, experienced, and acculturated academic legal writers, familiar with genre and analytical legal research paper writing. Liv, also a confident, experienced legal writer in her home country, scored high on the QAI (30.65%). For both Tory and Liv, the greatest assessment differences were for pre-writing and drafting, the cognitive learner-centered stages. Their quality assessment scores were a closer match to the writing teacher's for revising, however, the "writing to communicate" to the law school educated reader stage.

Table 6.9. *Quality Assessment Index (QAI):* Difference between students' SQAT and the teacher's TQAT evaluations for individual learners and across all six learners for the three stages of scholarly legal writing.

Student (N = 6)	Pre-writing 17 possible items		Drafting 17 possible items		Revising 28 possible items		SQAT/62	TQAT/62	QAI/62	
	SQAT	TQAT	SQAT	TQAT	SQAT	TQAT	cf	cf	difference	%
Gee	4 /17	7/17	11/17	9/17	15/28	9/28	30/62	25/62	5/62	8.07
Tory	16/17	6/17	17/17	11/17	28/28	24/28	61/62	41/62	20/62	32.26
Ferra	10/17	9/17	14/17	5/17	25/28	26/28	49/62	40/62	9/62	14.52
Liv	15/17	9/17	15/17	8/17	28/28	22/28	58/62	39/62	19/62	30.65
Anyo	13/17	8/17	15/17	15/17	25/28	20/28	53/62	43/62	10/62	16.13
Sam	17/17	16/17	14/17	11/17	23/28	28/28	54/62	55/62	<1/62>	1.61
Cumulative "yes"	75	55<20>	86	59<27>	144	129<15>	305/372	243/372	62	16.67

Ferra (14.52%) and Anyo (16.13%) scored in-between these extremes on the quality assessment continuum. The three blocks of learners, each containing an acculturated and an un-acculturated student participant, appear in Figure 6.3 below.

1.61% 8.07%|_____14.52% to 16.13%_____|30.65% **32.26%**
*Sam Gee   Ferra   *Anyo   *Liv   Tory

*denotes un-acculturated

Fig. 6.3. Blocks of learners % differences relative to *Quality Assessment*.

Individual results for each stage of scholarly writing show that both Tory and Liv had higher percentage (%) differences in assessment for stage 1, pre-writing and stage 2, drafting than for stage 3, revising. Both tended to overestimate the quality of their writing generally, with scores that ranged from 32.26% (Tory) to 30.65% (Liv). In contrast, Sam and Gee showed the lowest % differences in quality assessment. Sam underestimated the quality of his work product at the revising (reader-centered) stage, whereas Gee underestimated the quality of her work product at the pre-writing (writer-centered stage). Both may have lacked confidence in what they were producing – Gee from a substantive view and Sam from a communicative view. In-between were Ferra's percentage difference that was highest for drafting, and Anyo's percentage difference that was highest for pre-writing and for revising. Figure 6.4 below shows the blocks of stages relative to quality assessment.

Pre-writing |_____| **Drafting |** _____| **Revising**
Tory, *Liv, *Anyo   Gee, Tory, *Liv, Ferra   Gee, Tory, *Liv, *Anyo

*denotes acculturated

Fig. 6.4. Blocks of stages showing highest % differences relative to *Quality Assessment*.

Individual results describe the percentage differences for each student participant using the SQAT/TQAT phrasing for items and categories.

6.4.2 Individual Quantitative Results Across All 3 Stages for Case 1 – Gee

Pre-writing, stage 1: *"researching to learn."* Gee's checked items on the SQAT for pre-writing were less extensive than the writing teacher's checked items (TQAT). Gee's SQAT indicated four actions she had taken to prepare for writing her first draft. The TQAT showed agreement with Gee that the student had incorporated these actions in her paper; additionally, the TQAT showed Gee how she could be more explicit identifying the purpose for her paper with examples of purpose: that is, phrases from the TQAT that were highlighted for the student writer to reconsider. The TQAT further indicated that Gee had organized her research into a kind of outline, and that she had decided on an approach to writing. However, the TQAT questioned whether Gee had started with what she already knows and whether Gee had defined a topic that was interesting and authentic to her experience.

Drafting, stage 2: *"writing to learn."* In contrast to pre-writing, Gee's checked items on the SQAT for drafting and revising were more extensive than the writing teacher's checked items on the TQAT. Gee's SQAT indicated that she had executed one item in the Introduction section, all four in the Background section, four in the Analytical/ Discussion section, and two in the Conclusion section of the draft submitted for discussion and teacher review. Gee had executed 30 out of 62 possible items within the basic four-part structure of the paper. The TQAT showed accord with the student's assessment; in addition, the TQAT offered suggestions for improving each section, focusing on organization and explicit (versus implicit) communication. The difference in the checked SQAT/TQAT items for Gee was related more to issues of quality than to execution of the items satisfying the genre requirements for a typical legal research paper.

Revising, stage 3: *"writing to communicate."* Gee's SQAT indicated that she still had more work to do on this paper in some important areas like citation, but that she had met her objectives in terms of audience, organization, and clarity even if she had not achieved eloquence. The TQAT for this last stage indicated that the student's overall purpose was not evident throughout the paper and that the paper may not have included all the information needed by her law professor reader. The TQAT also indicated that (a) the structure will not be obvious to any reader because there was no roadmap in the Introduction, and that (b) the reader could misunderstand the content in the sub-headings and Conclusion section of the paper. After final revision, Gee submitted her twenty-five page paper for a one-credit independent study.

Content law professor's evaluation. "I thought your paper was relatively well-written. I wish you had had more time to develop some of the research themes you figured out late in the semester, but *c'est la vie.* I did not mark up that final paper." Grade: B+ (Gee, personal communication, February 2, 2009).

6.4.3 Individual Quantitative Results Across All 3 Stages for Case 2 – Tory

Pre-writing, stage 1: *"researching to learn."* Tory's checked items on the SQAT were more extensive than the writing teacher's checked items on the TQAT for all stages. For pre-writing, the TQAT indicated that the writer's purpose for legal research writing, "to make sense out of a confusing array of issues," was not as clearly stated in the student's "Introductory Outline" as it could be. The TQAT did show, however, that Tory's claim was clearly stated. Tory also made a "disclaimer" to her content law professor at the end of her outline that she "may discover sources that may alter" her claim, reserving the right to develop her paper and change the title of her paper accordingly. Tory considered her working title to be an "hypothesis" only.

Drafting, stage 2: *"writing to learn."* Tory's checklist of SQAT items was also more comprehensive than the writing teacher's TQAT checklist for this stage. The TQAT indicated that the student's draft explicitly stated the writer's purpose, but was missing a thesis or claim; in other words, Tory was still "writing to learn" and was not yet ready to commit to a thesis or claim. The second major difference between the quality assessments involved small-scale organization. The TQAT was in accord with the SQAT that very clear organizational paradigms existed in the paper, but the TQAT indicated that the student had not (a) introduced and concluded on each issue, or (b) rebutted any opposing argument, if relevant. One patterned error was also noted for the student writer at this stage: that is, improper use of the definite article for generalities.

Revising, stage 3: *"writing to communicate."* Tory's SQAT checklist was complete for this stage, indicating a high level of attention to revising. The open-ended SQAT student comment stated that "at this stage my paper is almost complete. I just rephrase and reorganize if needed (for clarity)." The TQAT was in accord with the student's quality assessment for all the categories and most of the items. Teacher feedback that accompanied the TQAT checklist indicated that the student had done an excellent job revising and that her footnotes were thorough and functioned properly. After final revision, Tory submitted her twenty-eight page paper to complete a three credit law course.

Content law professor's evaluation. Tory emailed her content law professor and asked why he had given her a B+. Her professor said that her ideas were not feasible economically ... and that if she had followed her original outline – the one she wanted to use as model – she would have had a better paper. Tory commented that she had wanted to follow her original outline, but that she ran into a problem when she tried locating a specific contract. She said that she "could not find supporting documents to write a good paper. In any case, thank God, it is over." (Tory, personal communication, February 1, 2009).

6.4.4 Individual Quantitative Results Across All 3 Stages for Case 3 – Ferra

Pre-writing, stage 1: *"researching to learn."* Ferra's checked items on the SQAT were only slightly more comprehensive than the writing teacher's checked items on the TQAT for the first two stages (pre-writing and drafting). The TQAT for stage 1 was a pre-drafting checklist, but the student had submitted a working draft for teacher assessment rather than an outline: that is, a draft that had not yet integrated or synthesized her legal sources into essay format for a "paper." Ferra's SQAT pre-writing checklist differed from the teacher's assessment on two important items. The TQAT showed that the student had identified the type of research paper she was writing but that she had not formulated a working thesis, whereas the student's SQAT indicated the opposite; Ferra indicated that she had formulated a working thesis but had not identified the type of research paper she was writing. This may be a difficult distinction to make without student-teacher consultation or explicit instruction before writing. In essence, Ferra did not have a working outline with an explicitly stated purpose and working thesis before she started drafting.

Drafting, stage 2: *"writing to learn."* Ferra's SCQ checklist for this stage was comprehensive. The small-scale organization items on the SCQ were unchecked, however, indicating that Ferra was unsure of her small-scale organization at the paragraph and sentence level and still had more work to do. The TQAT checklist for all categories were in accord with the SQAT although additional teacher comments on the TQAT indicated that Ferra needed more work on her Introduction and Conclusion sections in particular. The student had introduced and noted why her topic was important in her Introduction, for example, but she had done so implicitly – not explicitly. In addition, the TQAT indicated that Ferra needed to connect her purpose (that is, to examine a theme) in paragraph two with her thesis in the next paragraph.

Revising, stage 3: *"writing to communicate."* Three SQAT items were left unchecked by the student participant. The first two related to purpose: (a) whether the writer's overall purpose was evident throughout the paper, and (b) whether she had explicitly stated if her purpose was primarily persuasive or analytical. The third item had to do with clarity and whether the legal reader would misunderstand the content at any point in the paper. Under student comment, the SQAT reported (qualitative data) that "some of the answers above would require a deeper explanation of their reasons because the answer in some cases cannot be considered yes/no as well as not applicable to my case." From Ferra's point of view, some discussion was needed for her SQAT to be fully understood by the researcher-teacher. Individual consultation with the completed SQAT/TQAT forms was necessary for this student participant.

Under purpose, the TQAT checklist indicated that (a) the student writer had clearly identified her paper as historical/analytical – something the student participant had left unchecked in stage 1 (pre-writing), and that (b) the reader would not misunderstand the content. Other TQAT items indicated that the phrasing was clear, the text was readable, the writer had emphasized key points, and the wording changes flowed together to create an eloquent whole. The TQAT further indicated, however, that some comma errors remained, and that mechanical proofreading may still be required for citations and wrong or overused words.

Ferra commented in her individual consultation that she had no time for the latter revision even though she had checked this item on the SQAT. The TQAT indicated that in terms of content, the writer's footnotes functioned properly. After final revision, Ferra submitted her thirty page paper to complete a three credit law course.

Content law professor's evaluation. Ferra received an "A" for this paper, and then went on to publish a condensed version of a sixty page paper she had written for six credits the previous semester in an international law journal (using the SCQ, stage 4).

6.4.5 Individual Quantitative Results Across All 3 Stages for Case 4 – Liv

Pre-writing, stage 1: *"researching to learn."* Liv's checked items on the SQAT were more extensive than the writing teacher's checked items on the TQAT for all stages. For pre-writing, only some SQAT items applied to Liv because she had outline only cases: primary legal sources new to her. She reported that she had a "problem" with structure because, as she was reading more articles (secondary sources), she had to reorganize the structure of her draft. Liv reported that she had an idea of how to structure her paper after speaking about it with the teacher in her individual consultation for this stage.

Drafting, stage 2: *"writing to learn."* Liv's SQAT indicated that she had resolved issues with large-scale and small-scale organization in contrast to the TQAT which indicated that, although she had a "good draft here," she had not met any of the criteria for small-scale organization. TQAT feedback showed that she still needed to summarize the cases presented and write an appropriate Conclusion section.

Liv explained that, although she had written papers for law school in her home country, writing Introduction and Conclusion sections in a U.S. paper was different because they required original thinking. Another difference between the SQAT and the TQAT was that Liv had subsumed the Background section into her discussion of the cases, which worked because of the type of legal research paper she was writing.

Revising, stage 3: *"writing to communicate."* While the SQAT indicated that the student's paper was ready for submission, the TQAT indicated remaining issues with clarity and mechanics. In particular, the TQAT showed that Liv still had to make changes in phrasing, wording, English grammar, and punctuation. A student email indicated that Liv had sent the teacher-researcher an older version of her paper "...from before our last meeting," but that she would apply TQAT stage 3.a comments to her "newer version" (Liv, personal communication, December 7, 2008). The TQAT checked items for this stage were otherwise complete, indicating that Liv had done a good job with time management. After final revision, Liv was able to submit her twenty-five page paper early, before her three-credit law course ended for the semester.

Content law professor's evaluation. Liv received A- for her research paper. The law professor gave her no feedback.

6.4.6 Individual Quantitative Results Across All 3 Stages for Case 5 – Anyo

Pre-writing, stage 1: *"researching to learn."* Anyo's checked items on the SQAT were more extensive than the teacher's checked items on the TQAT for pre-writing and for revising, but they were the same for drafting. The SQAT showed that Anyo had not identified the purpose for his legal research at the outset. This issue was later discussed in student-teacher consultation at the revising stage. In contrast, the TQAT indicated that Anyo still had to work at formulating a thesis and that formulating research questions to reflect on what he thinks about his legal topic might help. Further, Anyo identified the type of research paper he was writing verbally but not on the checklist. Anyo had started to write his paper late in the semester, at the time of his "last class." This was his first attempt at writing an academic research paper for law school.

Drafting, stage 2: *"writing to learn."* The SQAT and the TQAT checked items matched for Anyo at this stage. Both the SQAT and the TQAT clearly identified that Anyo had not yet introduced and concluded on each issue (small-scale organization) and that he had not yet restated his thesis in the Conclusion section of his paper without being obviously redundant. He said that he would be able to do this before submitting his paper for course credit, however.

Revising, stage 3: *"writing to communicate."* Anyo's SQAT was more comprehensive than the TQAT for revising. The SQAT showed that Anyo had not ensured that his citations functioned properly (Content) or that they were correct (Mechanics). The TQAT added that his paper did not seem to include all the information needed by his audience, that his point of view was not clear in the Introduction section, that the structure of his paper needed more work, and that his phrasing did not always emphasize key points. The TQAT also showed that the English grammar corrections still needing to be made were minor. Anyo did not have enough time to complete these minor corrections before submitting his twenty-one page paper for law course credit.

Content law professor's evaluation. Anyo received A– for the research paper he submitted to complete his three-credit law course. His law professor commented that Anyo had written a good paper and that if he still wanted to publish this paper, Anyo could schedule a meeting with her.

6.4.7 Individual Quantitative Results Across All 3 Stages for Case 6 – Sam

Pre-writing, stage 1: *"researching to learn."* Sam's checked items on the SQAT were more extensive than the writing teacher's checked items on the TQAT for pre-writing and drafting, but less comprehensive for revising. The TQAT for pre-writing showed that Sam had almost finished organizing his research into a working outline. However, he had not submitted a working bibliography of his sources with his outline and SQAT checklist.

Drafting, stage 2: *"writing to learn."* Although Sam was able to submit a draft for researcher-teacher review at this stage, the SQAT needed to be explained to him individually, in person, as Sam was still unfamiliar with the basic structure of a legal research paper. He had never before been exposed to the idea of genre in academic writing or to the basic structure of an expository essay. Also, Sam started the semester later than the other students. He had been attending an English for Lawyers class but, given that he had research papers to write, he moved into the Academic Legal Writing class.

Sam was able to revise his draft with the SQAT, however, after his individual consultation with the teacher-researcher. At this stage, Sam's SQAT showed that he had not stated his thesis and had not always introduced or concluded on each issue (small-scale organization). The TQAT indicated that Sam had ordered his issues logically, while Sam's SQAT indicated that he had not. Logic and organization for writing seemed to be a culture-related literacy issue for Sam, as well as a disciplinary one, because discussion helped to clarify the issues relevant to this student's specific writing situation. A quantitative checklist was not enough.

Revising, stage 3: *"writing to communicate."* Sam's SQAT showed that he still was not comfortable accounting for his reader's background knowledge when revising. With respect to SQAT Content, Sam was unsure if he had presented all relevant views on his topic accurately or if his footnotes functioned properly. With respect to SQAT Organization, Sam indicated that he was unsure if his paper's organization was consistent and unified throughout the document. These unchecked items, along with Sam's SQAT comment that "for publication purposes," he would have to "work more on the gaps in the paper" signaled to the teacher what to look for when reviewing and discussing Sam's paper. The TQAT showed that Sam had made a good beginning addressing his SQAT's unchecked items and that he had also done a good job emphasizing key points in his paper, although he could have done more in the Introduction section by following the structure provided by the SQAT (Stage 2).

Content law professor's evaluation. After final revision, Sam's grade for his research paper was A-. The law professor did not give Sam feedback after he submitted his twenty-eight paper to complete a two-credit law course.

6.4.8 Summary of Results for Research Question 3

Quantitative analyses for nominal data to answer Research Question 3 showed overall and individual results across the three stages of writing (pre-writing, drafting, and revising). Overall, student participants overestimated the quality of their writing produced in the learner-centered (pre-writing and drafting) stages. Less of a difference in quality assessment was reported for revising, the reader-centered "writing to communicate" stage. One possible interpretation may be that the students had developed as writers and thinkers by this stage, and they were prepared with techniques and strategies for revising and editing from the writing intervention that had included formative assessment: that is, structured feedback from the teacher. The finding that one acculturated and one un-acculturated student appeared in each block of learners on the quality assessment continuum (Figure 6.3) lends support to writer development and preparedness for stage 3 revising.

Individual results for Research Question 3 ended with law professor summative evaluation for each case. The three un-acculturated student participants participating in the academic legal writing course at the time of the study each received A-. The two acculturated student participants with native-like English language proficiency each received B+. The third acculturated student participant, the advanced (Ph.D.) law student with less than native-like proficiency, received an A.

The SQAT/TQAT evaluations were formative assessments that took place at three different times during the writing process. The SQAT/TQAT checklists facilitated teacher feedback to student writers that was objective, structured, systematic, and timely. This feedback helped participants develop their thinking about language and the law while writing. In contrast, the law professors assigned grades and judged student learning based on participants' writing product, without in-depth comment. Individual findings suggest learner development relating to strategic competence (proficiency) in written communication during processes of writing a scholarly legal paper.

The next chapter fleshes out the quantitative findings with qualitative results. The chapter after that presents a synthesis of the qualitative and quantitative results with discussion that ends the book by answering Research Question 4: For each stage of the scholarly L2 legal writing process, what interrelationships can be seen among (a) learners' writing strategies and cognitive academic language skills, and (b) learners' and teacher quality ratings of the learners' scholarly L2 writing product.

From a teaching/learning perspective, evaluations at each stage of writing gave student writers objective, structured, and systematic feedback for developing their research writing rather than for assigning grades or judging the writers' learning based on their writing product. Individual findings relate to learner development and competence in communication during processes of writing a scholarly research paper.

Part III: **Learner-User Perspectives**

7 Profiles

7.1 Introduction to chapter 7, qualitative research results

This chapter presents the qualitative results from the *Interview Protocol* (IP) and the *Strategic Competence Questionnaire* (SCQ) for each student participant in three recursive stages of scholarly writing. Qualitative key theme analyses from (a) participant responses to the IP, (b) participant responses to the open-ended questions on the SCQ, and (c) relevant definitions from the questionnaire create profiles of the six multilingual graduate student writers. These profiles show (a) how the learners go about their legal research writing task, (b) how they use writing strategies and CALP skills to present research effectively in academic English using ABC style (for accuracy, brevity, and clarity), and (c) when they make the cognitive transition to knowledge-transforming from knowledge-telling (if at all) in their scholarly writing process.

Besides identifying main themes and unexpected findings, qualitative research results from the IP also identify underlying problems and issues for student participants, along with their most helpful strategies from the perspectives of the student writers themselves. These perspectives disclose variables related to strategic competence for each participant across three stages of scholarly writing (pre-writing, drafting, and revising).

The results are organized by case in the different stages of writing. These stages correspond to the sections on the SCQ which explore strategies, skills, and the following related strategic competence constructs of importance to professional-level language learners: (a) knowledge transforming (versus knowledge telling), (b) developing as a disciplinary thinker and writer across stages, (c) explicit strategies instruction, (d) feedback during writing, and (e) proficiency defining abilities for competence in scholarly legal writing. Information from the semi-structured IP and the open-ended SCQ questions, presented under the above-mentioned sub-headings, combine to answer the "why" in *Research Question 2*: For each stage of the scholarly L2 legal writing process, which writing strategies and CALP skills do the learners think are the most useful and why?

Cross-validating the results

Juxtaposition of the qualitative data with the quantitative data from the SQAT/ TQAT instruments (*Research Question 3*) provides triangulation at the end for each case. A member-check follows the summary of the learner and teacher quality ratings for each case, when reported: five student participants reviewed researcher analyses for both Research Question 2 and 3 and provided a written response.

Chapter overview

The chapter begins with six profiles describing how the student participants went about their research writing. Description is systematic, with the SCQ section headings serving as sub-headings for each profile. After the last profile, a summary of the qualitative findings follows for each case and for the two groups: acculturated and non-acculturated. A summary of the six cases follows that, highlighting main theses, kinds of knowledge, and unexpected findings. The validity check ends the chapter.

Definition of Terms

Writing strategies are actions or activities consciously chosen by learners from among language, literacy, and culture alternatives for the purpose of regulating their own writing in a specific sociocultural setting (adapted from Griffiths, 2008; Oxford, 2011). CALP refers to formal academic language proficiency (in contrast to informal, social language proficiency). CALP includes listening, speaking, reading, and writing about legal content material. In the SCQ, CALP skills are defined as skills for language processing: that is, paraphrasing, summarizing, synthesizing, and analyzing information from printed legal sources to communicate thinking and avoid plagiarizing.

7.2 Results case 1 – Gee

United States: native Urdu, English; foreign Spanish, Arabic

Areas of Concern before Writing (SCQ 1)
The SCQ (stage 1) showed that Gee's areas of concern before writing her major research paper for the (fall) semester had to do with language and composition skills (question 5) – not with writing knowledge (question 6). Gee was an experienced graduate student writer in L2 English. Even though she had already earned a J.D. degree in a U.S. law school, she was still "very" concerned with the following components of research writing: organization, meaning (content analysis), legal style (for accuracy, brevity and conciseness), references and citations to scholarly works, and stages in scholarly legal writing.

Pre-writing, "Researching to Learn" Stage (SCQ 1)
The SCQ (stage 1) and the interview showed that Gee found both conceptual and rhetorical legal reading strategies most helpful when reading to find a topic, thesis, or claim for her research paper. She (a) read for a purpose; (b) drew conclusions from the reading relevant to her topic; and (c) noted aspects of organizational structure for reuse in her writing. "Seeing how other people organize this type of paper" was helpful to her. She said she read other writers for modeling of style and organization, and to see who other authors cited as sources.

In terms of CALP skills used for pre-writing, the SCQ showed that Gee summarized information simply by reducing source text to prepare to write the first draft of this paper – not a typical analytical paper. In her interview, she said she wrote the Introduction without formulating a thesis, which she related to motivation and to writing purpose. Gee said she did not like writing this paper for many reasons, some personal. She did "not intend to publish it."

Drafting, "Writing to Learn" Stage (SCQ 2)
For getting words and concepts down effectively on paper while drafting, the SCQ (stage 2) and the interview found two strategies most helpful. First, Gee used her knowledge of audience and purpose for writing to guide her drafts. She said she focused on her professor who "re-iterated the purpose" for her: that is, to write a proposal for the new Obama administration rather than a "typical analytical paper." Second, she rejected irrelevant substantive content in the readings while she wrote. Because "few things [were] written" about her topic, Gee had to "disregard" most of the secondary source papers she had read to prepare for writing.

In terms of CALP skills for drafting, the SCQ and the interview showed that Gee used all the CALP skills; one language processing skill was not more helpful to her than another at this stage of writing. She (a) paraphrased information by putting source material (text) into her own words; (b) summarized information simply by reducing source text; (c) summarized information complexly by selecting and reorganizing source text; (d) synthesized information by combining and connecting source text; and (e) analyzed information by reflecting and breaking down source text into its parts. Her use of various CALP skills suggests different levels of writing purpose.

The SCQ showed that Gee used four broad levels of writing purpose for "effective drafting": (a) she wrote to state knowledge by listing, repeating, or paraphrasing source text; (b) she wrote to understand, remember, summarize simply, or extend notes to herself; (c) she wrote to learn, problem-solve, summarize complexly, or synthesize source text information; and (d) she wrote to critique, persuade, or interpret evidence selectively and appropriately. Gee said she did not use a language other than English in this (drafting) stage, or in any other, for writing her paper.

Revising, "Writing to Communicate" Stage (SCQ 3.a)
The interview showed two strategies particularly helpful for Gee to revise her paper. First, she re-ordered her writing as she revised. She "did this in a lot in different sections" and noticed that, when re-reading her own paper, most of the revision was "with respect to the ordering" of information. Second, Gee asked herself if she addressed the needs of her reader. In "writing for the new Obama administration, [she was] more focused on practical recommendations than analysis."

Gee found one strategy particularly helpful to edit effectively before submitting her paper to her professor for assessment at the end of the semester: that is, she proofread her legal writing for appearance (for example, spacing, and indentation). She said that she spent "half an hour on indentation" alone. Appearance was most important for her in this particular paper – more so than "word choice," for example.

Gee found one grammar strategy most helpful to communicate effectively in writing before submitting her paper for grading: that is, she made one point per sentence, preferring simple and complex sentence structures to compound sentence structures. Rather than combining ideas, Gee isolated an important idea by writing another sentence to emphasize its importance in an attempt to persuade the reader. She wanted readers to make "their own decision before I made it for them." This was a key grammar strategy for Gee. In her interview, Gee emphasized that (a) this was "one thing she used [from] last semester when she studied with [the teacher-researcher]", and (b) she used this grammar strategy "not just in the editing stage."

As in the drafting stage, the SCQ showed that Gee used all five CALP skills when revising to communicate to her law school educated reader and all four levels of writing purpose. She said she "tried to be very basic" in her use of language at this point in order to be persuasive. Gee would have liked four days to revise but she had to work within limiting time constraints. She said she "really did" two drafts; the second draft dealt more with recommendations in contrast to the first draft which had "too much" background information. Gee said that a third draft "would have been useful" but she would have needed not just time but also distance "to do" draft three. When re-reading her second draft and reviewing her citations, Gee noticed there were "a lot of things" she could have improved; she "could have tied it all up" in a third draft.

Knowledge Transforming (SCQ 3.a)
The SCQ (stage 3) showed that revising was not the most effective stage for transitioning her writing from *knowledge telling* (stating knowledge) to *knowledge trans-*

forming (deepening her level of understanding to include synthesis and evaluation of research). Gee emphasized in her interview that although synthesizing (composing by combining and connecting) was her most helpful strategy for writing her paper in the spring semester, this was not the case for writing her paper (a proposal) in the fall semester.

The particular SCQ knowledge transforming strategy that helped her the most to deepen her thinking was integrating propositions (statements, assertions) for comprehensiveness. The particular strategy group that helped her the most to deepen her thinking while revising was *rhetorical transforming* for binding her paper's overall structure. The particular *linguistic transforming* strategy that helped Gee the most to transform text information while revising, giving her authorship of her fall paper, was summarizing (composing by selecting and reorganizing).

Developing as a Legal Writer across Stages
In her interview, Gee said that neither previous legal writing activities (SCQ stage 1) nor her use of strategies for writing this proposal – an atypical paper – helped her develop competency as a legal writer. She said that the stage 2 (SCQ and SQAT) writing materials did help her develop competency as a legal writer, however, because she was unsure of genre or "the type of paper" she was writing. For example, she did not know if her paper "should have large or small-scale organization," and these (SCQ and SQAT) materials helped her problem-solve.

Explicit Strategies Instruction (SCQ 3.b)
Gee found direct (explicit) writing strategies instruction important at *all* stages (pre-writing, drafting, revising) to develop an *efficient writing process*. Gee said that strategies gave her a "roadmap of things to look for because [she] did not know how to edit" her own work before taking the writing course and using the materials. "I was very afraid to do it because I did not have the strategies to do it; they were very helpful."

Formal instruction was important for Gee at *all* levels (conceptual, rhetorical, and linguistic) to develop an *effective writing product*. The strategies "broke down the conceptual, rhetorical, and linguistic" for her so she was able to look at her work "differently at all those levels." She said she "wasn't aware before," and she is "able to look at work differently" now. Without feedback from her writing teacher (-researcher) and her professor, Gee said she "couldn't have moved on."

Writing Feedback (SCQ 3.b)
Gee reported that three kinds of direct (explicit) writing feedback helped her complete her fall paper, but the most important was interactive and substantive feedback from her law school professor: (quote)

> Professor …, here is a draft of my paper. I am having problems. It is only eleven pages long and I need to add more material but I am not sure what to add. I know that paper still needs more work – I need to include more of my own ideas in it. Also the footnotes need to be cleaned up. I really need your advise [sic] and recommendations. Thank you.

Feedback from her content law professor was more important to Gee than feedback from her writing teacher or peers because it helped "define purpose," especially at the beginning. Gee said it helped to talk to her professor at the beginning of the paper, but she said she did not understand her professor this semester. She said part of the problem was the new kind of paper she was writing, but part of it was that she should have "reached out more" to him to (a) "feel more confident in what you are doing; (b) not waste time doing something else; and (c) help define your purpose because they know the topic better than you." In order for Gee to thrive as a legitimate participant in her scholarly legal discourse community fall semester, Gee said in her interview that she needed "more feedback interaction with [her] professor during every stage of the writing process."

Proficiency Defining Abilities (SCQ 3.b)
When reflecting on her proficiency defining abilities near the end of the interview, Gee said that what she gained most was the ability "to self-edit" with "the strategies to do it" because she used to be "so afraid" to read her own writing:

> Now I know that you can read for content; you can read for grammar; you can read for many different things; and knowing that makes me feel better; and knowing that everyone does that makes me feel better … Knowing that professors [experts] read and re-read to edit their work helps me…makes me feel better … I have to study this more. I took your class but I did not study it enough. Sentence structures, using short and long sentences, require editing.

The ability to self-edit was helpful to Gee even when she knew she had "to work on sentence structures more" for a third draft, which she did not want to do or have time to do for this paper (proposal). Gee said that she did not feel like she had a professional identity related to writing because she had not yet started working as a lawyer.

Summary, Case 1
For each stage of the scholarly L2 legal writing process, the interview found which writing strategies and CALP skills were most useful to Gee and why. Conceptual and rhetorical pre-writing strategies were most helpful for researching her topic: that is, reading for a purpose, drawing conclusions relevant to her topic, and noting aspects of organizational structure for reuse in her writing. Two drafting strategies were most helpful for getting words and concepts down effectively on paper: (a) using her knowledge of audience and purpose to guide her drafts, and

(b) rejecting irrelevant content in the readings. Re-ordering her writing as she wrote, and asking herself if she met the needs of her reader, were most helpful for Gee to decide what should be changed, deleted, added, or retained while revising her fall paper (proposal).

Strategies analysis across SCQ stages showed that Gee moved from summarizing simply (in the pre-writing stage) to summarizing complexly (in the drafting and revising stages). Summarizing complexly became most helpful for Gee to write her proposal and show legal domain learning. When composing from multiple sources, knowledge transforming strategies helped her, especially the strategy of integrating for comprehensiveness. Another key strategy for Gee throughout was making one point per sentence to emphasize and persuade her legal reader. This strategy was a bridge to competence in communication in scholarly legal writing for Gee. In terms of related proficiency defining abilities, Gee said what she gained most was the ability "to self-edit" with the "strategies to do it." The ability to edit in English "for special legal purposes such as scholarly writing" is a characteristic of functionally native proficiency found in the SCQ.

In sum, writing strategies were a bridge to increased proficiency and to competence in communication for Gee. Time and motivation became key issues for her once she began her research writing because the task was atypical in form, and the topic was undeveloped in the legal research literature. "I think time and motivation are definitely linked. I think I would have gotten an A like I did on my paper last semester [if I had more time]" (Gee, personal communication, January 27, 2009).

Triangulation, Case 1

Comparison of the responses on the SQAT/TQAT instruments reveal that Gee had resolved, or was in the process of resolving, some issues of concern to her like organization, citations, and style but that some language and composition skills having to do with explicit versus implicit communication or meaning were left unresolved in her paper (proposal). More time spent on the "writing to communicate" (stage 3) to produce a third draft would likely have made a difference for Gee in this paper. Constraints on the time Gee needed to produce an excellent paper were de-motivating to her, however. Comparison of the SQAT/TQAT (stage 3, section b) reports on proficiency and instruction suggested that lack of time to produce an excellent research paper may not only decrease student confidence but also detract from professional identity.

Validating Member Check, Case 1

> Donna, I think your interpretation of my writing process in this last paper is very accurate. Your analysis encompasses all my comments and gathers all the information I filled out in the forms you handed me. It identifies the writing stages I most concentrated on and the

areas where I did not concentrate in the writing process. Also, you considered the time restraints that I endured as well as the lack of motivation aspect to writing this paper and how that affected the outcome. (Gee, personal communication, March 4, 2009).

Main Themes/Unexpected Results, Case 1
Salient themes for Gee's case center around the link between: (a) time, motivation, and outcome; (b) stages and the use of surface-level versus deeper level writing strategies; (c) knowledge of strategies, control of fear, and self-regulation in scholarly legal writing; (d) self-editing ability, self-confidence, and writing proficiency; (e) strategies as a "roadmap" for editing; and (f) expert feedback during (rather than after) writing. In Gee's case, scholarly legal writing was seen as a social interactive process that included the law school professor for whom her paper (proposal) was written.

7.3 Results case 2 – Tory

Republic of Moldava: native Romanian; foreign English, French, Russian

Areas of Concern before Writing (SCQ 1)
The SCQ (stage 1) showed that Tory's areas of concern before writing her major research paper fall semester had to do more with language and composition (question 5) than with writing knowledge (question 6). Tory was in her second semester of her graduate program, and she said she was "very" concerned with grammar and punctuation. Areas of concern in writing knowledge that were "somewhat important" included knowing more about: (a) "research writing as a process for effective legal writing"; (b) "the assessment criteria for scholarly legal writing"; and (c) her "academic world as material for L2 law (EAP) classroom discussion." Given that Tory originates from a different educational system and that she is a polyglot who can use four languages as a lawyer (Romanian, Russian, French, English), a concern with writing knowledge specific to process, genre, and cultural context is not surprising.

Pre-writing, "Researching to Learn" Stage (SCQ 1)
Out of seven possible "reading to write" conceptual strategies on the SCQ, Tory found five most helpful when reading to find a topic, thesis, or claim for her major analytical research paper – more than any other participant. In her interview, she emphasized that she would read and interpret the text, talk back to the text, and draw conclusions from various legal sources that she would integrate with her own conclusions.

Tory re-iterated in her interview that she also found CALP skills helpful at this stage to summarize from her reading; then she paraphrased; then she synthesized. Tory said that the use of CALP skills is one of the "most important things to plant ideas in your thinking … you can apply them [later and] come up with your own ideas … You can compare them, contrast them, get to the stage where you can do the proper analysis." Going back to re-read with the use of CALP skills helped Tory generate ideas. "Organization and planning helped me a lot in my writing; synthesizing and analyzing a text [with] notes helped me with the legal analysis."

Tory also explained that talking to experts and peers also helps because it "makes you ask yourself more questions"; however, she did not "have a chance with this paper." She considered general problems related to the law school educated audience anyway, and made the effort to write clearly. The "writing part" took less time for Tory than the reading and re-reading which she said took most of her time. "Preliminary preparation" weighed most heavily in her process of scholarly writing, she said.

Drafting, "Writing to Learn" Stage (SCQ 2)
For getting words and concepts down effectively while drafting her paper, Tory summarized information from persuasive legal sources as well as from "existing case law" to give her the foundation to begin writing. She focused on the Background section of her paper to get started. She monitored her text for errors while she wrote and looked for "patterned errors." She wrote six drafts, changed her organization as needed, and either changed her ideas or made her ideas clearer as she wrote more drafts. She said that "drafting helps to refine language and ideas." "Revising and re-drafting helped me a lot to communicate my ideas with clarity and brevity; it also helped me to reach a deep understanding of the issues and to build substance in my ideas."

Revising, "Writing to Communicate" Stage (SCQ3.a)
Tory found eleven SCQ strategies particularly helpful for revising her paper. First, she read critically and reflected on her own written drafts. She either read with a purpose in mind or she read for cohesion, making linguistic/grammar revisions for clarity and "aesthetics." She also asked herself if: (a) she repeated key words and phrases for cohesion and emphasis, (b) she included the right level of detail, (c) her purpose was clear, and (d) she used headings, subheadings, and logical connectors effectively. Tory revised her paper to ensure sentence to sentence (semantic) cohesiveness, and speaker to speaker (pragmatic) coherence. Although she does not usually add material at this stage, in this paper she said she did so. She also compared her paper to a model of scholarship when revising "just for or-

ganization." The interview showed that Tory had a clear idea of what she usually does and what she did with this paper and why.

After the first two drafts, Tory said she "typically edits at the end of each draft." For this paper, she found seven (out of eleven) SCQ editing strategies most helpful. She proofread her legal writing at least once for (a) form (e.g., paragraph structure); (b) sentence structure (syntax); (c) proper word choice (diction); (d) punctuation; (e) spelling; and (f) citation. Editing for citation "is a slow, painful" process for Tory that she said starts at the beginning.

Out of seventeen SCQ grammar strategies used, Tory found eleven most helpful. She checked whether her sentences contained concrete subjects and active verbs, she tried to avoid nominalizations, and she made one point per sentence, preferring either simple or complex sentence structures. She made her sentences affirmative, not negative; she preferred active voice to passive voice; she used parallel structures in sentences containing multiple elements; she used clear and logical lists with grammatically parallel elements; and she used familiar words instead of flowery language or ornate words. In addition, she used simple past tense for events that already occurred, she used quotations only when necessary, and she avoided long, multi-clause sentences.

As in the drafting stage, Tory used two specific CALP skills for revising: she paraphrased information by putting source material (text) into her own words, and she analyzed information by reflecting and breaking down source text into its parts. In addition, Tory synthesized information by combining and connecting source text in this (revising) stage.

Also as in the drafting stage, Tory used two broad levels of writing purpose. She wrote (a) to learn, problem-solve, summarize complexly, or synthesize information, and (b) to critique, persuade, or interpret evidence selectively and appropriately. In contrast to her writing purpose in the drafting stage, Tory also wrote (a) to state knowledge by listing, repeating, or paraphrasing source text, and (b) to understand, remember, summarize simply, or extend notes to herself in the revising stage.

Knowledge Transforming (SCQ 3.a)

The SCQ showed that revising was the most effective stage for transitioning Tory's writing from *knowledge telling* (stating knowledge) to *knowledge transforming* (deepening her level of understanding to include analysis, synthesis, evaluation of research). One knowledge-transforming strategy was particularly helpful to her: using analysis to generate original content – "a strong tool for contrasting ideas." The interview showed that conceptual transforming (for refining her working thesis) was the strategy group that helped deepen her thinking in English the most while revising her paper, and Tory emphasized the importance of revision to do this. "Revisions helped me refine my ideas, understand them better, come to new conclusions, and deepen my knowledge about the subject."

In her interview, Tory added that "definitely reading critically" was important to her when revising (stage 3) and at "every stage." Tory views " reading critically" as trying to see if she's conveying ideas in her own writing "in a brief and a clear way … Re-reading with a purpose in mind definitely helps make writing (a) clear for the audience; (b) cohesion with the next paragraph."

Tory said she normally "aims for ten drafts just to improve the paper," but due to time constraints associated with this paper, Tory wrote six drafts. In the first three drafts, she deepened the ideas, changed a few words, and added cohesion to achieve "liaison from one part to another" to improve her paper. In the final three drafts, she did "not change substance but made changes in the form and the clarity."

Strategic competence for Tory includes multiple drafts with the writer attending to substance before attending to form and clarity, although she generally tries to edit at the end of each draft. Citation is the "most painful" part of the process for Tory every time she writes because attention to citations "disrupts" train of thought; Tory tries to put her citations in order every time she writes "to get it right from the beginning."

Developing as a Legal Writer across Stages
Tory's written responses to the SCQ open-ended questions describe how the strategies she used in each stage were helping her develop competency as a legal writer. SCQ (stage 1) shows that "organization and planning" helped her "a lot" in her "writing," whereas "synthesizing and analyzing a text with notes helped" her with "the legal analysis" (question 8). SCQ (stage 2) shows that "revising and re-drafting helped [her] a lot to communicate" her "ideas with clarity and brevity …, to reach a deep understanding of the issues, and to build substance" in her ideas (question 5). SCQ (stage 3) shows that "revisions helped" her "refine" her ideas, understand them better, "come to new conclusions and deepen" her "knowledge about the subject" (question 11).

Tory's written responses to the SCQ open-ended questions across stages also describe how writing a research paper in U.S. law school context is "completely different" from writing a paper in her home university law school in Romania: "In my home country the audience is composed of academic experts, therefore the writing is complex and formal" (SCQ stage 1, question 9). Her open-ended response to SCQ (stage 3) clarifies what is expected of her when communicating to her law school educated reader in that system:

> The academic writing requires a formalistic approach; when revising a formal paper one had to make sure the paper was complex. I addressed to an audience of experts who approve [of] complex writing [and] use of legal terms and concepts without a prior explanation of the terms, as they [are] presumed to be known by the audience (question 12).

Tory elaborated in her interview that simple sentence structures are used by people with less education in her native academic culture and that she was expected to be "more pompous and complicated" in her [academic legal] writing.

> They don't teach you how to write anything; you're either a good writer or you're not ... Coming here, taking this course, you realize it can be a learned process ... definitely if you're innately a good writer, you can become better, which is good ... helps you a lot as a person and you can definitely see improvement.

Explicit Strategies Instruction (SCQ3.b)
The SCQ showed that direct (explicit) writing strategies instruction was "very important" in the pre-writing stage for Tory to develop an *efficient writing process*, but only "somewhat important" in the drafting stage. In terms of developing an *effective writing product*, direct instruction was important at the *early* conceptual level. In her interview, Tory explained that instruction was "most important in the early stages because you have to know how to proceed." Also in her interview, Tory said that initially she "underestimated the significance of the class" which was "important" for her, "coming from a civil law country where we have a completely opposite style of writing."

Writing Feedback (SCQ3.b)
Direct (explicit) writing feedback was important for Tory as an L2 legal writer to complete her research paper. Interactive and corrective feedback from her writing teacher and interactive, substantive feedback from her content law professor were very important for Tory although the latter was not available for her. Tory did not identify additional kinds of writing tools or support from the SCQ that she might need to survive or thrive as a legitimate participant in her scholarly legal discourse community. She simply emphasized in her interview that "paraphrasing is golden," as is planning and organization.

Proficiency Defining Abilities (SCQ3.b)
On the "Can Do List of Defining Abilities" for writing at the level of professional proficiency (and higher), Tory checked positive for almost every item. She could not say that she makes "more [Level 3] errors in the low-frequency complex structures" (gerunds and infinitives), however. From Tory's view, she "doesn't make many errors." Similarly, she could not say that she "can edit for special legal pur-

poses such as scholarly writing." She is "totally capable of doing it" but has "no training" other than editing her own work.

For Tory, the concept of "editing" in the context of professional proficiency implies skills leading to publishing, not a stage in writing. It implies "seeing (a) if a paper has any potential for a professional law review; (b) strengths and weaknesses; (c) citations (the technical part)"; and (d) shortening, re-phrasing, and re-formatting, all of which "helps to speak" ideas and writing in English. Here Tory connects speaking and writing. She said she believes that her strengths in L2 writing with academic legal English can be transferred to her native language.

Tory concluded her interview by saying that after the writing course had finished, she saw "substantial improvement": she had "improved confidence, was able to convey ideas better, and [was] confident that she can convey ideas." She said that "there's a whole technique … you can just follow … [to] convey your ideas better … Just like cleaning your house: if you know where every single book is, then you don't have to waste time looking for it and you feel in control … Same with this…I feel more in control" doing the research with summary and paraphrase and with citation. Tory said she knows she is "smart enough to compare and to know the conclusions: that is your original work, your input." CALP skills were "new knowledge" for Tory, as was the process of constructing knowledge from L2 legal sources:

> I think I came to master this and I think this is very good because it helps you in any field; it organizes you as a person, as a thinker … Gives you confidence because you think everything [in writing] is in your control.

Summary, Case 2

For each stage of the scholarly L2 legal writing process, the interview found which writing strategies were most useful to Tory and why. Strategies analysis across stages revealed a focus on the interrelation of "reading to write" conceptual strategies and CALP skills for pre-writing that contributed to a cognitive process that not only developed Tory's thinking but also generated new ideas for her paper. The interview found that strategic competence for Tory included multiple drafts; revisions helped her to refine ideas, understand them better, come to new conclusions, and deepen her knowledge about her legal research topic.

Although Tory was "very" concerned with grammar and punctuation before she started writing, her key issues deepened as she progressed with her research paper writing. In her interview, Tory mentioned the value of knowing (a) CALP skills for constructing knowledge from multiple sources; (b) the connection between speaking and writing (as productive skills); and (c) the feelings of confidence and control that come from knowing about writing strategies and CALP skills for scholarly writing.

Triangulation, Case 2

Comparison of the responses to the SQAT/TQAT instruments reveal that Tory had resolved most issues of concern to her before submitting her research paper for credit to her content law professor. Further comparison of the SQAT/TQAT (stage 3, section b) assessments shows general agreement between the learner and writing teacher with one difference being that, from the teacher's point of view, Tory had very much improved in her ability to revise in response to feedback. Both agreed that Tory had improved as a scholarly writer in areas other than fluency and grammatical accuracy, given her already strong command English – her third academic language after Russian and French (in which she had prepared to be an interpreter). In her interview, Tory commented that, above all, she "feels more in control [now] because things she doesn't know can be improved." From Tory's point of view, she may not have "dramatically" improved as a scholarly legal writer because she was "innately a good writer," but she "got a boost in confidence."

Validating Member Checks, Case 2

Below are two member checks. The first one followed Tory's review of the responses to Research Question 3 and Research Question 2. The second one followed her review of her case with all the analyses, including her first member check and *Main Themes/Unexpected Results* below.

> Dear Donna, Your summary and interpretation of my writing technique and process are very accurate. Your analysis captured all the phases I went through during my writing process and encompasses all my comments and information that I have given you when I filled out your questionnaires (after each writing stage.) In addition, you considered the time constraints that I experienced while writing my paper, which forced me to go through the writing stages a little faster than I would have preferred. Best,..(Tory, personal communication, Dec.17, 2009).

> Dear Donna, Your analysis addresses all the issues I experienced while writing the paper; it also addresses all the progress I've made grace to the techniques you suggested I implement in all stages of writing. Therefore, you assessment is very accurate and to the point. Best,...(Tory, personal communication, December 22, 2009).

Main Themes/Unexpected Results, Case 2

Salient themes for Tory's case center around: (a) time and stages for writing; (b) the confidence and control that come from knowing about writing strategies and CALP skills (that is, "control and doing the research with summary and paraphrase and with citation," thereby avoiding plagiarizing); (c) the interrelation of strategies and CALP skills for developing thinking, deepening knowledge, and generating new ideas; (d) the link between multiple drafts and strategic competence; (e) the importance of knowing about process, genre, and cultural contrast for L2 legal writers; (f) metacognitive writing strategies and the importance of planning and organizing (as "preliminary preparation"); and (g) the use of CALP skills for constructing new knowledge, with the CALP skill of paraphrasing as "golden" for highly proficient multilingual writers.

7.4 Results case 3 – Ferra

Italy: native Italian, foreign English

Areas of Concern before Writing (SCQ 1)
The SCQ (stage 1) showed that Ferra's areas of concern before writing her major research paper, fall semester, had to do with writing knowledge (question 6) as well as with language and composition (question 5). With respect to the former, Ferra indicated that it was "very important" for her to know more about (a) how to write in English from L2 legal sources and (b) the research writing process for effective legal writing. With respect to the latter, language and composition, Ferra checked the following "very important" areas of concern before writing her major analytical paper,: organization, grammar, meaning (content analysis), legal style (for accuracy, brevity, and conciseness), formal versus informal language (register), references and citations to scholarly legal works, and stages of writing. Of these, Ferra's interview isolated organization and legal style as her two most important concerns.

Pre-writing, "Researching to Learn" (SCQ1)
The SCQ and the interview showed two legal reading strategies most helpful for Ferra to find a topic, thesis, or claim for her paper. Both are in the "conceptual" strategies category, the most helpful strategy being that she read for a purpose. The second most helpful strategy was that she "talked back to the text" by problem posing while reading. Ferra said she also used texts or quotes from experts to stimulate thoughts and ideas. In this way, she combined reading, note-taking, and thinking to discover what was important or true for her about her research topic, thesis, or claim. She explained in her interview how re-using text can be very helpful: "the idea is to use that as the top of a part of your paper (a) to write immediately, without a plan, and (b) to find connections." In this way she can "put down many ideas to work and re-work them" and reduce the number of pages in her paper later. The most helpful CALP skill she used for pre-writing was paraphrasing information by putting source material (text) into her own words. Ferra

never used her L1 for "anything including CALP summarizing, paraphrasing, or making comments" in this pre-writing stage.

In response to the first open-ended question for pre-writing (stage 1, question 8), Ferra said the strategies she used in this stage helped her develop competency as an L2 legal writer:

> The strategies used in the pre-writing stage (1) helped me to be concise and select only the information which is relevant to the purpose of my paper. My key pre- writing starting strategy, in fact, has been to focus on the purpose and select my information according to this purpose (question 8).

Drafting, "Writing to Learn" (SCQ2)

In her interview, Ferra said she found eleven drafting strategies most helpful (out of seventeen used). First, she focused on what authority is predominant to begin writing. As she pointed out in the SCQ pre-writing section, Ferra paraphrased from legal sources to begin writing – a knowledge telling strategy. She said, however, that it is "sometimes better to quote when a statement is relevant." She also reordered information from legal source texts to use in her drafts, and she conferenced with her instructor/professor to refine and clarify her ideas. In addition, Ferra considered various ways of organizing ideas related to her purpose when her paper's structure was not clear to her yet.

Later in the drafting stage, Ferra said she rejected irrelevant substantive content while she wrote. She reassessed her purpose as needed and made her ideas clearer as she wrote more drafts – as many as ten. She used an American legal English dictionary to read but not to write, and she wrote in English, leaving gaps for missing English words. If there was a gap, she "wrote sentences in Italian."

Grammar was "absolutely" not important for Ferra in her drafting (reading and writing) process. She used CALP skills to synthesize and summarize in Italian. Combining and connecting source text (synthesis) was most helpful for Ferra in this (drafting) stage of writing in which she wrote (a) to learn and (b) to critique. In her interview, she added that "someone who does not know about the topic can be more useful at this point because you have to be more comprehensive." The interview also showed that "synthesizing" is the same as "summarizing" when translating from Italian; Ferra emphasized that "we [Italians] do not have this word."

Revising, "Writing to Communicate" (SCQ3.a)

The SCQ showed that ten revising strategies were most helpful to Ferra: "Here I can be more effective at this point." First, she read critically and reflected on her own drafts, not to change ideas but to "sharpen" her own thinking so she could be "clear, concise, comprehensive and more effective" as a legal writer. She re-ordered her writing as she revised, not changing the structure, only the paragraphs. She also made lexical and vocabulary revisions, asking herself if she repeated key words and phrases for cohesion and emphasis. She asked herself if her purpose and message would be clear to the reader, and she got feedback from her writing teacher (researcher). When revising, Ferra asked herself if she used logical connectors effectively. The SCQ showed that Ferra revised her paper to ensure (a) sentence to sentence (semantic) cohesiveness and (b) speaker to speaker (pragmatic) coherence.

Ferra reflected in her interview that editing was the "worst part" of the revising process for her. Although she used all the strategies except peer review with fellow classmates, she felt she was "not able" to edit well and got "upset" with the detail, especially with footnotes. "There is no issue about editing in Italy for [a] dissertation." Her Italian Ph.D. advisor did not ask her to edit her paper, and when "you write an article for a law review, they make the editing part." Each law review has its own style, so "there is no issue" of one standard, Ferra said.

Nevertheless, even though she "does not like this stage," Ferra tried to use all of the grammar strategies when revising but not always with success. She said she tried to make one point per sentence, make her sentences affirmative (not negative), and avoid long, multi-clause sentences. Her most helpful grammar strategies were those that addressed the contrast between Italian and American expository writing style. Her most helpful plain English writing strategies included the following: Ferra checked to see (a) whether she used short and medium-length sentences, and (b) whether her sentences contained concrete subjects and active verbs. "Short and medium-length sentences is my kind of problem" because Ferra said she can be unclear if she writes long sentences with two ideas instead of one. She also tried to avoid nominalizations. She preferred active voice to passive voice with some exceptions because "passive voice is sometimes more effective", and she used parallel structures in sentences containing multiple elements. She also used familiar words instead of flowery language or ornate words. She kept subjects and verbs, and verbs and objects, undivided – without interrupting phrases. In addition, she used precise transitions to convey exact connections.

In terms of the most helpful CALP skills used, analyzing information by reflecting and breaking down source text into its parts was Ferra's "way to be clear." Her purpose was to critique and "go beyond what others have said." Although Ferra thought that stage 3 (revising) was "too late" for knowledge transforming, which began for her in stage 2 (drafting), she did find that analysis to generate original content was a most helpful strategy for deepening her thinking in English in both the stages of drafting and revising. In addition, the use of plain English

(A,B,C style) strategies to revise for accuracy, brevity, and clarity in thought helped her the most in this revising stage.

Linguistic transforming was the one strategy group that Ferra said helped most to get away from the language of source texts when revising. However, both *conceptual transforming* (for refining her working thesis) and *rhetorical transforming* (for binding her overall structure) helped her the most in stage 2 (drafting). Although Ferra used a number of *linguistic transforming* strategies "at the end of stage 2" (drafting), the one that helped her the most to transform text information while revising, giving her authorship of her major analytical paper for the semester, was the use of lexical repetition (that is, repeating key legal terms and phrases). The SCQ showed how the strategies she used in this (revising) stage helped her develop competency (proficiency) as an L2 legal writer:

> The revising stage is the stage which allows [me to] make the purpose of the paper effective. I think that only at this stage it is in fact possible for the reader to see completely the transformation of his or her thoughts, making them coherent and cohesive. I found particularly effective to review the passage between the last paragraph of one section and the first paragraph of the following one. It is only through this process that the thesis pursued by the reader has the capability to be effectively proved and completely harmonized with the context. (question 11)

Developing as a Legal Writer across Stages

A review of the SCQ during the interview showed that writing a research paper in U.S. law school context clearly contrasts with Ferra's first legal language academic writing process and non-native English speaker background and experience. The SCQ (stage 1) showed how preparing to write a research paper in U.S. law school context is similar or different from preparing to write a research paper in her home university or law school:

> The process is completely different. Firstly, in my own country (Italy) there is no academic course which introduces students to writing skill. Mainly because all the exams are oral and students are not required write a paper. The approach to legal writing is required only at the end of the 4 years through the presentation of a dissertation which is usually no less than 200 pages long. This means that the kind of work required is completely different from writing a paper of 30-50 pages long. However, the pre-writing and the writing process are very personal. Each student is free to use his own strategies without any standardization. (question 9)

Ferra's responses to the first open-ended question for this (pre-writing) stage and for the next (drafting) stage both revealed that the strategies she used for writing helped her develop competency as an L2 legal writer. For drafting (stage 2), she said that:

As already pointed out …, Italian students do not follow this complex process in order to write their dissertation. As Ph.D. student I can say that it is the same also for academic writer. The different process I have followed for my U.S. writing experience helped me to focus on the scope of my writing. If the writer decides to fill a purpose which it states at the beginning, it is easy to make it clear through research, but it is not easy to change it. This means that you can change your thesis, but not your purpose. In other words, the question to be answered is always the same, but the answer can be different after completing the writing process. Maybe, the Italian writing process does not allow achieve the same goal. However, I feel that there is some kind of standardization in deciding to follow precise legal writing strategies. (question 12)

The second open-ended SCQ question for revising (stage 3) showed how revising a research paper in U.S. law school context is different from revising a research paper in Ferra's home university law school:

As I have already said in the other two stages there is no similar process in an Italian University even if I think that this stage is particularly important for an advanced writer in order to make effective the purpose of the paper. (question 12)

Explicit Strategies Instruction (SCQ3.b)

The SCQ revealed that direct (explicit) writing strategies instruction was very important at *all stages* and at *all levels* (conceptual, rhetorical, linguistic) for Ferra to develop an *efficient writing process* and an *effective writing product* respectively. In her interview, Ferra said that her experience learning scholarly L2 legal writing increased her proficiency level "partially." She explained that she had been building proficiency over time but that the ABC legal style [and strategies for] writing helped her improve the most "to be concise, to be effective, to be clear, and to be brief" within a limited number of pages.

She also said that she "doesn't really know what 'strategies' means": that the "idea to write an introduction is important" along with a thesis or claim of what she wants "to prove." She said she never thought of "purpose" when writing papers in the Italian "academy." Italian professors only asked her to write on a topic: not one with a specific [limited] purpose and not one with a thesis that moves in a specific direction. The cultural "issue" for Ferra is freedom in Italy versus a more focused approach in the U.S. where she was "not just writing" but thinking of what she was doing, saying to herself, "O.K. Now I am organized. I know what I am doing." She said she became conscious of her actions, "trying to make clear (a) facts of my paper, (b) scope of my paper, and (c) what I want to prove in my paper." Ferra was affected also by her L1 Italian – a "problem all non-U.S. students have" – as well as by time constraints. Exams in U.S. law school context, she elaborated, were a "physical task" for her, not a "mental task." She really did not understand what her L2 U.S. law school exams were trying to measure.

Writing Feedback (SCQ3.b)

Direct (explicit) writing feedback was also very important for Ferra as an L2 legal writer to complete her fall paper: that is, (a) interactive and corrective feedback from her legal English writing teacher; (b) correction and explanation from both peer native-English speakers and peer non-native English speakers (class-mates); and (c) interactive and substantive feedback from her content law professor. Her content law professor commented to the teacher (-researcher) that she was impressed with Ferra's ability to solicit feedback from her.

Proficiency Defining Abilities (SCQ3.b)

Ferra said she improved most in her ability to be concise, effective, and clear in writing. She reported that page limits and a focus on the Introduction and Conclusion when revising "helped a lot." Editing at the functionally native proficiency level was still not possible for Ferra, however. From her point of view, editing at a professional level of English is not simply a native/non-native speaker issue but one having to do with contrasting "academic systems, academic conventions, and [academic] standards ... Other students also have this issue."

Ferra did not identify any additional kinds of writing tools or support she might need to survive or thrive as a legitimate participant in her scholarly legal discourse community. She was the one student writer who went on to stage 4 to publish her paper in an international law journal (not part of this study). Ferra did say in her interview, however, that she "feels more comfortable" now, and is at a "higher level in writing than in speaking." When she speaks, Ferra said that she sees her mistakes (real-time), whereas in writing she can correct them.

Summary, Case 3

For each stage of the scholarly L2 legal writing process, the interview found which writing strategies and CALP skills were most useful to Ferra and why. Strategies analysis across stages showed that revising was a key stage for Ferra because "only at this stage it is in fact possible for the reader to see completely the transformation of his or her thoughts, making them coherent and cohesive." A revising strategy that Ferra found particularly effective was "to review the passage between the last paragraph of one section and the first paragraph of the following one." Other key strategies occurred in the pre-writing stage when she focused on purpose and selected information from source text according to this purpose; in other words, re-using language for constructing knowledge: "The strategies used in the pre-writing stage helped me to be concise and select only the information which is relevant to the purpose of my paper" (SCQ open-ended question 8).

Key issues for Ferra were the following: (a) international student writers can experience contrasting academic conventions, standards, and systems for assessment; (b) editing can be an affective issue as well as one related to knowledge and skill; and (c) the speaking-writing connection is important to explore for learners coming from different educational systems and cultures of scholarship.

Triangulation, Case 3
Comparison of the responses to the SQAT/TQAT instruments reveal that out of 15 items on Ferra's self-report on proficiency and instruction, Ferra checked 11 that show how she improved as a scholarly legal writer spring and fall semesters. Out of those 11, the teacher agreed with the student's self-assessment. Whereas the student checked an increase in fluency, her interview clarified that the student meant an increase in the proficiency level of her writing. The teacher noted increased fluency in both speaking and writing, however; Ferra was able to speak about her writing fluently at the time of the interview.

Two areas of strong agreement were a much more (a) efficient legal writing process, and (b) effective writing product compared to spring semester. In addition, Ferra checked that her motivation had very much improved, but that her confidence had only "somewhat" improved. She said she had somewhat improved her ability to revise in response to feedback and to self-edit. Overall, Ferra reported that she had a stronger professional identity now.

Validating Member Check, Case 3
Not available. Student participant returned to her home country to finish her Ph.D. dissertation.

Main Themes/Unexpected Results, Case 3
The Interview Protocol for Ferra's case revealed how strategic competence may be related to areas of student concern associated with (a) language and composition as well as with (b) knowledge, especially pre-writing as a stage in scholarly writing.

Salient themes include the links between: (a) the revising stage and transforming thoughts because "the answer can be different after completing the writing process"; (b) language re-use and *linguistic transforming* for constructing knowledge and developing competency in L2 legal writing; (c) editing as more than a native/non-native speaker issue: that is, one having to do with contrasting academic systems, academic conventions, and [academic] standards; (d) academic writing "style" and cultural contrast; (e) oral and written L2 academic speech, especially for revising (stage 3); (f) knowledge of editing skills, professional identity and proficiency; (g) metacognitive knowledge, cultural awareness, and conscious use of strategies as tools for L2 writer development; and (h) the concept of synthesis as part of L2 legal writing vocabulary (in contrast to L1 Italian); and (i) law school exams as a "physical task" in contrast to a "mental task" for L2 legal writers.

7.5 Results case 4 – Liv

Ukraine: native Ukrainian; foreign Russian, Polish, English

Areas of Concern before Writing (SCQ 1)
The SCQ (stage 1) showed that Liv's areas of concern before writing her major research paper, fall semester, had to do with both language and composition (question 5) and with writing knowledge (question 6). Liv checked each item in both these two categories as "very important." The SCQ and the interview showed that Liv had prior experience writing academic papers for law school in her native language as an undergraduate student.

Pre-writing, "Researching to Learn" (SCQ1)
The interview for Case 4 showed that Liv's "reading to write" strategies were most helpful, especially reading for a purpose. She said that she "browsed for content" without reading whole (secondary source) law journal articles. For Liv, pre-writing was "all about finding relevant cases and answers," adding that case law is not important in civil law countries.

The SCQ showed that she used CALP skills to (a) paraphrase information by putting source text into her own words, and (b) analyze information by reflecting and breaking down source text into its parts. The interview further revealed that rhetorical "reading to write" strategies were also helpful to Liv at this stage as she "read others for structure" and re-worked her headings and sub-headings.

Drafting, "Writing to Learn" (SCQ2)
In her interview, Liv said she found six drafting strategies most helpful (out of twenty-three used). She said she focused on her plan and then followed it by (a) summarizing and (b) paraphrasing information from persuasive legal sources, (c) focusing on the Discussion (Analysis) section to get started, (d) collaborating with her classmates and writing teacher (researcher) to discuss the Introduction and Discussion sections, (e) monitoring her text errors as she wrote, and (f) writing three or more drafts. The interview showed that she summarized and paraphrased material into paragraphs, focusing on the Discussion (Analysis) section but adding material to the Background section as she wrote "several" drafts of her paper.

Revising, "Writing to Communicate" (SCQ3.a)

Liv's most helpful revising strategies were somewhat evenly distributed across three categories: revising strategies, grammar strategies, and knowledge transforming strategies. The interview revealed that as she revised, she used summary, added material, and re-ordered "all her writing" to fit her plan and make it readable. She said that she tried to end each paragraph with a "small summary" or begin the next paragraph with a "small introduction." Liv also proofread her legal writing for proper word choice (diction) and consistent use of key terms. She used grammar strategies to avoid the passive voice and long, multi-clause sentences. Liv said she used parallel structures in sentences containing multiple elements and familiar words instead of flowery language or ornate words. She provided structural clues and repeated key structure words to improve readability (for example, "that").

Knowledge Transforming (SCQ 3.a)

Liv found revising to be the most effective stage for transitioning her writing from *knowledge telling* (stating knowledge) to *knowledge transforming*, thereby deepening her level of understanding to include analysis, synthesis, and evaluation of research. The interview found that Liv's most helpful strategies to deepen her thinking in English while revising were twofold: (a) using editing routines for clarity in thought and expression, and (b) using plain English writing strategies for accuracy, brevity, and clarity. Both the rhetorical and linguistic strategy groups helped her to deepen her thinking in English the most while revising her major analytical paper.

Her most helpful linguistic transforming strategies included the following: (a) using lexical repetition by repeating key legal terms and phrases, (b) using source texts or quotations to support her own text, and (c) summarizing to compose by selecting and reorganizing. Liv said that summarizing was perhaps the most important CALP skill but she used all CALP skills equally when writing this paper. Liv emphasized that she also used lexical repetition "through all the stages." Further, The SCQ for all stages shows that Liv never used a language other than English to write her analytical paper.

Developing as a Legal Writer across Stages

A review of the SCQ (stage 1) during Liv's interview showed that preparation for writing a research paper in U.S. law school context is similar to Ukraine, but the concept of cases in her civil law home country is different. She clarified in her interview that she wrote papers for law school (unlike the other participants in this study), but the Introduction and Conclusion sections were different because student writers were not required to show original thinking in her home country.

Liv's responses to the open-ended questions in the SCQ (stage 2) showed that the strategies she used for drafting helped her develop competency as a legal writer. She said, "The strategies helped me to organize my thinking in order to start writing…[and] to put my research in logical and clear structure" (question 5). Her SCQ (stage 2) open-ended response further described how drafting a research paper in U.S. law school context is different from drafting a research paper in Ukraine: "The major difficulty is the language. My writing skills in native language were based on 'intuition'. Writing in English involves much more thinking."

Liv's responses to the open-ended questions in the SCQ (stage 3.a) and the interview elaborated on how she dealt with the language when writing research. A number of grammar strategies were "most helpful" for her to write effectively. She said, "I made several revisions and learned that it is better to revise separately for grammar, punctuation, word choice and content" (question 11). In the interview, she said:

> I think self-revising improved a lot. Before I was not able to read critically … my own writing … And now with checklists, I started revising separately for grammar, separately for word choice, separately for structure in general … I was not able to concentrate on everything [at one time] … When you revise several times by concentrating only on one thing, it's much easier and better: read for a purpose.

The SCQ (stage 3) further showed that "English is not my native language, therefore revising takes much more time and work. Also I had to learn how to make [my] paper reader oriented, which in my previous experience was not a requirement" (question 12). In sum, the inclusion of original thinking and a reader orientation made writing a research paper in U.S. law school context different from writing a research paper in Liv's undergraduate law school.

Explicit Strategies Instruction (SCQ 3.b)

Both the SCQ (3.b) and the interview revealed that for Liv, direct (explicit) writing strategies instruction was important at all stages to develop an efficient writing process. She said in the interview that formal instruction helped her to organize her thinking, make a plan for herself, make deadlines, and "break the process into parts": "At the beginning I was overwhelmed with the broadness of the material and when I broke it into parts," it was easier. Liv also indicated on the SCQ that direct (explicit) writing strategies instruction was important to her at all levels (that is, conceptual, rhetorical, and linguistic) to develop an effective writing product. Additional writing tools or support Liv identified as most helpful on the SCQ were the following: (a) making a "table of contents" with "a draft deadline for each stage" of writing, and (b) using the writing class handouts and checklists for each stage of writing.

Writing Feedback (SCQ 3.b)
Liv said in the interview that she received no feedback from anyone other than the writing teacher (-researcher) to complete her major research paper fall semester. Her law professor was not available. She found the writing teacher interactive and corrective feedback "very important."

Proficiency Defining Abilities (SCQ 3.b)
Probes during the interview revealed more about how Liv had been building proficiency over time during the semester. She said that all her fall courses helped her in her writing for U.S. law school, but the structure for papers was different (for example, instrumental versus scholarly legal writing). She said also that she followed the same structure of papers she had read from (a) the writing class, and (b) other law school courses. The writing class checklists she said also helped her with structure, and she "started writing more precisely …, avoided general sentences …, and stated her purpose and main idea at the beginning."

When questioned about the few items on the Checklist of Defining Abilities for legal expository writing she reported she could not do, Liv explained that because English is not her native language, it is difficult to recognize different meanings for words and express subtleties and nuances (shades of meaning) in legal writing. From Liv's point of view, vocabulary is an issue for non-native English speakers, and "using precise words can be difficult." Liv does not think she can write with proficiency equal to that of a law school educated native English speaker (for example, writing clearly, explicitly, informatively, *and* persuasively in one document) "all at the same time." Liv emphasized that she can edit for special legal purposes, however.

Summary, Case 4
For each stage of the scholarly L2 legal writing process, the interview found which writing strategies and CALP skills were most useful to Liv and why. Strategies analysis across stages showed that Liv's most helpful strategies for writing in U.S. law school graduate context were (a) reading for a purpose and (b) revising with a purpose in mind (that is, "revise separately for grammar, punctuation, word choice and content"). Summarizing was considered the most important CALP skill for Liv.

Triangulation, Case 4
Comparison of her responses to the SQAT/TQAT instruments reveal that Liv benefited from speaking about the "problem" of structuring her paper perhaps more than she benefited from using the self-assessment measures to organize her research and writing. Working with legal cases was new to her, and writing Introduction and Conclusion sections was also different, she said, because these sections require original thinking. Because of the difficulty of having one set of generic

self-assessment measures for more than one kind of scholarly article or paper, discussion between student and teacher proved invaluable for both. Working with this student participant was a process of "constant negotiation." Liv never did get feedback from her law professor.

Validating Member Check, Case 4

> Dear Donna: All the information in your analysis is very accurate. I found your assistance and my participation in the project very helpful. With your help I was able to develop an effective individual strategy for writing legal research paper. Thank you, …
> (Liv, personal communication, December 16, 2009).

> Dear Donna: Everything seems very precise and I would not add/delete anything.
> (Liv, personal communication, December 23, 2009).

Main Themes/Unexpected Results, Case 4
Salient themes resulting from Liv's qualitative case study include the observation that even experienced L2 legal writers need to develop an effective individual strategy for writing research papers at the graduate level. Other main themes center around: (a) self-regulation which can mean "self-revising" with a purpose in mind; (b) cultural contrast in scholarly legal writing which can include original thinking and reader orientation; and (b) metacognition which can include planning at each stage, rhetorical strategies, and monitoring – all ways to manage the writing process.

7.6 Results case 5 – Anyo

Cameroon: native Mbo; foreign English, French

Areas of Concern before Writing (SCQ 1)
The SCQ (stage 1) showed that Anyo's areas of concern before writing his major research paper, fall semester, had to do with both language and composition skills (question 5) and writing knowledge (question 6). Anyo checked almost each item in both these two categories as "very important." The interview revealed that his main issue was being a novice. Anyo was unfamiliar with concepts of genre, academic English, objective stance, and (expository) legal writing style. Before taking the scholarly legal writing course, he self-diagnosed "problems" with (a) long sentences, and (b) lack of control of punctuation.

Pre-writing, "Researching to Learn" (SCQ1)
Out of seventeen possible "reading to write" (conceptual, rhetorical, and linguistic) strategies on the SCQ, Anyo found six most helpful to prepare for his major analytical research paper – more than any other participant. The interview showed that the rhetorical strategies helped him the most because his "problem" was organization. He said that he needed to know which section of his paper to write first and why because he was unsure of what he was doing. Anyo said he noted aspects of organizational structure (a) for reading comprehension and (b) for reuse in his writing. Four linguistic strategies affecting his comprehension and ability to paraphrase in English were also most helpful. Anyo noted key legal terms for reuse in his writing, as well as key English phrases for reading comprehension, and he paraphrased in English for both reading comprehension and language reuse in his writing.

The interview showed five (type 1b) pre-writing strategies Anyo found most helpful for reading, note-taking, and thinking. He (a) used texts or quotes from experts to stimulate thoughts and ideas; (b) exchanged ideas with others, one peer in particular, about his research project; (c) read others for modeling of style and organization; (d) made a preliminary outline; and (e) found a quiet place where he could concentrate on his legal writing. As for the two CALP skills that helped most for writing his first draft, Anyo said he (a) summarized information complexly by selecting and organizing source text, and (b) synthesized information by combining and connecting source text.

Drafting, "Writing to Learn" (SCQ2)
The interview showed that of twenty-seven possible SCQ strategies for drafting, Anyo found twelve "most useful" (more than any other participant). When probed in the interview, he emphasized that they were "all very important" but he could order "the most helpful." Fist, he said he paraphrased from legal sources to begin writing – a knowledge-telling strategy. Then he re-read legal texts that served as rhetorical models. Third, he summarized information from persuasive legal sources. Then he reordered information from legal source texts to use in his draft. Lastly, he said he conferenced with his content law professor, his writing teacher (researcher), and his peers to refine and clarify his ideas. He was thus able to gain input into "how to write and organize information" before changing the organization of his draft after a class presentation.

The SCQ found that Anyo used all the CALP skills for drafting, and in the interview he singled out paraphrase as "very helpful" for putting source information into his own words. Anyo stressed that he was always going back to edit, correct errors, and get new ideas for developing his research topic. He said was able "to develop ideas to continue" writing by re-reading his own text, "going back and forth" because he said he was writing as if he were in the "final stage....Time was against me."

Anyo used a language other than English in this drafting stage for writing his major analytical paper. He said, "I read articles and books written in French, then translated the materials and ideas into English which I used in discussion" (the Discussion section of his paper).

On the SCQ (stage 2), his DK response indicated he did not know if he used a language other than English for revising. The interview further showed that Anyo was always concerned about citations: "I was very afraid."

Revising, "Writing to Communicate" (SCQ3.a)

The interview found Anyo's eight "most helpful" strategies Anyo used for revising, six for editing, seven for grammar, and two for writing to communicate to the law school educated reader. Anyo knew his research topic well, and he used linguistic and grammar revisions to decide what should be changed, deleted, or retained at this (revising) stage. He also asked himself (a) if he repeated key words and phrases for cohesion and emphasis; (b) if his purpose and message were clear; and (c) if he used headings, subheadings, and logical connectors effectively. Anyo said he also found the strategies to solicit feedback "most helpful" for revising. He got feedback from his writing instructor (researcher) to assess how effectively he communicated his message and to build or re-construct his analysis, and he got expert legal opinion of his analysis from his content law professor.

The only two editing strategies Anyo did not find most helpful at this last stage were (a) proofreading at least once for form (for example, paragraph structure), and (b) proofreading for appearance (for example, spacing and indentation). Otherwise, Anyo found all the editing strategies "most helpful" for revising (stage 3).

Anyo's long sentences were "problematic" for him, so he found some grammar strategies more helpful than others. His "most helpful" grammar strategies included checking to see whether he used short and medium-length sentences, trying to avoid nominalizations (the practice of changing short verbs to longer nouns), and keeping subjects and verbs, and verbs and objects, undivided – without interrupting phrases. He also preferred familiar words instead of flowery language or ornate words, consistent wording and phrasing without changing words for variety, and consistent parallel word signals such as "first" and "second." Using accurate and adequate punctuation as "road signs" in his legal writing "helped a lot!"

The "most helpful" CALP skills Anyo identified at this (revising) stage continued to be paraphrasing information by putting source material (text) into his own words, and synthesizing information by combining and connecting source text. The SCQ showed that for effectively revising his paper, Anyo wrote primarily to (a) state knowledge by listing, repeating, or paraphrasing source text at this stage, and to (b) critique, persuade, or interpret evidence selectively and appropriately. Although the SCQ showed he operated with two other (learner-centered) levels of composing, the interview showed that Anyo did not find them "most helpful" for communicating to his law school educated reader.

Knowledge Transforming (SCQ3.a)
On the SCQ, Anyo identified revising as the most effective stage for transitioning his writing from *knowledge-telling* (stating knowledge) to *knowledge-transforming* (deepening his level of understanding to include analysis, synthesis, and evaluation of research). Among the knowledge-transforming strategies he used to deepen his thinking in English while revising, Anyo found two "most helpful": (a) using analysis to generate original content, and (b) using plain English writing strategies for accuracy, brevity, and clarity (legal writing style). The particular linguistic transforming strategies he found most helpful to transform text information while revising, giving him authorship of his paper, were the following four strategies: (a) using source texts or quotations to support his own text; (b) paraphrasing by stating knowledge, (c) summarizing by selecting and reorganizing, and (d) synthesizing by combining and connecting.

Developing as a Legal Writer across Stages
The SCQ (stage 1) revealed that writing memoranda and summary reports for his *American Legal Institutions* teacher was particularly useful for Anyo to develop his ability to write an analytical paper (question 4). The SCQ (stage 1) and the interview showed that writing activities for other law school classes also helped Anyo "a lot" to be aware and overcome his habit of using the first person personal pronoun for expository legal writing. It was "very easy" for him to write using "I" but not easy for him to write using the objective third person. He said this kind of correction eventually "became an instinct" for him when writing this paper.

The only SCQ (stage 1) area of concern Anyo did not check was knowing more about the assessment criteria for scholarly legal writing. His other concerns about writing knowledge and about language and legal composition were more pressing; this was Anyo's first experience writing a legal research paper in English or in any other language. His previous experience with expository legal writing was limited to writing exams for law school. When asked how the strategies he used in the pre-writing stage were helping him develop competency as an L2 legal writer, Anyo said they helped him "to assemble the same facts from different sources into a body of organized work." When probed about what writing from legal sources means to Anyo, he said it means "writing out of your head with authoritative sources as support."

In the SCQ (stage 2), Anyo described how the strategies he used in the drafting stage were helping him develop competency as an L2 legal writer. He said they helped him know "how to arrange ideas chronologically and how to select what ideas are necessary for the paper and what to leave out." In other words, the strategies for drafting (stage 2) helped him develop conceptually and rhetorically more than linguistically. When responding to the SCQ (stage 3.a), Anyo reiterated that the strategies he used for revising were helping him "to reorganize my sentences and paragraphs."

Explicit Strategies Instruction (SCQ 3.b)

Anyo "wanted to sound clear" in his paper. He said in the interview that he really had problems with punctuation and parallel word signals which he "can control" now and that the exercises "we did…in class many times" helped him.

For Anyo, direct (explicit) strategies instruction was important at all stages for him to develop (a) an efficient scholarly writing process, and (b) an effective scholarly writing product. This was his "first time doing this academic work," and he did not know about "levels" or stages of scholarly legal writing (that is, "where to start and where to stop"). To develop an effective product, he said, it is "important to go through all the stages."

> Now I'm confident. If I have something to write, I know exactly where to look for the topic, how to narrow the topic, how to start the research, how to [engage in] pre- writing, writing, and editing; I'm confident in that.

Anyo said he knows exactly what he has to do "to get the final product" using the quality assessment tools (Research Question 3).

Writing Feedback (SCQ 3.b)

Direct (explicit) writing feedback was "very important" for him as an L2 legal writer in three ways: (a) the legal English writing teacher gave him interactive as well as corrective feedback; (b) peer non-native English speaking classmates gave him correction as well as explanation; and (c) his content law professor gave him interactive as well as substantive feedback. Anyo felt that peer native-English speaker (non-teacher) correction and explanation were only "somewhat important." Anyo "did not feel the need" to collaborate with a peer who was a native English speaker.

Additional kinds of writing tools or support Anyo identified to survive or thrive as a legitimate participant in his scholarly legal discourse community focused on other writers and their writing styles: that is, "reading other writers and learning from their style." When probed, Anyo said that "style" means (a) "what is needed in the Introduction; (b) how to come up with headings; and (c) what is needed in your Conclusion." Anyo was making reference to genre for scholarly legal writing (Research Question 3).

Proficiency Defining Abilities (SCQ 3.b)
The SCQ (3.b) showed that Anyo checked almost all items defining abilities up to "functionally native proficiency" in legal (expository) writing. The only SCQ (3.b) item he did not check was the "advanced professional proficiency" ability to "express subtleties and nuances (shades of meaning) in legal writing". He said he did not understand this item and that he has "to refer to a dictionary when using some words in a sentence" to ensure he expresses his intended meaning to his audience. He said he does this "a lot". Now he is more "conscious" of how to express his meaning since "doing" the writing course, and he can see if his "use of certain words conveys the meaning" he wants "to send out."

> Generally I've improved in grammar ... makes a big difference. Increased knowledge makes a difference ... You must use the right language to express your point of view to another legal thinker. Otherwise, you could express another meaning.

Summary, Case 5
For each stage of the scholarly L2 legal writing process, the interview found Anyo to have more "most helpful" writing strategies and CALP skills than any other participant at almost every stage. For pre-writing, the interview found fourteen strategies most helpful to prepare for his major analytical research paper. For drafting, Anyo's interview found thirteen "most useful." For revising, the interview showed twenty-nine "most helpful" strategies. Strategies analysis across stages showed that Anyo's most helpful CALP skill overall was paraphrase, although he said all were important for him at each stage. This student participant used strategies as a roadmap for guiding his scholarly writing.

Triangulation, Case 5
Comparison of the responses to the SQAT/TQAT instruments reveal that Anyo's checked items on the SQAT were more comprehensive than the writing teacher-researcher's checked items for pre-writing and revising, but the same for drafting. This match is important because additional TQAT comments that accompanied Anyo's last draft showed that he may have succeeded under severe time constraints by heeding the writing teacher's advice below: (TQAT quote 12/26/08)

> Anyo, My advice is to finish the revisions you wanted to make in drafting (stage 2) using the SQAT I gave you, then revise again using comments I gave you on this draft (stage 3.a).

> In this culture, an abstract is a summary containing the thesis which needs to be made clear in the Introduction also. Write the abstract at the end – not at the beginning of a paper. This

> may help you with structure – outlined in the stage 2 SQAT doc. I gave you. Email me if I have not been clear or if you have a question. All the best, Donna.

Surprisingly, a general summary or "abstract" substituted for an introduction in Anyo's final draft. The SQAT/TQAT tools for stage 2 helped the student writer revise for structure (that is, the scholarly legal writing genre), and the SQAT/TQAT tools for stage 3 helped him make revisions related to purpose and content that included footnotes functioning properly. Time-consuming corrections having to do with "mechanics" were less important for both student and writing teacher in this case although Anyo clearly stated in his interview that he constantly monitored his writing for errors as if he were writing his final draft.

Validating Member Check, Case 5

> Hi Donna, Your analysis are [*sic*] accurate. You have correctly stated the stages and experiences during my writing process. From being a novice to how I learned and developed the writing strategies. You stated the problems encountered during the writing process, what I found interesting to develop my writing skills, what I did to produce a final academic research paper and the reaction of my law professor. I think this is a perfect analysis from all the comments in the questionnaires and the interviews we did during and after the course. I will gladly welcome any further feedback you request. Best, …
> (Anyo, personal communication, December 17, 2009).

Main Themes/Unexpected Results, Case 5

Anyo's case centers around the following themes: (a) control and self-regulation allow for "writing out of your head with authorative sources as support"; (b) critically re-reading one's own text helps "to develop ideas to continue" writing; (c) writing with constant monitoring is useful when pressured by time constraints; (d) going through all of the stages develops an effective legal writing product; (e) conditional knowledge of strategies is related to developing an efficient writing process; (f) strategies instruction develops confidence and ACB academic writing style; and (f) increased knowledge [and use] of grammar affects the L2 writer's expression of meaning. Important to note is that when the student writer used the quality assessment tool for stage 2 and implemented suggested changes, the writing teacher did not have to edit.

7.7 Results case 6 – Sam

Palestine, native Arabic; foreign English, French

Areas of Concern before Writing (SCQ 1)
The SCQ (stage 1) showed that Sam's areas of concern before writing his major research paper, fall semester, had to do with both language and composition skills (question 5) and with writing knowledge (question 6). From a skills standpoint, Sam was particularly concerned with meaning (content analysis), legal style (for accuracy, brevity, and conciseness), social-cultural appropriateness for the U.S. law school educated reader, references and citations to scholarly legal works, and stages in legal writing (for example, writing to learn before writing to communicate). From a knowledge standpoint, Sam was especially concerned with (a) knowing more about American law school conventions, (b) knowing more about research writing as a process for effective legal writing, and (c) knowing more about the assessment criteria for scholarly legal writing.

Pre-writing, "Researching to Learn" (SCQ1)
Out of seventeen possible "reading to write" (conceptual, rhetorical, and linguistic) strategies on the SCQ, Sam found two most helpful to prepare for his major analytical research paper. His most helpful conceptual strategy was reading for a purpose. The interview showed that he "was looking for the argument" he wanted to use in his "paper" by reading, making "notes on his research documents on the computer to save time," and "marking the parts of the articles" he wanted to use. He "did not take more than one paragraph" from each document which included research articles, reports and some research papers – no books, he said. Sam made (tentative) headings and sub-headings from his notes, summarizing what he wanted to write "subject to changes." Sam's most helpful linguistic strategy was paraphrasing in English for reading comprehension. He used no Arabic at all, he said, because it would have been too time consuming to take notes and then translate.

Sam's most helpful pre-writing strategies for combining reading, note-taking, and thinking to discover what was important or true for him about his research topic was brainstorming and exchanging ideas with friends about his research project. Whether peers agreed or disagreed with him, Sam found their feedback very helpful. His second most helpful (Type 1b) strategy was starting to write immediately, without a plan:

> You need to do that because sometimes you think of the paper not only when you are on the table and writing...[but when] you are on the bus, [in] the car, walking ... and you can go back home and write it ... Sometimes you can write about your paper and you don't cite any authority.

He also paraphrased information by putting source material (text) into his own words. Even though he summarized and analyzed information at this stage, paraphrase was his most helpful CALP skill to prepare to write the first draft of his paper.

Sam stressed at the outset of his interview that he had time to just "read and write," that he had no time for revisions. He also said that he had never written "a paper" before and the experience was new for him. To go through the process was difficult, he said, because he had to do this research along with other readings for various law courses. However, Sam knew his topic well, and he went on to describe how the process was recursive for him. He said he "can go from beginning" (Introduction) "to end" (Conclusion) and then "to the middle" (Discussion/Analysis): "When you are writing, you know new things and you can go and combine it in your paper [in the different sections]." Recursiveness for Sam, therefore, seemed to have more to do with genre and conceptual development than with stages in writing.

Drafting, "Writing to Learn" (SCQ2)

Sam did not isolate any specific "most helpful" strategies for drafting his paper: "To have a draft is the most important thing. You can come up with the rest later." Sam thought he applied most of the strategies for this stage, but he found the Student's Quality Assessment Tool (SQAT) and the feedback he received from the Teacher's Quality Assessment Tool (TQAT) most helpful when drafting. Sam said he "likes feedback best" because sometimes he knew he made a point that "was not illustrated or expanded."

In the interview, he dismissed the issue of organization at the drafting stage, although he acknowledged its importance for his Introduction section. He focused more on the content; "you can just go to each point and discuss it." He said it is important to introduce each point before discussing it, and comment or conclude on each point even though he did not always do this when drafting. He said he "made some points but didn't go over them in the Discussion [section] or [he] didn't expand on them." He assumed that his law professor would do that for him.

Revising, "Writing to Communicate" (SCQ3.a)

In the interview, Sam focused on one "most helpful" strategy for the revising stage: that is, he read critically and reflected on his own written drafts. Sam determined at this stage that he needed more expansion of legal content because the paper consisted of only two parts. He said he was aware that he used only headings and sub-headings and that maybe his paper was not developed beyond this. He acknowledged he could do more "to make the paper flow in a better way." He said that writing for him was not just about ideas but about developing conceptually with cohesion and coherence. Sam also considered "the order" of his writing in the revising stage. Further, he "mentioned the point" his law professor wanted to see in his paper and found the feedback he had received helpful for writing effectively.

Sam did not think he had "serious problems" with punctuation, capitalization, spelling, *et cetera*, but he wanted to know more about logical connectors like "however." Because he did not see himself as having serious problems with editing, he did not find one revising strategy in this category more helpful than another.

Sam said the grammar strategies were useful to "make the writing clearer, plainer, and more persuasive." He said he "broke up" some sentences in the editing process and explained how he used the various methods he had been taught in the writing course. He felt he was strategic in his use of grammar at the revising stages and that he varied the length of his sentences to be persuasive. He found all the CALP skills useful for revising and communicating to his law school educated reader, especially paraphrase and the two kinds of summary: (a) reducing source text, and (b) selecting and reorganizing source text.

Knowledge Transforming (SCQ3.a)
The SCQ (3.a) showed that revising was the most effective stage for transitioning Sam's writing from *knowledge telling* (stating knowledge) to *knowledge transforming* (deepening his level of understanding to include analysis, synthesis, and evaluation of research). Using plain English writing strategies for accuracy, brevity, and clarity (ABC legal writing style) helped him the most to deepen his thinking in English while revising. The SCQ (3.a) also showed that conceptual transforming for refining his working thesis and paraphrasing helped him the most to transform text information while revising, giving Sam authorship of his paper.

Developing as a Legal Writer across Stages
The SCQ (stage 1) showed that writing memoranda and summary reports for *American Legal Institutions* helped Sam develop his ability to write an analytical paper (question 4). His SCQ (stage 1) areas of concern in language and legal composition (question 5) were the following: meaning (content analysis), legal style (for accuracy, brevity, and conciseness), social-cultural appropriateness, references and citations to scholarly works, and stages of legal writing (for example, writing to learn before writing to communicate to the U.S. law school educated reader). His SCQ (stage 1) areas of concern in writing knowledge (question 6) were: (a) knowing

more about American law school conventions, (b) knowing more about research writing as a process for effective legal writing, and (c) knowing more about the assessment criteria for scholarly legal writing. In terms of the strategies he used at the pre-writing (stage 1) that helped him develop competency as an L2 legal writer, Sam said:

> My writing process is slow but once I have established the thesis statement and the problem I am tackling, I started writing. The presentation of my topic [in class] helped me identify key areas that empower the message I communicate. I did research for the paper from the beginning of the semester, but writing started a month ago [December 2, 2008].

The SCQ (stage 2) and the interview showed that the strategies Sam used for the process of drafting helped him develop competency as an L2 legal writer (question 5): "These [drafting] strategies will help me refine my thoughts and look at the writing process from another angle. I have encountered problems with the logic and organization in the paper." When asked about how drafting research papers in U.S. law school context is similar to or different from drafting a research paper in his home country (SCQ stage 2, question 6), Sam said, "I think there is consideration [in the U.S.] given to authority and citations. Sometimes it may limit [versus expand] your thinking if you have experience in the field of study."

The SCQ (stage 3) and the interview also showed that the strategies Sam used for revising helped him develop competency as an L2 legal writer (question 11):

> The strategies for citations, limiting the subject, developing the structure of the paper all helped me improve the paper. However, there is still an opportunity to develop these skills. There is no wrong or right process in writing.

As an Arabic native speaker, Sam said that he was expected to be both descriptive and loquacious: "Sometimes one paragraph could be one sentence or two sentences ... Writing in Arabic is different from writing in English." Further, Sam said he could not compare writing in legal English with writing in legal Arabic because he has no legal writing experience in Arabic. In Sam's law school, he said, students learn only through lectures, and in class exams "you would have... three or four essay questions to complete; you write whatever comes in your mind ... [T]his cannot be considered as an academic writing exercise to be compared to writing a research paper" (Sam, personal communication, December 16, 2009). Genre in legal writing, however, does share some "common things" according to Sam such as "introduction, summary of the abstract, and you have your discussion, headings, and subheadings... [but] it's different regarding the citations – how you give authority and maybe how to be selective about your subject ... "

Explicit Strategies Instruction (SCQ 3.b)

For Sam, direct (explicit) strategies instruction was important for him at both the early (pre-writing – drafting) and the later (drafting – revising) stages to develop an efficient writing process. To develop an effective writing product, direct writing strategies instruction was important at all levels (conceptual, rhetorical, and linguistic). As am L2 legal writer, the SCQ (3.b) showed that (a) legal English writing teacher interactive and corrective feedback were important; (b) peer non-native English speaker (class-mate) correction and explanation were important; and (c) content law professor interactive and substantive feedback were important. The interview showed "drafting and revising ... helpful as far as instruction is concerned because of feedback." Sam said, "It was a very good learning experience. I learned a lot. Hopefully I can apply the knowledge."

Writing Feedback (SCQ 3.b)

Sam said in the interview that the writing "intervention was different from one process [stage] to another." For pre-writing, he said the writing teacher (researcher) "just gave instructions how to do it." For drafting and revising, he said "it was very helpful" to receive feedback [during the process] from someone other than the law professor, indicating that Teachers' Quality Assessment Tools (TQAT) for those stages were "important" and "good." Feedback from his peers was important to Sam as well, he said. The quality assessment tools in the course helped him in the "overall evaluation ...; I learned how I can shift from pre-writing to drafting to revising." The key point he would want to emphasize with students is "have a draft as soon as possible while researching." He said he needs to work on planning more time for revising.

Proficiency Defining Abilities (SCQ 3.b)

Sam self-reported more strengths than weaknesses on the SCQ (3.b) checklist of defining abilities for professional proficiency in legal (expository) writing. The SCQ (3.b) indicates general professional proficiency (level 3) overall, but gaps in advanced professional proficiency (level 4). Sam did not check that he can (a) write on all topics normally pertinent to professional school needs, (b) consistently tailor his legal writing to suit his reader's needs, or (c) write with relatively few grammatical errors in English, including those in low-frequency complex structures (e.g., passive voice, gerunds/infinitives, conditional/future perfect/and compound tenses such as past perfect progressive, etc.). At the functionally native proficiency (level 5), Sam checked that he (a) can write and edit both formal and informal professional correspondence, (b) can write clearly, explicitly, informatively, *and* persuasively in one document, and (c) can employ a wide range of stylistic devices known as plain English writing strategies to enhance clarity and readability (for example, keeping the subject and verb undivided and focused on your point; using precise transitions to convey exact connections).

Summary, Case 6
For only two stages of the scholarly L2 legal writing process did Sam's interview show "most useful" writing strategies and CALP skills for this paper: that is, the pre-writing and revising stages. His most helpful pre-writing strategies were (a) reading for a purpose (conceptual strategy) and (b) paraphrasing in English for reading comprehension (linguistic strategy). Further, exchanging ideas with others about his research project to get feedback and starting to write immediately, without a plan, were Sam's most helpful strategies. Paraphrasing information by putting source information (text) into his own words was Sam's most helpful CALP skill (a) to comprehend before writing, and (b) to start the actual process of writing. For revising and deciding what should be changed, deleted, added or retained, the interview found Sam's most helpful strategy to be reading critically and reflecting on his own written drafts.

Triangulation, Case 6
Comparison of the responses to the SQAT/TQAT instruments reveal that Sam felt more comfortable using the stage 1 and stage 3 quality assessment tools than the stage 2 quality assessment tool that dealt with genre. Researcher notes revealed that the SQAT tool for stage 2 (drafting) needed further explanation for this student participant. Specifically, the writing teacher-researcher needed to explain to Sam how each of the four sections typical of a legal research paper work together for his particular paper, the approximate number of pages in each given his law professor's requirements for the research paper, and how and where to add critical comment in his draft (#1 in this student participant's file).

Validating Member Check, Case 6

> Dear Donna, Many thanks to the supportive learning atmosphere at ....Your help was always impressive, and I highly appreciate the time and effort you put into supervising my writing throughout last year. You worked on weekends helping me meeting deadlines and devoted time from your family to help me and other students do well. Good luck on your academic research and I hope I have been a good student.
>
> Attached is the document where I copied the [member check] summary that you sent. I made some editings which are traced in the document. I further made a comment in another area. Here is my comment on your analysis copied from the document:
>
> "This is a comprehensive diagnosis and analysis of the writing process of my first legal research paper at the law school. I think the way I wrote my four other papers was different and more time efficient. At your class and thanks to your assistance I learned an important skill which is the transition from the "write to learn" to the "write to communicate". I can

remember that you told me more than one time how I should engage the reader in my cause and to make the message readable, understandable and clear to the extent that it would not be misinterpreted or its meanings confused.

In addition your feedback was very important in setting up the background of my paper to an audience who are not aware about the topic of my paper. I learned where I would need to define an idea or a term and elaborate on ideas where the reader would require more information or have questions. I used these skills in my other papers, but still there are still prospects for improvement. One more thing I want to note is the selection of sentences and the range between the long and short ones which I developed through my writings.

I can remember that I added a legal argument to my paper on the last day before the submission of the paper. Sometimes this happens, but I avoided that in my other papers. It appeared to me that I devoted much time to some parts of my paper and less time for others. I think this is an important skill that I learned and developed, which is to make the research specific and narrow to the thesis statement and to know what kind of research is required to address the question or the problem the paper is addressing. The failure to do that will lead to some problems in the revision stage. I overcame this in my other papers and managed to score progress in this area. I managed to submit four papers in the Spring semester." Thank you again for your help. I will let you know of my new adventures and on [*sic*] my future writings ...
(Sam, personal communication, December 16, 2009).

Sam's additional comment (above) revealed that the way he wrote his subsequent research papers was "different and more time efficient," suggesting that he was able to learn from and tailor his research writing process as time went on. Sam's email attachment to his *Member Check* (personal communication above) also showed that he was able to correct both native speaker and non-native speaker errors and use plain English strategies for accurate written expression. In other words, Sam's *Member Check* gave him the opportunity to make corrections to the text and to self-edit.

Main Themes/Unexpected Results, Case 6
Salient interrelated themes emerging from Sam's case highlight the value of the following: metacognitive knowledge (Flavell 1979), genre knowledge, and process knowledge; self-regulation with stages in writing leading to demonstration of expertise in the final (reader-centered) presentation as well as increased proficiency (for example, the ability to self-edit); feedback and strategies instruction that foster learning; and transfer of "process knowledge" to other L2 legal research papers.

7.8 Summary of the qualitative findings

7.8.1 Acculturated student participants

Gee, Tory, and Ferra were acculturated, exit-level student participants who had completed the academic legal writing course the previous semester. Their overall qualitative results revealed how scholarly legal writing is both a learner-centered cognitive process (for pre-writing and drafting) and a sociocultural reader-centered process (for revising). Related to the scholarly legal writing process is strategic competence, with writing strategies and CALP skills impacting each stage of participants' academic legal writing. These were social and cognitive tools shown to impact learner confidence, motivation, and self-regulation in disciplinary academic writing at every stage. Individual results are summarized below.

Case 1 – Gee
Qualitative findings reveal that Gee concentrated on the drafting stage of her writing process: the writer-centered stage. She did not move deeply into the reader-centered stage of revising even though she had the ability "to self-edit" with the "strategies to do it" which gave her confidence. Stage 2 drafting became problematic even though English was Gee's first academic language and she had been socialized as an American (J.D.) legal writer. Missing was content knowledge and knowledge of genre structure and genre constraints. Gee did not know how a proposal should be written. She had no models, and she was unsure of her law professor's expectations until after the paper had been written. Further, little had been written about her research topic. Time and motivation emerged as key issues for Gee who saw scholarly legal writing as a social interactive process that necessarily included the law professor for whom the paper was written.

The interview found which writing strategies were most useful to Gee and why. Conceptual and rhetorical pre-writing strategies were most helpful for researching her topic: that is, reading for a purpose, drawing conclusions relevant to her topic, and noting aspects of organizational structure for reuse in her writing. Two drafting strategies were most helpful for getting words and concepts down effectively on paper: (a) using her knowledge of audience and purpose to guide her drafts, and (b) rejecting irrelevant content in the readings while she wrote. Re-ordering her writing as she wrote and asking herself if she met the needs of her reader were most helpful for Gee to decide what should be changed, deleted, added, or retained while revising her paper (proposal). In sum, Gee's most useful strategies helped her eliminate revising as a separate stage when writing her proposal.

Case 2 – Tory

In contrast to Gee who lacked the necessary genre-related knowledge for expert performance in her written proposal, knowledge of CALP skills for constructing knowledge in the revising stage boosted Tory's confidence "as a person, [and] as a thinker." For her, confidence stemmed from self-regulation and knowledge of transformation in writing. In addition to literacy strategies and language skills as tools for learning and communicating, strategic competence for Tory included multiple drafts that allowed her to refine and define her ideas to arrive at new conclusions and deepen her legal knowledge.

Strategies analysis across stages revealed a focus on the interrelation of "reading to write" conceptual strategies and CALP skills for pre-writing that, above all, contributed to a cognitive process that both developed this student participant's thinking and generated new ideas for her paper. This is the same process that, when applied to the writer's own writing (drafting, stage 2), combines literacy strategies and language skills for revising (stage 3) to construct new knowledge from multiple sources. Recursiveness in scholarly writing was thus disclosed and emphasized, as were the benefits of explicit strategies instruction for academic legal writers who cross linguistic and cultural borders.

Case 3 – Ferra

Ferra's qualitative results highlighted how sophisticated and appropriate use of writing strategies promotes success in academic writing and how they relate to sociocultural knowledge of the writing process, sociolinguistic knowledge of academic language skills, and discourse knowledge of academic legal composition. Awareness of (socio-) cultural differences in the academic writing process and (socio-) linguistic differences in discourse skills such as synthesizing contributed to expert performance in her research paper.

Strategies analysis across stages revealed key strategies used in the pre-writing and revising stages. Language re-use was particularly helpful to Ferra as an L2 legal writer and English language learner who had working knowledge of citation for scholarly legal writing. Revising was a key stage for her because "only at this stage it is in fact possible for the reader to see completely the transformation of his or her thoughts, making them coherent and cohesive." A revising strategy that Ferra found particularly effective was "to review the passage between the last paragraph of one section and the first paragraph of the following one." Thus, strategies analysis showed that Ferra had acquired discourse knowledge of inferencing (bridging, elaborating) in addition to discourse skills through explicit strategies instruction that included the following kinds of feedback during the writing process: (a) interactive and corrective feedback from the writing teacher-researcher; (b) correction and explanation from both peer native-English speakers and peer non-native English speakers (class-mates); and (c) interactive and substantive feedback from the content law professor. Her content law professor commented to the writing teacher-researcher that she was impressed with Ferra's ability to solicit feedback from her. Ferra's case disclosed how she had used the cognitive and social tools she needed to demonstrate both competence and professionalism as an L2 legal writer and thinker.

Summary: acculturated student participants

In addition to confidence, motivation, and self-regulation in academic writing for law school (summative) assessment, Ferra's case links strategic competence with professionalism and professional identity.

7.8.2 Non-acculturated student participants

Liv, Anyo, and Sam were non-acculturated, entrance-level student participants actively engaged in the academic legal writing course. As such, they were strategically making the "transition from EFL learners to ESL users" (Zhou, 2010, p. 75) at the graduate level by taking the non-credit academic legal writing course in their first semester. Their overall qualitative results further revealed how scholarly legal writing is both a learner-centered cognitive process (for pre-writing and drafting) and a sociocultural reader-centered process (for revising) at different levels. Strategic competence for these participants focused more on knowledge and skills development, however, than on the confidence-boosting, self-regulating effect of informed strategies' use for efficient (Gee) or effective (Tory, Ferra) academic legal writing.

Case 4 – Liv

Qualitative findings for Liv, as for Ferra, revealed that strategic competence for professional performance in scholarly writing is related to process and to culture. Speaking about problems in writing, such as structuring, was therefore important to Liv as an English language proficient academic legal writer. Text structure, a disciplinary culture-specific feature of writing (like grammar and vocabulary), can cause problems for L2 academic writers. Second language awareness – which includes cultural awareness of contrasting rhetorical patterns and genres of writing – is therefore necessary for graduate-level academic writers because the American academic legal writing style differs significantly from writing styles of international students who come from contrasting academic traditions and cultures of scholarship. Whereas Ferra's case points to the contrasting academic conventions, standards, and systems for assessment that international student writers can face, Liv's case highlights basic differences in the presentation of the main point and choice of approach to research problems in a paper. "These differences do not signal lack of language competence but lack of focus, logic, and coherence in academic legal writing" (Marina Ageyeva, legal English personal communication, January 2005).

For Liv, self-regulation in academic legal writing was associated with purposeful academic literacy strategies such as reading and revising with a purpose in mind: for example, revising separately for grammar and punctuation, word choice and content. Further, explicit instruction that included the opportunity for student-teacher interaction helped Liv "develop an effective individual strategy for writing [a] legal research paper."

Case 5 – Anyo

Qualitative results for Anyo highlighted that stages in scholarly writing can be seen as levels for developing an effective work product. Stages in scholarly writing, then, can be seen by learners as levels of development that move the academic legal writer through stages of conceptual, rhetorical, and linguistic development with strategies and skills that anticipate transfer to like work products. Knowledge of process strategies and product assessment tools developed the scholarly L2 legal writer from both a cultural and a disciplinary view: that is, they provided focus, logic, and coherence in academic L2 legal writing as well as confidence and self-regulation.

Evidence from Anyo's SCQ (stage 2) showed that the strategies he used in the drafting stage helped him develop competency as an L2 legal writer. He said they helped him know "how to arrange ideas chronologically and how to select what ideas are necessary for the paper and what to leave out." In other words, the strategies for drafting (in stage 2) helped him develop conceptually and rhetorically. When responding to the SCQ (stage 3.a), Anyo reiterated that the strategies he used for revising were helping him "to reorganize my sentences and paragraphs." Anyo's interview disclosed twenty-nine most helpful revising strategies that included use of plain English linguistic strategies for accuracy, brevity, and clarity in academic legal writing style.

Case 6 – Sam

Qualitative findings for Sam suggested that transitioning from the drafting (writing to learn) stage to the revising (writing to communicate) stage requires knowledge, skills, and explicit instruction for students and scholars who may be culturally distanced from the U.S. and the American writing habit. Metacognitive awareness as it relates to process in academic, disciplinary, or scholarly writing may be the step, stage, or level that transforms conscious use of a strategy into a skill for the L2 legal writer who is a foreign-trained professional.

Sam's interview showed "most useful" writing strategies and CALP skills for only two stages of scholarly L2 legal writing: that is, for pre-writing and revising. He relied on the SQAT with writing teacher-researcher feedback for drafting and rhetorical structuring. His most helpful pre-writing strategies were (a) reading for a purpose (conceptual strategy) and (b) paraphrasing in English for reading comprehension (linguistic strategy). For revising and deciding what should be changed, deleted, added or retained, the interview found Sam's most helpful strategy was reading critically and reflecting on his own written drafts.

Summary: non-acculturated student participants

Strategic competence for these participants focused on (a) knowledge of writing strategies and (b) development of language skills. Through strategic knowledge and use of culturally appropriate writing strategies and academic language skills, participants were able to transition successfully from their (EFL) learner-centered pre-writing and drafting stages to a more linguistically complex (ESL) reader-centered revising stage for effective communication in their first L2 legal research paper for a U.S. law school professor.

7.8.3 Summary across the six cases

The following summarizes main themes, kinds of knowledge, and unexpected findings from the six cases.

Main themes

Qualitative findings revealed that confidence, motivation, self-regulation, and professional identity were all associated with strategic competence for the socialized L2 legal academic writers. For the un-socialized writer participants, qualitative findings emphasized sociocultural/sociolinguistic awareness and conditional knowledge of appropriate strategies leading to professional (or higher) proficiency in disciplinary academic English writing.

Qualitative findings also disclosed the possibility for positive transfer, depending on knowledge and use, with the possibility for negative transfer (that is, of culturally inappropriate strategies such as language reuse with no citation) without this knowledge or understanding.

Kinds of knowledge

Different kinds of knowledge developed through sophisticated, culturally appropriate use of writing strategies in disciplinary academic context. These comprise *conditional knowledge* for competence or expertise in scholarly legal writing and were revealed as: discourse knowledge, metacognitive knowledge, process knowledge, product (genre) knowledge, sociocultural knowledge, sociolinguistic knowledge, and second language awareness. All are associated with metacognition, or thinking about thinking, for student participants at some level in their writing: that is, planning, organization, and grammar use as an element of style for "high communicative precision" in academic legal writing (Engberg, 2009, p. 223).

Unexpected findings

These include the time-motivation link for Gee; the relation between confidence and self-regulation or control in writing for Tory; the speaking-writing connection for Ferra (sociolinguistic) and Liv (sociocultural); stages as levels of product development that transfer with strategies and skills for Anyo; and the use of quality assessment tools that eliminate the need for native-speaker (or writing teacher) editing for Sam.

Peer debriefing of 15% of the data validated these qualitative findings, the research instruments, and the research design for collecting data in stages that correspond to the writing process (that is pre-writing, drafting, and revising). In other words, Zhou's (2009) validity check linked stages of writing with cognitive, metacognitive, and social-affective learning strategies occurring together, in different combinations, for different student participants with different cultural and linguistic backgrounds. Themes identified across stages of scholarly writing relate to:

- selective attention with metacognitive strategies such as planning and setting goals for *pre-writing*;
- self-management, procedural knowledge, and non-native-English speaker (NNES) consciousness for *drafting*;

- evaluating, monitoring, and centering learning with quality assessment checklists to reach a deep understanding of the argument, claim, or thesis for both *drafting* and *revising*; and
- *self-editing* in the latter stage with selective attention to (linguistic) forms and (legal) meaning.

These themes associate participants' use of metacognitive strategies (to develop their own thinking in L2 legal writing at each stage of the writing process), quality assessment checklists (to learn from the processes of drafting and revising in the latter stages of writing), and self-editing in the final stage of writing that links linguistic forms with clear meaning.

Metacognitive Strategies for Strategic Competence

With respect to the metacognitive strategies' theme, there is a conceptual link between developing thought in writing and language use, one interpretation being that participants developed cognitively as they worked with L2 English in academic legal context. The link between developing thought and language use suggests a theoretical framework that views L2 legal scholarly writing as developmental learning in two domains, language and law.

Quality Assessment in Stages for Strategic Competence

With respect to centering learning with quality assessment checklists for research writing, a conceptual link is made between the research instruments and learning from the processes of writing, thus validating the instruments as effective tools for: (a) self-assessment and self-regulation in scholarly legal writing, and (b) teacher feedback for revising and editing. The importance of teacher feedback during students' processes of writing, rather than at the end of a paper, cannot be overstated.

Self-Editing for Strategic Competence

With respect to self-editing in the final revising stage, selective attention to linguistic forms as they relate to clear meaning and communication contrasts with surface-level editing of grammar and punctuation as a quick fix for L2 writer issues in a paper. A grammatically correct sentence does not necessarily communicate L2 (or L1) legal writers' intended meaning. In addition to editing for clarity, effective legal writers must "make an extra effort to edit for precision and conciseness" (Oates & Enquist, 2009, p. 19). Native-speaker editing of L2 text, therefore, may be a waste of time and money for L2 academic writers. Rather, social interaction – with the opportunity to speak with a "more competent other" about unclear expression and relation of ideas in text – may be a first step toward self-editing. Re-phrasing to clarify or communicate ideas from L2 writers' text in individual consultation, for example, was a productive form of editing and language learning. Social interaction provided "teachable moments" with learners' authentic text regarding sentence structure and word choice, smaller issues in writing. After editing for clarity with a knowledgeable other, the L2 text could be turned over to a native-speaker or peer reviewer for correction of surface errors, but that was not necessary. Anyo's case illustrates that surface error correction may not be necessary for an L2 writer to show proficiency in language and law in a legal research paper for law professor summative assessment. "[E]ffective writing requires attention to both the process of working with text and the output which conveys the intentions and ideas of the writer" (Grabe & Kaplan, 1996, p. 313).

In sum, the validity check identified metacognitive strategies, self-assessment checklists, and self-editing consistent with Distinguished-level proficiency (Leaver & Shekhtman, 2002) and strategic competence. Peer debriefer interpretation of data validates this study in two ways: first, with a description of how strategic competence consists of more than just compensation strategies (Ehrman, 2002); and second, with a description of how sophisticated choices of strategies combine with goals for self-assessment of writing in stages that may "characterize the SD (Superior-Distinguished) threshold": that is, where L2 legal writers "become linguistically an equal partner with native speakers" (Ehrman, 2002, p. 251).

The next chapter discusses interrelations among strategies, skills, and quality assessment for each stage of the scholarly writers' process. The major synthesized research findings from the mixed methods show how academic legal writing was both developmental and socially interactive for learners as they moved from the writer-centered activity of drafting to the reader-centered activity of revising and constructing knowledge.

8 Developing Learner-User Agency

8.1 Interrelations for strategic competence (proficiency)

> "Thought development is determined by language i.e., by the linguistic tools of thought and by the sociocultural experience of the writer." (Vygotsky, 1986, p. 94).

This chapter discusses meta-level linkages from the first three research questions, connecting the quantitative findings with the qualitative findings, to answer Research Question 4. A macro-conceptual, theoretical understanding of the mixed methods results is presented through tables, with an explanation beneath each table. Theory and practice related to assessment and instruction are considered, and the critical connection between empirical research and L2 writing instruction is made.

8.2 Overview of the study and findings

The research questions explored strategic competence as a repertoire building factor for developing international graduate student writing at the level of professional (or higher) proficiency. This competency is important because research writing mediates "scientific" knowledge and concepts for the writer so he or she may have conscious awareness of relations (based on Piaget in Kozulin, 1986). Second language acquisition and production is a content domain of learning and, in academic legal context, language was substantive subject matter for the L2 legal writer participants. Language was both a tool for learning law and a tool for communicating ideas about the law through scholarly research and writing. In addition, L2 legal use was a sociocultural mediated activity that crossed disciplines of learning, with scholarly L2 legal writing seen as developmental learning in two domains – language and law – as well as social-cultural practice.

To answer the research questions, four research instruments were developed for each stage of the study (that is, pre-writing, drafting, and revising). The Strategic Competence Questionnaire was task-specific, the Interview Protocol was writer-specific, and the matching pair of Quality Assessment Tools was genre-specific. Figure 8.1 below summarizes the instruments used within the context of the academic legal writing intervention for student writer participants.

These descriptive research instruments were found to be useful tools for (1) providing a roadmap of strategies for scholarly legal writing with the possibility for learning and teaching; (2) stimulating critical reflection and cross-cultural dis-

1.	QUAN Strategic Competence Questionnaire (SCQ)
2.	QUAL Interview Protocol (IP
3.	QUAN Student's Quality Assessment Tool (SQAT)
4.	QUAN Teacher's Quality Assessment Tool (TQAT)
	Pre-writing <> Drafting <> Revising

Fig. 8.1. Research instruments developed for the study.

cussion about the nature and purpose of recursive stages in the scholarly writing process; (3) (self-) assessing the writing product at key intervals during the scholarly writing process with critical reflection and feedback.

The research tools disclosed interrelationships among the following: (1) writers' academic literacy strategies and academic language skills, (2) writers' and teacher's quality ratings of learners' scholarly L2 writing (product), and (3) stages in writers' scholarly legal writing (process). The dynamic interplay among student participants' strategies, skills, quality assessment, and stages shows that strategic competence for L2 participants acted as a catalyst for increasing proficiency in an academic research paper.

The research questions addressed interrelating problems in EFL/ESL education and legal education: that is, the complex and multidisciplinary nature of L2 academic legal writing, and international student writer assessment in a graduate program. As classroom-based research, the study addressed the "dearth of extensive discussion of, and explicit guidelines for, the practices and processes of *teaching* L2 writing" (Hedgcock, 2005, p. 609) at higher ranges of proficiency, in academic domain, professional school context. Table 8.1 below briefly summarizes findings from each of the three interrelated research questions to show what the research instruments revealed.

From a micro-perspective, the research tools disclosed the dynamic, changing nature of strategies, skills, and goals for (self-) assessment and feedback in stages that influenced strategic competence, a component of communicative competence (Canale & Swain, 1980) impacting EFL and ESL student writer development. Strategic competence, therefore, can be seen as a critical factor for achieving professional (or higher) writing proficiency in a graduate level paper because it expanded student participants' existing repertoire of strategies and knowledge base for academic writing.

From a macro-perspective, the research tools disclosed that cultural proficiency, disciplinary proficiency, and language proficiency overlapped for L2 student writer participants, most of whom were international graduate students with diverse cultural, educational, legal, and linguistic backgrounds. All participants were engaged in processes of acquiring lexical and syntactic competence in aca-

Table 8.1. Overview of findings from interrelated research questions (RQ).

RQ 1	QUAN results	The SCQ results for each stage of writing (process) showed an interrelation between writing strategies and CALP skills: tools for writer-centered learning and reader-centered communicating that bridged sociocultural and sociolinguistic gaps in L2 writers' academic legal backgrounds.
RQ 2	QUAL results	The IP results for each stage of writing (process) emphasized the interrelation of academic literacy strategies and academic language skills, revealing such themes as self-regulation and professional identity for acculturated writers; increased knowledge and development of language skills for un-acculturated writers; and confidence in writing for both.
RQ 3	QUAN results	The SQAT/TQAT results for each stage of writing showed an interrelation between the learners' L2 academic legal writing process and L2 English product mediated by teacher-student-peer social interaction.

QUAN = quantitative
QUAL = qualitative

demic English writing context. The use of L2 English for purposes of academic legal writing defined advanced literacy and disciplinary proficiency (competence) for international student participants. Figure 8.2 below illustrates the overlap, showing that language and culture interrelate as academic and disciplinary literacy variables.

L2 legal context

(trans) academic/
disciplinary
language
proficiency

Fig. 8.2. Interrelation of language and culture for academic and disciplinary literacy.

Although language proficiency may be the most visible variable for L2 academic writers and speakers in an English-medium professional school program, this research stressed how sociocultural context and disciplinary proficiency merged for competence in L2 academic legal writing. "[T]he L2 writer is writing from his or her own familiar culture and the L1 reader is reading from another context" (Hyland,

2003, p. 47): that is, another sociocultural context. Disciplinary proficiency therefore includes explicit knowledge of appropriate written language use in L2 academic context that international student L2 writers cannot be expected to have before studying in the host country where student voices and learner experiences vary. One or two academic semesters, furthermore, is not enough time for implicit acquisition.

The research tools disclosed that learner (internal and external) variables for achieving disciplinary proficiency interrelated with their strategic competence: (a) reading to write strategies; (b) CALP skills; (c) knowledge of genre and cultural expectation; (d) formal instruction and useful feedback at the advanced (sociolinguistic and sociocultural) level; (e) time and motivation. Table 8.2 below highlights these interrelating variables, showing formal instruction as a necessary disciplinary literacy variable "that affects CALP in direct ways" (Gunderson, D'Silva & Odo, 2014, p. 42).

Table 8.2. Interrelating variables for appropriate written language use.

- reading to write strategies
- CALP skills
- knowledge of genre and cultural expectation
- formal (sociolinguistic, sociocultural) instruction and feedback
- time and motivation

Advanced literacy strategies such as reading to write strategies, and cognitive academic language skills such as summary, synthesis, and paraphrase were found to interconnect with each other, as well as with the demands of research writing. Participants' strategic shift from L2 writer-centered to L1 reader-centered scholarly legal writing was emphasized. See Appendix G for the process of scholarly writing illustrating this shift by Fajans and Falk (2005).

8.3 Synthesis of data analyses

A synthesis of quantitative and qualitative data analyses, based on all the instruments for all the learners, follows for each research question. This discussion reconsiders the SCQ (stage 1) open-ended questions, providing sociocultural setting to anchor the interpretations and ensure that they are meaningful (Oxford, 2011). The discussion also reconsiders (SCQ 3.b) self-reports on proficiency and formal instruction with items describing how learners achieved at professional levels of writing proficiency, the primary range of interest in this learner-centered study. Recalling Swales (1990) and Hyland (2003), the interactive social-cultural nature of writing and thinking, the role of language and text structure in disciplinary writing context, and the cognitive development of the L2 academic legal writer through text work are recognized and explored.

8.3.1 What research question 1 showed

Overall findings from the first research question showed that strategies and skills at each stage of writing interrelate; they were used together in different combinations at different stages for different purposes. Use of some strategies and skills overlapped, and understanding deepened for the participants as they wrote. Individual findings showed that social-cultural (learner-external) variables such as legal education culture and background knowledge likely influence internal variables such as frequency and use of writing strategies and CALP skills, as well as academic domain (legal) learning.

Strategies and CALP skills increased at the writer-focused drafting/learning stage for three participants in the study, and they continued to increase at the reader-focused revising/communicating stage for the other three participants. Two blocks of writers emerged: Sam, Ferra, and Tory gave more attention to editing, grammar, and/or knowledge-transforming than Gee, Liv, or Anyo. At this point, acculturation did not distinguish the student writer participants.

Triangulating product quality assessment data for Research Question 3 informed participants' revising processes. For example, Tory's SQAT checklist was complete for this stage indicating a high level of attention to revising. Ferra and Sam's SQAT/TQAT checklists showed similar attention to revising although Sam's SQAT showed that he was not comfortable accounting for the reader's background knowledge as an un-acculturated writer.

Interview data for Research Question 2 further revealed that Gee, Liv, and Anyo were concerned with managing their time; they did not have enough time or motivation (in Gee's case) to attend to all aspects of revising in this paper. For Gee, the only U.S. student participant, time and motivation were linked. She relied on surface-level editing strategies to prepare her paper for final submission rather than on deeper transforming strategies for constructing knowledge from her text.

Like background knowledge and sociocultural orientation, stages in scholarly writing influenced frequency of strategies and CALP skills as participants moved through the scholarly writing process. The study revealed that stages in writing interrelate, like literacy strategies and language skills. Although this may not be surprising given the recursive nature of writing, this interrelation suggests integration or merging of the cognitive and the sociocultural for some student participants. This also may not be surprising given that all participants underwent an academic writing intervention with explicit strategies instruction. However, qualitative data analysis for the acculturated participants shows how the cognitive and the sociocultural integrated. Ferra's case, for example, shows that transforming disciplinary knowledge can begin in the drafting "writing to learn" stage; Gee's case shows that reader-awareness is also possible in the drafting "writing to learn" stage; and Tory's case shows that implementing a well-conceived strategic (stage 1) plan is as important as advanced writing techniques in the (stage 3) "writing to communicate stage."

Qualitative data analysis for participants shows that rather than integrating, a strategic shift may occur from the cognitive to the sociocultural when consciously choosing to (a) focus on analyzing legal research during (stage 2) drafting, and (b) reflect on the use of L2 English during (stage 3) revising. This conscious shift may strategically lighten the cognitive load for the L2 legal research writer.

To miss a stage from the point of view of all participants was to miss a "level, "step" or opportunity for one or more of the following: (a) deciding what should be changed, deleted, added, or retained in the legal analysis; (b) polishing and checking for (sociocultural) writing conventions; (c) writing clearly and accurately in L2 English for (sociocultural) academic writing style; (d) deepening understanding by analyzing, synthesizing, or evaluating the research (the highest level in Bloom's taxonomy of learning); and (e) using linguistic transforming as a knowledge-transforming strategy for constructing knowledge from the writer's own text, giving the L2 writer authorship and voice as a legal thinker in L2 English.

In sum, findings from Research Question 1 highlight the important (conscious) use of literacy strategies for legal writer development while drafting and of (conscious or unconscious) use of CALP skills for L2 writer communication while revising. Writing strategies seem to associate more with writers' (internal) cognitive development, and CALP skills seem to associate more with writers' (external) disciplinary and social-cultural development in this study. This was previously mentioned as an important finding insofar as writing strategies helped law students learn, and CALP skills helped law students write from multiple L2 legal sources without plagiarizing.

In addition, the above-mentioned interrelations allow for the reverse possibility as participants were engaged with two academic domains of learning while writing: language and law. Acculturated student participants were reflecting on their legal research writing process while learning about their legal research paper topic. Un-acculturated student participants were learning about both their legal research writing process and their legal research paper topic concurrently. All were learning language explicitly and implicitly given their L2 immersion experience. In other words, participants were living the languaculture (Agar, 1994) of the U.S. professional school with an informal register but performing the language consciously in writing with a formal, L2 academic register. Academic legal writing was a conscious act for both the acculturated and non-acculturated student participants. All had to meet the cultural expectations of U.S. native English speaking legal writers trained with an instrumental or technical orientation to writing.

Based on Hinds (1987), the American cultural expectation for legal writing is that it be writer-responsible (Oates & Enquist, 2009). This means that the writer is primarily responsible for successful communication and reader comprehension. Being writer-responsible in U.S.legal education culture means that the student writer is at fault if the highly educated, native English legal reader does not immediately comprehend at every level of text organization: that is, sentence, paragraph, and composition levels of writing. The writing must be clear enough to reflect students' critical thinking and legal analysis, even if the research topic is complex. This means also that grammatical errors must not interrupt reader flow or affect writer meaning. Accuracy and fluency are both important. Further, grammar use at the professional level becomes an issue of "style" in U.S. academic culture, and legal writers are expected to (re-)work their writing for accuracy, brevity, clarity (ABC style), directness, and explicitness to achieve a stated purpose. Professors (lawyers and judges) are known to value their time more than their students' (or interns') time and will not labor to understand writer meaning or logic in organization. Writers at this professional level are expected to be critical readers who place themselves in the position of the reader during the final stages of revising. This writer-centered to reader-centered switch requires cognitive dexterity as well as sociocultural awareness and understanding on the part of the L2 legal writer. Through this shift, the L2 legal writer is elevated from undergraduate to graduate-level performance (competence).

8.3.2 What research question 2 showed

Overall, findings showed how post-intervention participants went about their legal research writing task and how student participants in the academic legal writing course were learning to write in U.S. academic legal culture. All participants were able to tell why they made certain choices by identifying their most useful academic legal writing strategies and elaborating why these strategies were helpful. Further, participants identified if/when they made the cognitive transition to knowledge-transforming from knowledge-telling in their scholarly legal writing.

Quantitatively

Participants found Type 1a and Type 1b "reading to write" strategies most helpful for stage 1 pre-writing. These were literacy strategies associating more with writers' conceptual development than with writers' rhetorical or linguistic development when planning to write. Participants found Type 2a drafting strategies more helpful than Type 2b CALP skills when starting to write a scholarly legal research paper, however. Type 2a drafting strategies helped the writer get words and concepts down effectively on paper whereas Type 2b CALP skills helped the writer process academic legal text when drafting, highlighting the cognitive role of academic language skills for writing. Findings for stage 3 revising further revealed that deeper-level revising strategies, rather than surface-level editing strategies, were most helpful to participants.

Qualitatively

Qualitative data analysis deepened understanding of the research participants' strategic shift from writer-centeredness to reader-centeredness in scholarly legal writing and when it occurred. The SCQ disclosed that, in addition to above-mentioned interrelations (of pre-writing, drafting, revising, knowledge transforming, and developing as a legal writer), formal strategies instruction and in-process interactive feedback contributed to participants' cognitive and sociocultural development.

Triangulating SCQ-based interview data revealed that the ability to self-edit "with the strategies to do it" (Gee) was a proficiency-defining ability for "control" or self-regulation in scholarly legal writing – a common theme in research participants' interviews. The idea of deliberate, planful, goal-directed thinking and writing is deeply embedded in Piaget's formal operations.

Related to the theme of control and self-regulation is metacognitive knowledge (Flavell, 1979) through which participants showed awareness of (a) themselves as L2 academic legal writers, (b) their individual academic writing process using L2 English, and (c) academic writing strategies and techniques skilled legal writers are known to use for clear and accurate expression. With metacognitive and sociocultural knowledge of scholarly writing strategies, participants found they could self-manage their process and their product quality. Metacognition for participants therefore included the conscious ability to monitor the process and regulate production quality, as well as self-knowledge (Hacker, 1998).

Metalinguistically

This study revealed that student participants had the "metalanguage" (Hacker, Dunklosky, & Graesser, 1998) to discuss their most helpful strategies: that is, their reports on language use revealed knowledge of themselves as L2 academic writers, their L2 academic legal tasks, and their L2 English writing strategies. These interrelating variables affected participants' L2 English performance in academic legal writing. For example, Ferra clearly articulated difficulties with L2 writer knowledge and L2 academic culture; Gee expressed frustration with L1 task (proposal) knowledge; and Sam demonstrated satisfaction with L2 strategies knowledge: "The [SCQ strategies] questionnaire opens eyes on different things" (personal communication, December 12, 2008). See Figure 8.3.

Metacognitive with Sociocultural Knowledge

- L2 academic writer
- L2 academic legal task
- L2 English writing strategies

Fig. 8.3. Interrelating variables influenced L2 writer performance (based on Flavell, 1979).

In addition to interrelating strategies, skills, and stages (Research Question 1), Research Question 2 showed that strategic competence included participants' knowledge of themselves, their tasks, and their strategies as interrelating variables that affected their L2 English performance as writers, thinkers, and graduate students in professional school context. Strategic competence acted as a catalyst for participants' scholarly legal writing. The SCQ-based interviews showed how participants confronted individual problems in knowledge, language, composition, and culture with variations of a problem-solving repertoire to show competence or expertise in a legal research paper that met the performance expectations of their law school professors. See Figure 8.4 below.

RQ 1	Interrelating strategies, skills, and stages produced a (cognitive → sociocultural) shift.
RQ 2	Interrelating (metacognitive – sociocultural) knowledge of writer, task, and strategies affected L2 performance.

Fig. 8.4. Dynamic nature of strategic competence in scholarly L2 legal writing.

8.3.3 What research question 3 showed

Quantitatively

Quantitative analyses for nominal data to answer Research Question 3 showed overall and individual results across the three stages of writing (pre-writing, drafting, and revising). Overall quantitative findings showed that student participants overestimated the quality of their writing in the learner-centered pre-writing and drafting stages especially. Less of a difference in quality assessment was revealed for revising, the reader-centered "writing to communicate" stage. One possible interpretation may be that the students had not only developed as writers and thinkers by this stage but also they were prepared with techniques and strategies for revising and editing from the writing intervention that included formative assessment or structured feedback from the teacher-researcher. The finding that one acculturated and one un-acculturated student appeared in each block of learners on the quality assessment continuum lends support to writer development and preparedness for stage 3 revising. For all participants, competence in research writing included the ability to revise ideas and self-edit their scholarly writing product.

Qualitatively

Individual findings were triangulated with law professors' summative evaluation for each case according to standards in the disciplinary community. The three un-acculturated students participating in the academic legal writing intervention at the time of the study each received A-. The two acculturated student participants who showed native-like English language proficiency each received B+. The third acculturated student participant, the Ph.D. law student with developing intermediate proficiency, received an A. See Table 8.3 below for law professors' summative evaluations and the two groups.

Table 8.3. Law professors' summative evaluations.

N = 6	Student participants	Research paper grades
Acculturated	Gee	B+
	Tory	B+
	Ferra	A
Non-acculturated	Liv	A-
	Anyo	A-
	Sam	A-

The non-acculturated student participants ($N = 3$) achieved as high, or higher than, the acculturated student participants ($N = 3$). The acculturated participants had taken the academic legal writing course the previous semester but did not seek structured support or "scaffolding" from the teacher-researcher in the semester of data collection except for Ferra, the least proficient student participant. Writing teacher feedback was especially important to her. She was the Italian doctoral student, intent on developing language proficiency. Her taped interview disclosed that Ferra still considered herself to be very much an English language learner. Highly motivated, Ferra took more than one legal English course during her master's program, enhancing her own L2 learning and preventing fossilization of errors in L2 production. Ferra's case highlights the value of L2 (socio)linguistic and (socio)cultural support through situated or contextualized writing instruction as an important component of graduate-level L2 writing, in addition to learner motivation and content domain knowledge. Situated learning (Wenger & Lave, 1991) states the importance of knowledge acquisition in a cultural context and integration in a community of practice.

Language and literacy acquisition in disciplinary context was supported through the SQAT/TQAT evaluations that, in contrast to the law professors' summative evaluations, were formative – taking place at different times during the writing process. The student (SQAT) evaluations provided opportunity for L2 writer self-reflection, and the teacher (TQAT) evaluations provided objective, structured, and systematic (controlled) feedback for participants to develop their writing and thinking in L2 English. The efficacy of supporting student learning with reflection and attainable goals throughout a semester contrasts with judging student learning at the end of a semester based on a research product that may confound writing proficiency with domain knowledge for both student and professor. Individual findings highlight learner development and increased competence in written communication through formative assessment during processes of writing a legal research paper.

8.3.4 What all three showed together to answer research question 4

Figure 8.5 below shows the dynamic nature of the interrelationships from the first three research questions that answer Research Question (RQ) 4. Not only did findings emphasize the interrelation among building, self-assessing, and evaluating competence at each stage of writing to increase proficiency through knowledge of scholarship and social interaction, but the findings underscored the role of metacognition for higher levels of proficiency in writing, as for speaking (Leaver & Shekhtman, 2002).

RQ 1	Interrelating strategies, skills, and stages produced a (cognitive → sociocultural) shift.
RQ 2	Interrelating (metacognitive with sociocultural) knowledge of writer, task, and strategies affected L2 writer performance.
RQ 3	Interrelating ability to revise and self-edit with social interaction affected L2 product quality.

Fig. 8.5. Dynamic nature of strategic competence in scholarly L2 legal writing.

Strategic competence acted as a catalyst for development in participants' scholarly L2 writing.

8.4 Strategic competence as catalyst for development

For all participants, strategic competence evolved into a traveling toolkit of interrelating literacy strategies, iterative language skills, stages or levels of performance, L2 knowledge of person, tasks, and strategies, and quality assessment goals that affected their performance and helped them develop competence (proficiency, expertise) in scholarly writing. Overall qualitative results emphasized how scholarly writing was both a learner-centered, cognitive process (for prewriting and drafting) and a sociocultural, reader-centered process (for revising). Building strategic competence for scholarly writing impacted (a) acculturated student participants' confidence, motivation, and self-regulation at each stage, and (b) and non-acculturated student participants' L2 knowledge and skills development across stages. With respect to transfer, all participants reported that they had the necessary disciplinary or sociocultural knowledge for self-regulating production of other legal research papers or scholarly articles. Member checks with five participants, after data analyses had been made available to them, validated this finding.

Revising for specific purposes was a key component of the strategic competence toolkit described by one participant as a "roadmap" of carefully defined strategies, skills, and levels for building competence or expertise. The revision stage, in particular, was seen as a level of academic English performance that acted as a catalyst for high communicative precision.

The scholarly writers' toolkit included quality assessment criteria for evaluating the disciplinary research product at key intervals. The interactional SQAT/ TQAT process was formative for participants because they not only self-assessed but also discussed how to build competence at the level of professional (or higher) writing proficiency at each stage of writing: conceptually, rhetorically, and linguistically. Through planned, individual consultations with their teacher-researcher, participants learned by reflecting and gaining contextual knowledge of themselves, their tasks, and in-depth strategies that enhanced their existing competences in stages, at three levels: that is, planning competence, genre competence, and communication competence. Student self-reassessment with teacher-researcher evaluation at key intervals thus promoted writing proficiency (competence or expertise) in a legal research paper with multiple opportunities for revising ideas and self-editing text. This metacognitive, social-interactive view of learning and writing, interesting and productive for L2 graduate student writers from diverse cultures of scholarship and traditions of legal education, contrasts with static assessment of academic writing as a one-dimensional form of editing by faculty (Woodward-Kron, 2007). Planning and (re)evaluating were key metacognitive strategies that assisted participants in developing their analytical thinking and enhancing their existing competences. Also associated with learner development was knowledge of how to manage the scholarly writing process, facilitating control of complex cognitive and social processes involved in academic text production to meet disciplinary standards.

The mixed-methods findings suggested that, in addition to knowledge of genre, register, and cultural expectation (Hyland, 2003), knowledge of scholarly writing as a dynamic, interactive, strategic process for text construction has to be received as declarative (substantive) knowledge before it can be produced by students as procedural (rhetorical) knowledge. Development happened through increased knowledge and use of language in disciplinary writing context, with conditional knowledge of strategies for problem-solving bridging declarative and procedural knowledge for participants – culturally and linguistically. Findings conclude that (a) building strategic competence positively influences writing proficiency, and (b) developing writers in academic domain context promotes learning and achievement.

More than one kind of knowledge is necessary for international graduate student writers to meet their goals and challenges in this 21st century of globalization: that is, declarative, conditional, and procedural. In their shift from language learners to language producers – a shift from the cognitive to the sociocultural – EFL/ESL graduate student writers need to understand the conditional (contextual) dimensions for competent performance so they can use what they know more flexibly (Newell & Simon, 1972) and learn what they do not know more effectively. Strategies, skills, goals, and levels for academic writing comprise knowledge of situated performance.

Table 8.4 below shows how L2 use of dynamic SCQ skills and strategies built competence at the level of professional (or higher) proficiency at each stage of recursive scholarly writing.

Table 8.4. SCQ strategies and skills for building competence.

Stage 1	Pre-writing strategies (for legal reading and researching) +CALP skills (for legal language processing: summary, paraphrase, and synthesis)
Stage 2	Drafting strategies (for getting words and concepts down on paper) +CALP skills (for academic/ legal language processing) +CALP skills (associated with levels of writing purpose)
Stage 3	Revising, editing, and plain English grammar strategies (related to legal style) +CALP skills (for academic/ legal language processing) +CALP skills (associated with levels of writing purpose) +Knowledge transforming strategies (for getting away from language of source text and to avoid plagiarizing)

The word "dynamic" connotes overlap of strategies, skills, and stages as well as re-cursiveness of cognitive, metacognitive, and social-affective strategies and CALP skills for each stage.

The table below shows how use of the interactional SQAT/TQAT process facil-itated quality assessment, oral discussion, and insider knowledge of how to build competence at the professional level at each stage of recursive scholarly writing. With each individual consultation, the student writer learned from his/her own work and became more adept by gaining the knowledge needed to enhance exist-ing competences (Table 8.5).

Table 8.5. SQAT/TQAT interactive process for building competence.

Stage 1	Pre-writing (learner-centered) – planning competence, 17 items
Stage2	Drafting (writer-centered) – genre competence, 17 items
Stage 3	Revising (reader-centered) – communication competence, 28 items

Student self-assessment, teacher evaluation, planned and focused social inter-action at each stage promoted mastery (expertise) in scholarly legal writing with informed opportunities for revising and self-editing. This (meta-) cognitive (so-cial-) interactive view of writing and instruction was interesting and productive for L2 legal writer participants originating from contrasting academic cultures and traditions of legal education that may privilege speaking over academic writing for summative evaluation of learner knowledge. An engaged, interactive view of learning and formative assessment contrasts with static assessment of L2 academic writing that may not be a valid measure of international graduate student learning.

Also important to consider is that a (meta-)cognitive, (social-)interactive approach for developing graduate-level L2 academic writers does not require disciplinary content knowledge on the part of a writing teacher. Her focus with students is on language use in disciplinary writing context which requires (a) in-depth knowledge of the L2 graduate writer, culturally and linguistically, (b) awareness of learners' agency while adapting to the demands of their research discipline, and (c) knowledge of student learning: that is, how learners acquire disciplinary content knowledge, genre knowledge, and strategies for textual borrowing (Silva, McMartin-Miller, Jayne, & Pelaez-Morales, 2010). Learner agency for professionalization, and various kinds of knowledge for academic development, can be mediated through an understanding of the cognitive and sociocultural processes involved in learning to write L2 graduate research papers and journal articles. Research writing teachers and advisors must probe deeper than surface-level grammar so L2 English graduate students can clarify their research interests and writing challenges. International student writers operating at the pre-professional level can enhance their existing competences for effective communication with knowledge of scholarship and advanced literacy in a paper or article, as this study shows.

Table 8.6 below illustrates what was needed for the L2 academic legal writers in this study to make the shift from writer-centered to reader-centered scholarly writing.

These interrelations for developing L2 academic writers comprised conditional knowledge of situated performance (Alexander, 2006). Student participants needed to know about and understand contextual dimensions for performing disciplinary-related literacy tasks to produce a legal research paper for U.S. law school credit. "Because strategic processing entails the effective and intentional selection of appropriate actions and problem-solving responses, it encompasses conditional knowledge–when and where knowledge" (Alexander, personal communication, 1/11/2013). This knowledge helps students integrate procedural with declarative knowledge.

"Achieving disciplinary literacy," according to Berkenkotter, Huckin, and Ackerman (1988, p. 9), "requires that the writer be able to integrate procedural with substantive/declarative knowledge, in this case knowledge of appropriate discourse conventions with his developing knowledge of a disciplinary community's issues and research methodology." Conditional knowledge of cognitive and socially-culturally appropriate (disciplinary) writing strategies is important,

Table 8.6. Interrelations for developing L2 academic (scholarly) writers.

Interrelating kinds of writing knowledge	Interrelating kinds of literacy strategies	Interrelating kinds of language skills	Interrelating levels or purposes for composing (based on Grabe, 2001)	Interrelating social-interactive competences

– U.S. cultural conventions
– Criteria for assessment
– Writing from L2 legal sources
– Linguistic system SVO
– Process management
– Product genre
– Metacognitive Knowledge of process and content:
  – planning
  – organizing
  – evaluating
  – monitoring
– Revising
	– Reading
	– Drafting
	– Revising
	– Editing
	– Grammar
	– Knowledge transforming
	  – conceptual
	  – rhetorical
	  – linguistic
		– Reading to learn
		– Writing to learn
		– Writing to commun-icate
			– Stating knowledge by listing, re-peating, or paraphrasing source text
			– Understanding, remembering, summarizing simply, or extend-ing notes to oneself
			– Learning, problem-solving, summarizing complexly, or syn-thesizing information
			– Critiquing, persuading, or inter-preting evidence selectively and appropriately
				– Planning (stage 1)
				– Genre (stage 2)
				– Communication (stage 3)

but interrelations for strategic competence, a component of communicative competence (Canale & Swain, 1980) that includes CALP skills, was needed for L2 student writers in this study to communicate effectively. Developing writing proficiency with conditional knowledge of literacy strategies, language skills, and levels/stages for writing advances academic literacy (Braine, 2002), moving graduate writers toward disciplinary literacy. The benefit for student writer participants was confidence, self-regulation, and professional identity, maximizing their potential for domain learning, professional voice and graduate-level scholarship.

The "bottom line" for this discussion is an understanding of strategic competence that is more than compensatory. For highly motivated international graduate students working at or toward professional levels of writing proficiency in a content domain, *strategic competence* centers on the ability to apply appropriate disciplinary literacy strategies and language skills for knowledge acquisition and language production, and for coping with the unknown in North American research writing habit (process) and cultural expectation (product).

Thus, strategic competence may be viewed from an additive (versus deficit) cultural and linguistic perspective. Without L2 strategic competence, attempts to transfer competence from L1 academic writing to L2 academic legal writing may be socioculturally inappropriate; international graduate students may fail or drop out (Hu, 2001), or their transcripts may not accurately reflect content domain learning. This is because linguistic and rhetorical conventions from L1 academic writing may interfere with L2 academic legal writing (Connor, 1996). "There is ample evidence that L1 writing processes, for better or worse, are likely to be transferred to L2 to the extent that the writer's knowledge of the L2 permits" (Caudery, 2002, p. 183).

Proficiency developed from a strategic, goal-directed, process-oriented approach to writing as a scholar that focused the learner on what each needed to know and do to achieve communicative competence in a graduate research paper. Learners developed from appropriate actions and problem-solving responses in L2 academic legal English across stages (pre-writing, drafting, revising) or "levels of writing" and thinking for development: conceptually, rhetorically, and linguistically.

Stage 1, Conceptually

The literacy strategies used in Stage 1 (pre-writing) helped participants students plan, monitor, and evaluate their understanding of legal research and scholarly writing. Students learned from researching multilingual legal sources and reworking thoughts in L2 English with discourse synthesis among other strategies.

Metacognitive strategies for writing such as self-monitoring thinking extended to composing when participants reflected on their learning and expressed their ideas explicitly – without copying or translating source text inappropriately. Planning and organizing helped participants limit the scope of their research and tailor their writing by defining and developing a controlling idea (argument, claim, or thesis). Some linguistic actions for problem-solving that required explicit instruction were research problem/issue, purpose, and thesis statements in academic legal English, acting as a global positioning system (GPS) for limiting legal research. Stage 1 learning strategies, with use of the quality checklist, proved efficient for time management and effective for draft creation.

Stage 2, Rhetorically
The literacy strategies used in Stage 2 (drafting) helped the writers learn from their legal research while writing. Participants interacted with their legal research and with their language production, relating to what they know and organizing material to understand and appreciate it in terms of their legal problem/issue, purpose, and thesis (from Stage 1). Conscious use of strategies helped participants consider goal directed actions they may take more than once while drafting a scholarly paper. The drafting strategies helped participants create text from legal sources without plagiarizing, summary or discourse synthesis being a key cognitive strategy. The quality assessment checklist, with teacher feedback, helped students achieve genre competence in a non-linear progression, focusing learner attention on legal analysis and large-scale rhetorical organization. Key actions for problem-solving that required explicit instruction were (a) the application of CALP skills (summarizing, paraphrasing, synthesizing) for long quotations, especially when students were unsure of how to get words and concepts down on paper without re-using language from source text inappropriately; and (b) scholarly knowledge of citation to integrate evidence from source text.

Stage 3, Linguistically
The revising strategies used in Stage 3 helped student participants develop their thinking about the law and academic legal English by deciding what should be changed, deleted, added, or retained. Attention to small-scale organization (paragraphs and sentences) with knowledge-transforming strategies was required. Editing strategies helped the student participants make the shift from the cognitive to the socio-cultural when refining and checking for linguistic conventions. The plain language grammar strategies helped make students' expression clear, accurate, and concise – accommodating their level of language proficiency. Key

actions for problem-solving requiring explicit instruction were coherence devices that reinforce connections among ideas, like parallel structures and dovetails that begin a sentence by repeating key words or phrases used at the end of a previous sentence or paragraph, making a connection and providing new content. These substantive transitions allow student writers to show cognition (logic) and deeper levels of understanding within their own text by making the relation between sentences and paragraphs clear and explicit, to themselves and to their law educated reader.

Thus, revising strategies helped student participants (a) process legal domain knowledge, and (b) develop their L2 English communication to express original thinking about a legal problem or issue. The end result was text construction that contributed to the literature rather than re-tell it. In addition, reader-centered (revising, editing, and grammar) strategies were needed for EFL participants who assumed that responsibility for successful communication lay with the reader, not with the writer, as in U.S. academic legal culture.

Iterative Use of Strategies, Skills, Stages, and Goals

The use of literacy strategies, language skills, stages/levels for writing, and quality assessment goals was iterative when student writers' role shifted to being critical readers of their own texts. "All work can be reviewed, evaluated, and revised," (Hyland, 2003, p. 11). Strategies and iterative CALP skills across stages, combined with self-regulating goals at each stage, contributed to developing writers' cognitive-linguistic and sociocultural proficiency. In other words, learning about and using self-regulating actions and goals for scholarly writing acted as a mechanism for EFL and ESL graduate writer development (assimilation and accommodation) in legal domain context.

8.5 Learner assessment and writing instruction

Learning and assessment become an ethical responsibility for language teachers, university professors, and academic deans when research papers are used to assess international graduate student learning through summative assessment of L2 writer product. By definition, "education" means the process of receiving or giving systematic instruction, so educating international graduate student learners means more than a severe warning against plagiarism, a PowerPoint presentation, or a workshop on U.S. academic (legal) writing culture. It means (a) adding to graduate students' repertoire of academic literacy strategies; (b) giving them socially-culturally appropriate tools for developing thought, language, and content domain knowledge; (c) elevating them from undergraduate to graduate level "knowledge-building" (Coulson, 2009, p. 165); and (d) expecting them to transform as learners through their research and writing.

At its core, this learner-centered study shows how strategic competence facilitates the graduate writer shift from the cognitive to the sociocultural "with the strategies to do it." Figure 8.6 below illustrates interrelating strategic shifts for competence in scholarly writing.

- academic literacy strategies shift across stages
- academic language skills shift across stages
- goals for assessment shift across stages
- roles of writer and reader shift across stages
- roles of composing shift across stages (from knowledge-telling to knowledge-transforming)
- roles of revising shift to include techniques for self-editing and clear communication
- proficiency shifts across stages: acclimation (stage 1, pre-writing) → competence (stage 2, drafting) → expertise (stage 3, revising).

Fig. 8.6. Interrelating strategic shifts for competence → expertise in scholarly writing.

The dynamic processes of scholarly writing reflect the dynamic nature of strategic competence for participants learning to be more skilled writers. Disciplinary literacy, writing proficiency, and L2 academic language use are interrelated.

International graduate students in U.S. law schools are required to show individual competence (proficiency) that satisfies performance expectations of highly literate native-English speakers who are not required to have training in L2 writing pedagogy or second language development "and who may not devise adequately clear assignments, scaffold these assignments effectively in the classroom, provide helpful feedback, or fairly assess students' written products" (Ferris & Hedgcock, 2014, p. 47). Without explicit instruction relevant to learners' cultural and linguistic backgrounds, there may be no significant progress for international graduate students. Their writing challenges may remain unseen by uninformed native English speakers, legal writing instructors, or law school professors whose focus is more on the law than on the learner. Indeed, graduate study-abroad without formal language instruction may not advance learning or writing proficiency, not to be confused with speaking fluency or accuracy.

This research study suggests a systematic, self-regulating approach for developing professional levels of proficiency in written language use that includes formal instruction for international graduate student writers. Explicit strategies instruction, quality assessment, and feedback during writing helped research participants develop their thinking, legal analysis, and written communication. Lack of linguistic and cultural knowledge may be at the heart of writing problems for other graduate writers and teachers as well (Caudery, 2002).

8.6 Theory and professional practice

Academic writing contributes to developing competence in a high literacy academic domain like law. From a learning perspective, student participants moved along the novice-expert continuum in a legal research paper from (a) writer-centered learning in the early stages of research writing, to (b) reader-centered communication in the revising stage. Although both surface-level and deeper-level strategies were used at each stage, a progressive non-linear movement was seen from research topic *acclimation* (in pre-writing, stage 1) to *competence* (in drafting, stage 2) to scholarly legal discourse and content *knowledge* about a legal topic (in revising, stage 3). Conditional knowledge of strategies helped scholarly writer participants learn by impacting their interest, motivation, engagement, and achievement.

This finding is in line with Alexander's Model of Domain Learning (MDL). The extensively researched MDL explains how subject matter knowledge, strategic processing, and interest provide foundation for developing competence and expertise. According to Alexander (1997, 2003), expertise develops across three stages of (1) acclimation, (2) competence, and (3) proficiency. These stages articulate "a sound foundation for understanding the development of academic writing expertise" (Lasssig, Lincoln, Dillon, Diezmann, Fox, & Neofa, 2009, pp. 3–4). For participants, both quantitative and qualitative changes took place during the learning process; affective and motivational factors with "dialogic processes" supported their success; and (c) "a progressive blurring of the lines" occurred among the student writers who had "variable expertise" (Lassig et al., 2009, p. 3). In other words, the following three factors contributed to developing L2 academic writer competence: (1) strategies developed strategic performance, (2) motivation developed self-efficacy and confidence, and (3) knowledge developed mental operations. Increased knowledge of language use in U.S. academic legal context, with goals for learning and assessment in stages, contributed to L2 learner development.

From a teaching perspective, enhancement of competences is a higher-order goal in U.S. education. Higher order learning outcomes met by participants in this study include (a) creativity in problem solving in a manner that expresses originality of thought; (b) critical thinking and academic inquiry that utilizes writing from sources and evidence; (c) depth of knowledge demonstrated in a disciplinary research area; (d) effective written communication that presents research results for a specific audience and purpose and that expresses ideas and information logically and clearly; and (e) cultural competency that recognizes and understands different academic perspectives and writing experiences. Recursiveness through Vygotsky's notion of the Zone of Proximal Development (ZPD), the distance between the learner's individual competence and the capacity to perform and meet learning outcomes with assistance, requires assisting international student performance as a preeminent responsibility of teachers and institutions (Gallimore & Tharpe, 1998). At the very least, knowledge of culture and discourse synthesis is necessary for competent performance by international graduate student writers. In the U.S. academic context, this means that international student writers have to learn how to connect various elements of discourse appropriately and how to engage in direct and explicit interaction – an analytic communication style that contrasts with holistic and implicit learning found in the East (Nisbett, 2003). This study, therefore, underscores "draft-and-revision" (Afflerbach, 1990) with in-process social interaction and teacher feedback as especially useful strategies for international graduate student writers. Teaching learning strategies for planning, drafting, revising (and publishing), and regulating strategic processing with attainable goals for writing quality, is part of learner-centered instruction that acknowledges the difficulty of academic writing "often situated on the far end of a perceived trajectory of difficulty in terms of language learning and use" (Lillis & Curry, 2010, p. 62). Knowledge of strategies developed L2 academic writers' processes, and knowledge of goals developed L2 writers' product, transforming learner-centered writing into reader-centered communication. The research tools contributed to student learning by facilitating a graduate writer shift from learner to scholar with (a) explicit strategies assessment for process, and (b) goals assessment for product quality across three stages of writing. Clarity, explicitness, and directness are sociocultural elements of style that imply moving along the novice–expert continuum as much as moving along the cultural language learning–producing continuum.

8.7 Implications

The mixed methods design for this research is deeply triangulated, and its procedures are replicable. The two sets of tools for developing graduate student writers' strategic processes and product quality predict enhanced performance in two ways. First, the Strategic Competence Questionnaire predicts high communicative precision and communicative competence measured by the study's (formative) assessment tools, triangulated in part by content law professors' (summative) grades. Second, the Students'/Teacher's Quality Assessment Tools predict planning competence (stage 1), genre competence (stage 2), and communication competence (stage 3) in stages or levels of text construction. Research results suggest that strategy (self-) assessment for guiding writers' cognitive and social-cultural processes, and quality assessment for (self-) checking student writers' product *in-situ* transforms learner-centered writing into reader-centered communication. The contribution to knowledge for graduate students is the distinction between "writing to learn" and "writing to communicate ideas" with advanced literacy techniques in a research paper or journal article. "The book's added knowledge value lies in its empirical validation" of the effectiveness of a largely self-regulated, strategy-based, professional writing program for foreign-trained graduate students in a U.S. university (Brendel, G., personal communication, January 20, 2014).

From a teaching perspective, a transformative approach to learning is advocated "in which teachers facilitate experiences for students who make use of them to transform information into knowledge" (Ebsworth, 2010, p. 322). The research instruments guiding students' engagement with their own thinking and research writing can be (a) adapted for other disciplinary/academic writers, and (b) generalized across academic languages. The benefit is self-regulation or control for international graduate student writers and a systematic approach to L2 writer development that offers more than surface-level editing by faculty, peers, or tutors. A transformative approach supports thought development in L2 academic writing through effective, efficient problem-solving that goes beyond knowledge-telling from sources or translating from the L1. With interactive and corrective feedback, L2 academic writers can make the critical connection between process and product at each stage, gaining cognitive linguistic and sociocultural knowledge that includes "knowledge of discourse" for text construction and communication (Gee, 1996, p. 134). Knowledge of discourse may need to be taught or made explicit in the L2 academic/disciplinary writing situation. Based on Grabe and Kaplan (1996, pp. 220–221), Figure 8.7 below defines this kind of knowledge.

Thought development and communication in academic writing can be mediated by instructional intervention through which international graduate student writers interact (textually and socially) to reflect critically about what they are doing while they are doing it, stimulating teacher reflection for meaningful feedback in stages: conceptually (stage 1), rhetorically (stage 2), and linguistically (stage 3).

Discourse knowledge

A. Knowledge of cohesion and syntactic parallelism
B. Knowledge of informational structuring (topic/comment, old/new)
C. Knowledge of semantic relations across clauses
D. Knowledge to recognize main topics
E. Knowledge of genre structure and genre constraints
F. Knowledge of organizing themes (top-level discourse structure)
G. Knowledge of inferencing (bridging, elaborating)
H. Awareness of differences in features of L2 vs. L1 discourse structuring
I. Awareness of discourse skills in L2 vs. L1 (legal) language

---

Fig. 8.7. What may need to be taught or made explicit for international graduate student writers.

Part IV: **Learner-User Centered Pedagogy**

9 Connecting Learning with Teaching

9.1 How prior knowledge and learning interact

International students' conceptualizations of scholarly and academic writing, and knowing how to write, directly influence their approaches to writing from sources, academic success, personal investment in learning, and motivation (based on Alexander, 2006). Teachers' conceptualizations of writing and knowing how to write are evident in their instructional goals, pedagogical decisions, and assessment practices (based on Alexander, 2006). However, because of the number of assignments and complexity of assignments in a disciplinary legal writing classroom, for example, there may not be enough time to address processes for writing and thinking explicitly. This omission can be highly problematic for multilingual graduate student writers, whether their writing knowledge is proceduralized (automatic) or not.

The purpose of this chapter is to bridge research perspectives on learning (Alexander, 2006) and language learning strategies (Oxford, 2011) to explain why explicit strategies instruction works for learning and development in L2 academic and disciplinary writing. It shows how teachers can implement strategies and goals to foster growth for international EFL/ESL student writers beyond their current capacities. Research perspectives move the focus from teaching (teacher) to learning (learner) and learner agency.

The bottom line is that prior (background) knowledge is a significant factor for learning and development. It exists in three states: declarative (what) knowledge, procedural (how to) knowledge, and conditional (when, where, and why) knowledge (Alexander, 2006; Oxford, 2010). "Anything that is known well is known declaratively, procedurally, and conditionally" (Alexander, 2006, p. 73). Declarative knowledge is factual and conscious, procedural knowledge is unconscious or automatic, and conditional knowledge of learning strategies helps transform conscious declarative knowledge into procedural writing habit. In other words, when EFL/ESL student writers become conscious of what they do and why, they can change their writing habits with learning strategies.

Being a conscious act, writing performance encompasses both declarative and conditional knowledge. Attending only to the basic elements of language like vocabulary and syntax is not helping international students write better in an academic discipline or solve problems in it through academic or disciplinary writing. Teachers and students must attend to the conditions for language use – the context for writing. In other words, when the basic declarative building blocks of writing knowledge become part of an integrated system in terms of (a) classifications and categories, (b) principles and generalizations, or (c) theories, models and structures, competence or proficiency results (Alexander, 2006). International student writers, therefore, need awareness of interrelationships among the basic elements of writing within a larger structure, like a research paper or journal article, that enable them to function together: conceptually, rhetorically, and linguistically. When learners become aware of the interrelationships among the larger writing structure, components of prior writing knowledge and learning may interact rather quickly for more highly literate performance. Interrelations for strategic competence become crucial for international graduate student writers whose background knowledge contrasts across cultures, languages, educational systems, and approaches to language learning.

Oxford (2010) defines the conditional or contextual dimensions of L2 strategies use for international student writers and their teachers that may otherwise remain implicit (complex, unanalyzed, or uncommunicated). These are *L1* (self) knowledge, *L2* (culture) knowledge, *task* knowledge, *whole process* knowledge, and *strategies* knowledge which is multidimensional: cognitive, affective, and sociocultural-interactive (Oxford, 2011). With language learners in mind, Oxford (2011) refers to these contextual dimensions as "metaknowledge" (p. 20). This context for L2 strategies use is culturally, linguistically, and affectively sensitive compared to knowledge of cognition only, often referred to as "metacognitive knowledge" after Wenden (1991) and Flavell (1978; 1979) (as cited in Oxford, 2011, p. 19). Awareness of *metaknowledge* contributes to conditional knowledge for L2 strategies use (Oxford, 2011), and building *meta*(cognitive) *knowledge* helps transform declarative into procedural knowledge for both native and non-native English learners. These typically unseen contextual (conditional) dimensions for language learning and written language use are juxtaposed in the figure below. Note how *metaknowledge* is context-sensitive in contrast to *metacognitive knowledge* which is context-reduced.

Metaknowledge	Metacognitive knowledge
1. L1 person	1. self-knowledge
2. L2 culture	
3. task	2. task knowledge
4. whole [writing] process	
5. strategies:	
(a) cognitive [and linguistic]	
(b) affective	
(c) sociocultural-interactive	3. strategic knowledge

Fig. 9.1. Dimensions of meta (cognitive) knowledge for consciousness raising.

Understanding and use of *metaknowledge* by academic and disciplinary writing teachers facilitates learning for international EFL/ESL student writers – explicit knowledge being the primary focus of all teachers (Alexander, 2006). International EFL/ESL student writers may acquire (a) self-knowledge in the context of big (scholarly) culture and small (disciplinary) culture; (b) task knowledge with explicit criteria for reflection and assessment in stages, and (c) strategic knowledge with explicit strategies for different conditions, purposes, situations, and settings (Ehrman, Leaver, & Oxford, 2003).

Learning and teaching L2 academic writing does not have to be taxing if explicit knowledge of written language use is adopted within the context of scholarly and disciplinary writing practice. "Development involves not only learning of new strategies for generating meaning through print. It also involves increasing the range of materials and contexts in which the cognitive, linguistic, and sociocultural [interactive] strategies can be employed" (Kucer, 2014, p. 287). So, understanding the linguistic, cognitive, and sociocultural dimensions for advancing literacy and language use is important to developing L2 academic writing and individual growth. "Development typically continues throughout the course of one's life as long as literacy is encountered and used in new or novel ways" (Kucer, 2014, p. 287). The goal for learning and teaching international graduate student writers, then, must be self-regulation pertaining not just to EFL/ESL learners' management of cognition and academic/disciplinary writing tasks. Based on Oxford (2011) and Alexander, Graham, & Harris (1998), autonomy also involves regulation of affective states and the social environment in which the written communication or discourse occurs. Teaching new strategies within the context of conditional (when, where, and why) knowledge means addressing individual differences within the advanced academic setting and disciplinary writing situation as well as new ideas about scholarship. The outcome for international graduate student writers may be learning or change in behavior. The outcome for teachers may be high performance reviews from international students who claim new "knowledge" and understanding of what it means to be a scholarly writer, even in a short paper.

Strategic knowledge facilitates learning for all international graduate student writers. Strategic knowledge implies reflection, important for all (L1 and L2) learners at high levels (Anderson, Lorin & Krathwohl, 2001). It is especially important for multilingual academic writers connecting factual knowledge of L2 scholarly writing production with procedural knowledge of discipline-specific skills and techniques. Communicative practice in rich disciplinary writing context can be a catalyst for transforming conscious, declarative knowledge of written language use into procedural knowledge. Teaching scholarly communication strategies like paraphrasing with citation are foundational for knowledge transforming in a professional paper or article. This kind of learner-centered teaching contrasts with teaching a style manual or other textbook, for example. International graduate students can read and they can study. Language use, composition skills, and writing knowledge, however, are important for international EFL/ESL writer development. Direct (explicit) teaching of process, strategic (reflective) knowledge, and use of (research-based) quality checklists can mediate L2 academic writer knowledge and behavior which, in turn, mediate content domain learning. "Learning textual practices in a given discipline is closely intertwined with one's personal development as a scholar" (Lonka, Chow, Keskinen, Hakkarainen, Sandström, & Phyältö, 2014, p. 247). However, "learning academic writing is not easy because of the challenges concerning how to transform knowledge into a comprehensible and disciplinarily acceptable entity for a specific audience (Lonka et al, 2014, p. 249). Writing to transform knowledge from source text, rather than reproduce information from source text, is a learning process that needs to be supported by building on prior knowledge, L1 academic and disciplinary writing experience, and L2 learning experience.

Alexander (2006) identifies many factors that contribute to student learning and effective teaching, but two are key for developing international EFL/ESL students as writers. These are construction of knowledge and strategic thinking. The successful learner can (1) link new (L2 writer) information with existing (L1 writer) knowledge in meaningful ways, and (2) and use a repertoire of disciplinary thinking and reasoning strategies to achieve complex learning goals in research and writing. Construction of knowledge and strategic thinking are both important in a learner-centered writing classroom because (1) international students' existing knowledge base serves as foundation for all subsequent learning, and (2) the ability to reflect on and regulate one's thoughts and research writing behaviors contributes to learning and development (Alexander, 2006).

9.2 The strategic learner and the student-centered classroom

Educational research suggests ways to create a learning environment that addresses strategic thinking in an explicit and integrated manner with a focus on the writer rather than on the writing product. The following guidelines, based on Alexander's (2006) synthesis of research, promote self-monitoring and self-regulation (control) in L2 academic writing. Although presented linearly, they overlap and are interactive. Most can be incorporated into any classroom or writing situation, flipping it from being "teacher-centered" to "student-centered" learning and instruction.

9.2.1 Advice for teachers

First, teachers should identify the nature and purpose of all writing tasks and language use situations. Students can articulate their perceptions of what is being asked and what results they should demonstrate so teachers and students are "on the same page." Teachers should do this even if the writing task is for a third party, as in the writing intervention for this learner–centered research. For example, in the author's L2 academic writing classroom, international students are given time to find out from their content law professors what is required and when, with interaction (email and face to face) strategies discussed for individual student situations. It is important to know what law school writing tasks students are expected to do with the scaffolding provided in the L2 academic writing course. After two weeks or so, students articulate their perceived requirements in a round-table classroom setting. Similarities and differences surface for students to probe deeper and begin to think what they might have to (learn to) do to prepare for a graduate level research paper (thesis or dissertation). Checklists for reflection (e.g., Appendix B) provide language for identifying the kinds of knowledge students might need to perform various research and writing tasks, and how they might characterize improvement in their disciplinary academic writing. Self-reflection and discussion provide rich, authentic context for international EFL/ESL student writer development.

Second, teachers should engage in task (problem) analysis. Teachers can show students how to take a large research writing or disciplinary reading task apart so they can deal more effectively with the various components and language use dimensions. For example, scholarly writing students need to identify their research problem, purpose for research and writing, and thesis or research question(s) before they can begin drafting a paper. A pedagogical tool like Appendix G shows how the three component stages of the writing process are recursive and interactive in terms of research and writing, and how student writers may be expected to revise their written analysis from an audience perspective in the final stage(s) of writing. It is imperative to note that international student writers may have multiple audiences in mind simultaneously, so discussion of how the same research (data) can be re-visited and presented from multiple (cultural and disciplinary) perspectives is interesting and useful to international graduate student writers and visiting scholars. From a language use perspective, Appendix D (stage 4) is useful for showing students where they are headed and what makes a good paper in L2 academic English context. It is also important to note that explication of genre, with strategies for writing the basic components of a scholarly paper or article (Introduction, Background, Analysis, and Conclusion), is reserved for when students are ready to write in stage 2, drafting.

Third, teachers should describe criteria that could be used to judge various learning outcomes and show students workable models to make the assessment criteria concrete. A grading rubric with use of models saves a lot of time and energy for everyone, making teaching concrete, effective, and efficient. In the author's L2 academic writing classroom, for example, a model of a student's substantive outline from the previous semester shows how statements of purpose, problem, and thesis are conceptual tools for limiting research and preparing to write – different from a skeletal outline or Table of Contents required in stage 2, drafting. Simply looking at a successful student's work from a previous class makes the abstract concrete for learners. Discourse analysis helps learners break down the components of a journal article: a useful tool for discovering genre in the L2 academic writing situation. Students need to know what an effective work product may look like, how it may be organized, what the key elements are that must be present in each section, and how transitions may function. Semantic (sentence-to-sentence) cohesiveness and pragmatic (speaker-to-speaker) coherence may need to be taught, though, along with syntactic parallelism to increase student writer proficiency. Criteria for assessment thus overlap with task analysis in significant ways, contributing to L2 learner-user development.

Following teacher explication and modeling, students may want the opportunity to generate other criteria for use in evaluation, depending on the nature of instruction. Teachers can give students opportunities to create (individual or collective) criteria for evaluating disciplinary writing and language use tasks. In the author's L2 academic writing classroom, for example, students reflect on a Can-Do Checklist that defines proficiency (competence) in academic legal writing. This checklist was contextualized to make it relevant to L2 legal learners, but the statements describe competence for both native and non-native English writers. They can be re-contextualized for other kinds of disciplinary writing. Like the ACTFL Can-Do Statements' progress indicators for language learners,[1] the checklist in this text supports competence-based writing instruction (Appendix D, SCQ 3.b). It shows defining abilities for expository writers and how international student writers need to be concerned with effectiveness in written language use rather than pure literary style that may contrast across cultures and kinds of writing.

Because choice and personal outcomes contribute to student investment in learning, teachers can also help students formulate their own personal goals for select learning tasks. In the author's L2 academic writing classroom, students get research-based examples of writing purpose so they can (re-) use the phrasing to formulate their own purpose statements for a three slide PowerPoint (ppt)

---

[1] http://www.actfl.org/sites/default/files/pdfs/Can-Do_Statements.pdf

oral presentation. The purpose of professional speaking with technology is to prepare students for writing a substantive (conceptual) outline that includes focused statements of problem, purpose, and thesis. Giving international graduate students and visiting scholars guided opportunities to speak about their disciplinary research interest, answer questions, receive (conceptual and linguistic) feedback, and process information in L2 English helps make abstract thinking concrete. It also helps limit research writers' topics when they are too broad. Thus, presentational speaking with feedback is formative for international graduate students trying to formulate clear statements of purpose, problem, and thesis in an L2 academic research paper (thesis or dissertation). Developing international graduate student thinking and communication with teacher monitoring and self-evaluation contributes to self-monitoring and self-regulation.

9.2.2 Advice for students

Empirical research in learning and instruction informs professional practice. You should know that research writing in a second language requires both factual (declarative) knowledge and contextual (conditional) knowledge of written language use. Writing research is a linguistic problem-solving activity in intercultural literacy context, far more involved than English grammar and vocabulary. You must understand the problem you aim to solve through your academic or disciplinary research writing, and you must communicate it effectively to a highly educated reader from another academic culture. Therefore, you must demonstrate conscious, declarative knowledge of purpose, audience, and level of formality (register) when writing a research paper (thesis or dissertation). Style is less important because there are many different kinds of writing styles across cultures. Professors in North American academic culture simply want to know what you think (critical thinking) and why you think that way (documented evidence). They will not judge you according to cultural, literary standards. Clarity, not beauty, is therefore the guiding principle in writing for academic and professional purposes. This principle should guide your writing because the onus for communication is on you, the thinker and writer. It is not your professors' responsibility to infer what you mean in your writing. Clarity, accuracy, and brevity are characteristics of professional writing style that can be achieved in any paper through feedback and revision. A research-based checklist for clarity in academic English writing is at-

tached[2] (Appendix H). This is a self-editing checklist that breaks down what you need to do for effective communication in academic English writing. Use it for revising your writing before submitting a paper to a teacher, professor, or editor for review.

You should also know that a process approach to academic and/or disciplinary writing is a routine approach to solving problems in a paper or article. The process approach for writing is familiar to proficient writers internationally. Linguistic processes of draft and revision help limit the challenges all writers face that seem overwhelming initially. While drafting and revising more than once, you will internalize what you are reading and writing about, gaining more control over your thinking and written language output. You can draft for (content) accuracy first and revise for (language) clarity second. To be efficient, though, you are advised not to do both at the same time. Also, to be effective, find out how you will be evaluated. If your professors cannot give you explicit criteria for evaluating your research product objectively, you should ask them questions during the research and writing processes. Individual consultation is expected in our educational system. Interaction with more knowledgeable others is always advisable, especially when you have a substantive outline so professors can target your problem area(s) quickly. You should not expect them to read long tracts of your writing. Your outline should include a preliminary search of the research literature so they can tell you what you may be missing in your working bibliography. Academic writing does not have to be a solitary (cognitive) endeavor; it is known in the research literature to be a social-cultural practice and both professors and students should treat it that way. This means that academic writing, like disciplinary writing, is a learned process requiring knowledge and support from your professors and peers. Native-English is not a requirement and can be a determent if your advisors are untrained or limited by their personal experience. Be selective in your choice of advisors.

Above all, take lots of time for preliminary research and planning in stage 1, problem and task analysis in stage 2, and interacting with your own text through revising in stage 3. Your teachers and more experienced peers can give you useful feedback if you ask them specific questions at each stage. Do not assume that native speakers have factual knowledge and understanding of multilingual writing to edit papers for you. They may not even have pedagogical knowledge of gram-

---

2 First published in "Essential Legal Skills: Legal Writing from an Academic Perspective" by Donna Bain Butler in the *Journal of the Russian Academy of Legal Sciences* RUSSIAN LAW: THEORY AND PRACTICE, Issue No. 1, 2012 and is republished with permission. Subsequently published in *Clarity 70* (2014).

mar to understand what you are doing or why. Allowing time for reflection and revision are more likely to improve your final research product than sending your paper out for review. The research writing schedule in Appendix C shows how you might plan your process for writing an academic paper or journal article.

9.3 Process pedagogy and evaluation

Process writing and process pedagogy can be transformative. "Process pedagogy is based on investigations of how successful writers produce texts" with best practices for "producing entire papers – not on grammar, parts of papers, or rhetorical modes, such a comparison/contrast and definition" (Williams, 2014, pp. 219–223). The process pedagogy and international graduate student writer perspectives in this book suggest that (a) formative assessment during the writing process advances L2 writer competence, academic success, and professional goals; and (b) researching and writing from disciplinary sources using L2 academic English defines authentic text acquisition and production for language learners. In other words, research writing provides meaningful, content-focused language use in disciplinary context. Systematic writing intervention, with formative assessment and feedback, advances disciplinary literacy with strategic self-control of L2 written language use across stages of writing.

Formative assessments are learning-oriented. They are "ongoing assessments designed to make students' thinking visible to both teachers and students ... They permit the teacher to grasp the students' preconceptions, understand where the students are in the 'developmental corridor' and design instruction accordingly" (Commission on Behavioral and Social Sciences and Education National Research Council, 2004, p. 24). In a diversified instructional setting, they allow the teacher to tailor instruction to meet individual student writer needs. They provide students with opportunities to use language meaningfully, clarify thinking, revise writing, and deal with any other problems they may be encountering that may not be visible without the assessments.

To produce full text, students must engage in various language tasks associated with different "phases" of composing (pre-writing, drafting, revising), pausing "to reflect on whether the draft is achieving its rhetorical aim, how activities and evidence are supporting that aim, and whether the draft is addressing audience needs and expectations" (Williams, 2014, p. 223). Best practices include L2 academic writer reflection on their aims – with process strategies and product goals that make their academic English writing clearer in stages or phases. Formative assessment during the writing process contributes to L2 academic writer development by encouraging ongoing student-teacher interaction with corrective input and formative feedback that may result in high achievement during summative assessment.

Best practice involves (a) learning about scholarship through disciplinary research and drafting, and (b) learning about language and discourse above the sentence level. Sociolinguistic contrasts with L2 writers' first academic and disciplinary language(s), educational culture(s) and product assessment(s) become clear with strategies questionnaires and quality checklists. Such instructional tools help international EFL/ESL writers become aware of individual variations and literacy strategies they bring with them from their home countries and prior disciplinary/language learning experiences. Dialogic teaching and learning (Vygotsky, 1978) take place in which the learner interacts with the writing teacher, content professor, and peers at different stages of writing to produce quality text that meets disciplinary standards. Learning objectives may include any of the following:

- generating and conveying disciplinary research ideas effectively and efficiently;
- acquiring knowledge of discourse/strategies for writing in cultural/disciplinary context;
- developing existing competencies for integration of form, content, and meaning;
- expressing analytical thinking clearly, concisely, and accurately in L2 academic English;
- learning to use plain English techniques for conveying and editing complex ideas;
- developing a critical, independent voice as an L2 academic writer; and
- developing confidence to assume a professional identity in L2 academic English.

In problem-solving activities associated with L2 writing from disciplinary sources – as in an article, thesis, or dissertation – different kinds of competence can be dealt with in a writing intervention that address these learning objectives and that interact for communicative competence: that is, (a) discourse competence, (b) grammar competence, (c) strategic competence, and (d) sociolinguistic competence (Oxford, 1990).

To exhibit competence, international scholarly writers need (a) a foundation of declarative (factual) knowledge in academic English writing and in disciplinary research, (b) understanding of facts and ideas within a conceptual framework for L2 academic discourse (communication to a highly educated reader), and (c) organized knowledge that facilitates retrieval and application to a disciplinary research problem or issue. Paying attention to L2 academic writer needs during the research writing process is therefore very important for learning and development. These needs are not remedial; needs analysis is known to be a keystone in teaching English for Specific and Academic Purposes requiring knowledge and a methodological approach. This research shows that even highly proficient graduate student writers may have needs at various stages of writing. A process approach shifts (teacher and student) focus on phrasing, sentence structures, and grammar forms toward the end of each stage of writing when writer-reader communication becomes important. Linguistic focus at this point becomes relevant for reader concentration on content, formative and/or summative assessment.

Conceptual vocabulary, on the other hand, is especially needed by the L2 academic writer at beginning stages of writing, along with (a) critical thinking for evaluating arguments, issues, and ideas, and (b) analysis skills for examining relevant information, sources, and evidence. International EFL/ESL writers can think in more than one language, so English only is not a pre-requisite for drafting and citing international or domestic sources. Because linguistic translation can be highly problematic and inefficient, a multilingual approach for getting ideas down in the first draft, with citation from the original source text in the original language, may be helpful.

When breaking down the research writing process into tasks and components – with an emphasis on recursiveness in research and writing – complexity is decreased, a process approach is learned, and L2 writer self-reflection is promoted. Research-based instruction therefore operates on two levels attending to L2 writers' prior knowledge and cultural experience in writing. The first level deals with writers' *processes*: that is, strategies and skills student writers employ as novices contrasted with those that a more competent writer might use. The second level deals with *goals* for production that advance writing proficiency (competence) across stages: that is, (a) planning competence for thinking and organizing in the pre-writing stage; (b) rhetorical or genre competence for learning and problem-solving in the drafting stage; and (c) communication competence for presenting research results from a reader point of view in the revising stage.

Instructional intervention may include student-centered agendas featuring oral presentation of research and language points taught by selected students with the use of technology. For example, when discussing elements of style for accuracy, brevity, and clarity in academic legal English writing, the teacher may select a native Spanish speaker habituated to very long sentences (with increased possibility for L2 English error) to address brevity or concision as a teaching/learning/writing point. Or when a student is prone to serious patterned errors that may interfere with meaning like comma splices, run-on sentences, or fragments, the teacher may feature that student for grammar review and class presentation of appropriate grammar form(s) with punctuation. Punctuation, formatting, and usage (structures used) work together as "matters of convention" and are part of advancing literacy for international student writers as for native English writers (Williams, 2014, p. 136). However, the difference between "usage" and "use" is that the latter considers the communicative meaning of language. Teaching usage with a form manual as in a law school doctoral program, for example, is not teaching international EFL/ESL students to write.

Instructional intervention is interactive. It should include dialogic question and answer (Q&A) sessions following student presentations. Peer and teacher feedback help shape student understanding of scholarly research, writing, and contextualized language use. Q&A involves interaction and negotiation of meaning with conventions like punctuation, for example, as it does with conceptual presentations of problem, purpose, and thesis. Course tools in the form of questionnaires and checklists across stages of writing center learners on their processes and goals for writing. They help students take control of their own writing by managing their processes and monitoring their production while learning new, advanced techniques like parallel structuring and substantive transitioning that advance literacy. Self- and teacher- assessment at different stages of writing prompt students to revise with increased awareness of written language use and usage. In sum, formative assessment is learning-oriented assessment. When nested within stages of writing for organized feedback, formative assessment promotes international EFL/ESL writer development as students learn how to revise for professional performance in a research paper or article. Through process pedagogy and formative (vs. critical) feedback, students acquire metalinguistic (reflective) awareness and knowledge of writing with different conventions for various audiences. Learning and knowledge interact to develop competence.

9.3.1 Knowledge transforming literacy strategies

An important purpose of instructional intervention is for international graduate students to learn how to develop L2 academic English writing beyond *knowledge telling,* or stating knowledge from source text. International graduate students may be expected implicitly to engage in *knowledge transforming* or deepening the level of understanding to include analysis, synthesis, and evaluation of research that crosses languages, disciplines, cultures of learning, and traditions of scholarship.

International EFL/ESL writer perspectives from the Strategic Competence Questionnaire discussed earlier suggest that two of Grabe's (2001) broad levels of writing purpose are useful for knowledge telling in early stages of drafting. These are (a) stating knowledge by listing, repeating, or paraphrasing source text (with citation); and (b) summarizing simply by reducing source text and extending notes to oneself in the L1 or L2 (with citation). Building on these levels of writing, L2 writers may add knowledge transforming in various ways. Writers may (a) summarize complexly by selecting and reorganizing source and draft text, (b) synthesize by combining and connecting source and draft text information, and (c) interpret evidence previously cited and analyzed.

Academic writing becomes self-regulating from a learner perspective when language skills, like summary and paraphrase, are consciously used as transformational strategies. By shifting the role of composing from knowledge telling to knowledge transforming, L2 writers may re-use language skills for the purpose of constructing knowledge in their own text. Language skills like summary and paraphrase become literacy strategies for deepening learning when writing with (rather than from) disciplinary sources. Other strategies for knowledge transforming, as they relate to the pedagogical intervention for this research, include the following: (a) conceptual transforming in stage 1 pre-writing by formulating and refining a problem, purpose, and thesis statement for a substantive outline; (b) rhetorical transforming in stage 2 drafting by providing a format that supports the thesis or claim with a Table of Contents and first draft; and (c) linguistic transforming in stage 3 revising by getting away from the language of source texts. Rather than retaining long quotations, for example, use of language skills like summary and paraphrase helps transform L2 academic writers' text, giving authorship.

9.3.2 Knowledge transforming language skills

Students' use of language skills, based on Cummins' notion of cognitive academic language proficiency, deepens and develops L2 academic discourse. Through use and re-use of paraphrasing and summarizing, for example, students can construct discourse at different stages of research and writing (pre-writing, drafting, and revising). They can also learn how to cite authoritatively early in the scholarly writing process by summarizing and paraphrasing source text to prepare for writing with an annotated bibliography or literature review. Practice exercises for knowledge transforming might include rephrasing and summarizing from journal articles with citation so that use and usage are illustrated. Convention is emphasized when students become aware of (a) how to introduce the source, (b) how/when/where/why to cite direct quotation or paraphrase, (c) when/where to provide commentary on the source to discuss the research writer's understanding of the source, and (d) where the quote or paraphrase was taken from. Awareness *and use* of convention is part of conditional knowledge: how, when, where, and why knowledge for written language use that international graduate writers typically do not have and may not get in abridged study abroad programs. International EFL/ESL writers transform or create when they move beyond simply generating content in L2 English to re-working thoughts, changing both text and ideas, and avoiding plagiarism: a linguistic issue associated with advanced cross-cultural literacy – not simply an ethical issue associated with cheating.

The next section describes three in-process tools for learning, formative assessment, and instruction that have been revised based on findings from this research. They are pedagogical tools that help international graduate student writers (a) link new information with existing knowledge, and (b) create a repertoire of strategies to achieve strategic self-control in L2 academic and disciplinary writing. These pedagogical tools are (1) strategies questionnaires for academic English writers, and (2) checklists for formative assessment during the writing process that are valid and reliable, and (3) a sample syllabus for in-class or on-line instruction that can be adapted by teachers across disciplines and genres. These are systematic tools for instruction and feedback that develop self-regulation or control for L2 academic English writers.

9.4 Tools for learning, teaching, and formative assessment

The questionnaires and checklists developed for this research and revised for pedagogy facilitate international graduate student L2 writer development and engagement at different levels of proficiency by taking into account cultural, rhetorical, and linguistic differences between L1 and L2 academic writers. They are performance enhancing tools that tap into international student L2 academic writer perceptions with a view to enhancing critical thinking in L2 academic writing and appropriate language use when translating and writing from disciplinary source text. Such questionnaires and checklists perform the function of ESP/EAP needs analysis by (a) helping linguistically and culturally diverse academic writers discover what is appropriate and conventional when writing across academic languages, and (b) disclosing contrasting ideas about academic writing, written language use, and text attribution. This kind of research-based pedagogy discloses the impact of academic culture on international students' formation of writing knowledge – basis for intellectual growth and development in a professional school program or graduate field of study. Transitioning to a more professional program, with a more rigorous level of expectation regarding performance in L2 written language use and composition, means (a) comprehensible input for learners within the context of L2 academic culture, and (b) strategies for problem-solving in L2 English writing like knowledge transforming that help develop language use and academic proficiency (Krashen 2011).

As international graduate students write from multilingual sources in an academic discipline requiring advanced literacy and conventions for scholarship, they acquire language and re-use it, appropriately or inappropriately, depending on their background knowledge, writing experience, and academic literacy training. Direct, explicit teaching of processes and skills for scholarly writing deepens and expands L2 academic writer knowledge, mediating disciplinary content and language learning. Language use, composition, and writing knowledge are all important for developing international graduate student L2 writers. The problem is that L2 written language use is not proceduralized (automatic, habitualized) for international EFL/ESL students generally, as it is for native-English graduate students writers. The latter have likely integrated procedural (how to) knowledge with declarative (what) knowledge, and have acquired implicit knowledge of appropriate academic discourse conventions through extended socialization in undergraduate programs which vary across academic disciplines. This is not to say that all native English graduate students entering U.S. professional schools write well. Literacy is known to be a developmental process for both native and non-native English writers (Kucer, 2014). U.S. law schools, for example, invest heavily in the disciplinary literacy process for native English speakers without attention to how non-native English writers may be different.

Second language writing pedagogy with this study's tools necessarily operates at two levels for each stage of writing. Both address issues of quality. The first level deals with quality in *L2 writers' strategic processes*, and the second level deals with quality in *L2 writers' goals for production* that advance competence: that is, (a) planning competence, (b) rhetorical/genre competence, and (c) communication/language competence. Criteria for (formative or summative) assessment likewise fall into three (conceptual, rhetorical, and linguistic) categories that parallel the writing processes for pre-writing, drafting, and revising. Reflective thinking, teacher feedback, and revision in stages promote learner development and text transformation.

As previously mentioned, the strategies questionnaires (Appendix D) and quality goals checklists (Appendix F) used to collect the data for this research have been revised for in-process writing intervention in other domains of learning and research writing. Revisions made to these instruments are based on the learner-user perspectives in this book: that is, research participants' most helpful strategies and assessment goals for producing quality in an L2 academic English paper or article. The revised questionnaires and checklists are pedagogical tools that promote self-regulated learning and strategic production in a writer-centered (versus teacher-centered) classroom. The aim is to develop the writer so he/she can develop his/her own writing product. The benefit to teachers is a lightened work load because the L2 writer becomes responsible for editing his or her own research product as part of the writing process with the knowledge, literacy strategies, and language skills needed to revise and edit. Through teacher-regulated reading and feedback (stages 1, 2, 3), understanding deepens and appreciation mounts as to what international graduate student researchers have to say and how they say it. Descriptive (vs. prescriptive) guidelines for teachers follow. They accompany the two sets of pedagogical tools described below for each stage of academic English writing (pre-writing, drafting, and revising).

Stage 1 (Pre-drafting)

Formal instruction, a socially mediated process with the Stage 1 strategy questionnaires and quality checklists, directs learner attention to conceptual concerns such as research problem, purpose for research and writing, thesis/claim/argument or research question(s), and key definitions and terms. Presentational speaking, with feedback for revision, helps learners produce the product goal for the pre-writing stage: (a) a conceptual outline, and (b) an annotated bibliography if the writing teacher acts as writing advisor for an independent study or research project.

Pre-writing strategies are defined on the stage 1 questionnaire as "conscious, goal directed actions successful research writers may take more than once while preparing to write a scholarly (academic) paper." These actions are intentionally used to prepare for writing effectively and efficiently in L2 academic English. Critically reflecting on strategic actions in the questionnaire helps bridge the gap between declarative and procedural knowledge for graduate student L2 academic writers. Checking to make sure goals are met for a conceptual outline ensures a quality product. The revised, research-based production tools for stage 1, pre-drafting follow.

- *Strategies for Academic English Writers,* Stage 1 (Appendix I)
- *Pre-Drafting Checklist of Goals for Academic English Writers* (Appendix J)

Stage 2 (Drafting)

Formal instruction at this stage directs learner attention to macro- and micro-level rhetorical arrangement. The product goal for this stage is a first draft in English with headings, sub-headings, and structure flowing from substance. The draft begins with a skeletal outline or "Table of Contents" followed by the previously defined statements of problem, purpose, and thesis (or research question) in the Introduction section. From the L2 academic writers' view, these three key elements limit the research and writing for the rest of the paper. Also, the teacher can begin to understand the logic and check to see if there is a link between the Introduction and Conclusion sections to help the student writer move into the next stage for developing discourse.

Drafting strategies are defined on the stage 2 questionnaire as "conscious, goal directed actions successful research writers may take more than once while drafting a scholarly (academic) paper." These actions are intentionally used for preparing a preliminary version of a research paper effectively and efficiently in L2 academic English. Reflecting on strategic actions in the questionnaire helps bridge the gap between declarative and procedural knowledge, as it does in stage 1. Checking to make sure quality goals are met for writing a first draft ensure a quality product. Teachers can revise the drafting checklist from the viewpoint of other genres. The revised, research-based production tools for stage 2, drafting follow.

- *Strategies for Academic English Writers*, Stage 2 (Appendix I)
- *Drafting Checklist of Goals for Academic English Writers* (Appendix J)

Stage 3 (Revising)

Formal instruction at this stage directs learner attention to audience expectation, lexicogrammatical concerns, accuracy, and clarity. Revision, interaction, and explicit instruction help learners synthesize research to produce academic discourse that is analytical, clear, and readable. By this stage, the teacher and international graduate student writers have already dealt with culturally based logic and disciplinary thinking in terms of what counts as primary and secondary sources. The final draft should therefore exhibit cohesiveness (internal connections between paragraphs and sentences) and coherence (logical presentation of ideas to the reader).

Revising strategies are defined on the stage 3 questionnaire as "conscious, goal directed actions successful research writers may take more than once while revising a scholarly (academic) research paper." These actions are intentionally used for revising effectively and efficiently using L2 academic English. The revised, research-based production tools for stage 3, revising follow.

- *Strategies for Academic English Writers*, Stage 3 (Appendix I)
- *Revising Checklist of Goals for Academic English Writers* (Appendix J)

It is important to note that the revising checklist includes goals for editing that focus on clarity and correctness. Editing thus becomes a strategic tool for self-regulating L2 academic writing that operates on two levels: (1) clear communication, and (2) correct language use.

In terms of development, these two sets of production tools (a) guide L2 academic writers' processes, and (b) develop L2 academic writers' existing competencies in language use and communication. The role of the teacher is to support learning and development by (a) comparing teacher assessment with students' self-assessment at each stage of writing, and (b) giving constructive feedback at each stage of writing for students to know how to revise. Teacher (formative) assessment and feedback build on L2 academic writers' existing competencies for revising purposes at each stage of writing. Students and teachers both engage in systematically developing self-regulation (control) and quality in L2 academic writing.

Teaching international graduate students to communicate in L2 academic writing can be viewed from a task-based learning and teaching (TBLT) perspective, a branch of Communicative Language Teaching emphasizing development of meaningful tasks for learners using the L2. The focus of the learning process is on the L2 academic writer, with critical reflection built into the writing process. Tasks for each stage of writing focus on meaning before grammatical forms, like the (stage 1) substantive or conceptual outline. International EFL/ESL student writers in the intervention associated with this research, for example, were expected to engage with legal meaning and legal purpose in all stages of writing before focusing on linguistic forms. However, they all needed and wanted advanced techniques for clear communication in writing, especially in stage 3. Instruction, therefore, should be tailored to student learning and authentic to each student's L2 academic writing experience for learning (change) and development to occur, the outcome of formative assessment.

9.4.1 Syllabus with formative assessment tools

The revised questionnaires and checklists (in Appendices I and J) for teaching academic English writers comprise formative assessments. They can provide important information to teachers about what students do not know and what classroom instruction should focus on. The formative assessment tools also provide important information for students to know how to revise. Ongoing feedback – while the writing process is happening – allows students and teacher to find and fix issues pertaining to scholarly composition and language use.

Appendix K is a sample syllabus that incorporates use of the formative assessment tools. It outlines an academic English writing course for international graduate student writers, indicating how the two sets of tools may be used. The important issue for teachers is to have students submit completed checklists *with* their work product (outline or draft) at each stage of academic writing. This facilitates targeted assessment and feedback, in addition to any comments the teacher wants to make on student drafts.

This core syllabus is for a seven week (content-adjunct or stand-alone) course, adaptable across research disciplines. It can be used in face-to face or on-line teaching or extended into a full semester course. It can also be embedded into a research methods course so that issues pertaining to disciplinary research and advanced literacy become part of scholarly writing instruction. The purpose of the syllabus is descriptive, not prescriptive. The aim is to build on teachers' existing competencies for course design and writing pedagogy. No matter how the syllabus and course tools are used, they will foster learner-centered instruction and L2 writer development.

9.5 What every educator can do

Content professors, writing teachers, and language specialists can do three things to support international academic English writers: (1) guide student learning, (2) connect learning outcomes with assessment, and (3) shift pedagogical priorities from a focus on the thing being taught, researched, or discussed to the learner undergoing change. For teachers of writing and written language use, this means teaching the writer – not the writing text. For content (subject) professors and advisors, this means directing the research and writing processes and engaging with the student writer at planned intervals. For learning to occur, a mutual paradigm shift is required of both teachers and professors, as well as of international EFL/ESL student writers responsible for their own learning.

9.5.1 Guide student learning with strategies

Guiding international EFL/ESL students and scholars with a process approach for writing and tools for self-regulation helps the L2 academic writer focus on form and language use in stages to express clear meaning without being lost in the complexity of the writing process. In-process (speaking and writing) intervention through self-assessment and structured feedback helps avoid inauthentic "template-production," a common approach among lawyers and U.S. legal writing teachers (Hoffman, 2011). Pedagogical strategies for disciplinary writing teachers and content professors include the following:
- presenting key terms and concepts visually, before lectures;
- wrapping-up with the same key terms and concepts;
- using models, visual schemes, formats, and/or examples whenever possible;

- providing context and making links explicit;
- constructing hierarchies of information and timelines (visually, if possible);
- recombining new material throughout course;
- using formative assessment during the course;
- categorizing student writer feedback: (a) conceptually, (b) rhetorically, and (c) linguistically;
- employing a grading rubric with criteria for student (learner/writer) assessment; and
- making the grading rubric part of your course syllabus so students know outright what they are expected to do to succeed.

All are effective tools for knowledge construction and learner transformation. All support (native and non-native English) graduate student writers acquiring (a) *self-knowledge* in the context of academic and disciplinary culture; (b) *task knowledge* with explicit criteria for reflection and assessment, and (c) *strategic knowledge* with explicit strategies for different conditions, purposes, situations, and settings (Ehrman, Leaver, & Oxford, 2003).

9.5.2 Connect learning outcomes and assessment

Connecting learning outcomes with learner assessment through grading rubrics makes explicit (a) what students are expected to do in a professional school (content or skills) course, and (b) how their mastery of course material will be assessed. Writing teachers and content professors can discern learning outcomes by articulating (a) the most important *content* topics for students to learn, and (b) the specific *skills* students need to acquire and develop through their course. Clearly stated learning outcomes with action verbs link the learning outcomes to the assessment measure, as in Figure 9.2 below that uses academic writing to assess higher level student learning.

Making the purpose of academic writing assignments explicit in a discipline promotes learning for both native and non-native academic English writers. "The design of assignments, as well as their assessment, then, can be critical factors in determining the student representation of the assignment [as in Gee's ESL case]. The relationship between assessment and writing context presents various obstacles to be negotiated in deciding on an ethical approach" (Bloch, 2012, p. 172).

Scholarly writing ethic and western views on plagiarism are examples of the need to re-align ethical teaching practices that connect international student learning outcomes with assessment. The study of writing and language use suggests that the onus for plagiarism needs to be on the changing instructional

Learning Outcome(s)	Assessment Measure(s)
Students will be able to **investigate, critique, evaluate**	Research paper
Students will be able to **analyze, synthesize, evaluate**	Research paper, exam question, or research project
Students will be able to **describe, compare/contrast, critically examine**	Research paper, exam question, demonstration, or group project
Students will be able to **research, read, critically examine, evaluate,** and **write critically** about multilingual authorities in the context of a disciplinary research problem	Annotated bibliography
Students will be able to **paraphrase, summarize, synthesize,** and **analyze** primary and secondary sources, with citation, in the context of a disciplinary research problem or paper	Annotated bibliography Research paper with well-defined research problem, purpose, and thesis

Fig. 9.2. Learning outcomes connected with assessment.

contexts international graduate student writers face – not on learners who have no prior knowledge or exposure to academic English writing before entering an English-medium institution or graduate program of study. This shifts the focus to the educational sociocultural setting because the culture of learning plays a role in academic English writing (Bain Butler, Wei, & Zhou, 2013). Professional school programs in the U.S. need to do more than give the appearance of educating international graduate student writers. If the common purpose of educators is to teach and assess student learning, professors and teaching practitioners need to know how to do it. A portion of income generating revenue from international student tuition may need to be put back into education and professional development. Resources may need to be re-allocated: for example, research-based collaboration across disciplines may be more cost effective than re-inventing the wheel in a professional domain of learning like law school.

This shift from the cognitive to the sociocultural is required in all matters dealing with international education and international graduate student assessment with the academic research paper. Reducing the stakes and lowering the standards are not options for international graduate students who are serious about their investment in study abroad. From the point of view of learning and development, international graduate student L2 writers can learn quickly through informed teaching practices, and they can be evaluated objectively with academic writing through formative and summative assessment when goals for learning are set. Assessment measures, like those in this study, can be valid and reliable.

Conclusion

9.5.3 Shift pedagogical priorities and fund professional development

If our intention is to hold international graduate students responsible for L2 academic writing like we do native English academic writers, current pedagogical practices and attitudes toward collaboration and professional development need to upgrade with transfer of knowledge from empirical research across academic disciplines. Ethically responsible teaching entails student learning connected to learner assessment at all levels in the professional school hierarchy. At the very least, L2 academic writers need more time for writing a paper, as they do for writing an examination. They also need access to informed research and writing professionals – beyond those providing remediation or surface-level editing – to help learners become aware of their (socio) cognitive processes and preferences for academic writing.

One alternative to remediation is mediation of learning through systematic instruction and formative assessment with the pedagogical tools from this research linking teaching and learning. Learner-user centered pedagogy increases international EFL/ESL academic writers' (a) awareness of processes for knowledge construction that are scholarly first, and that avoid textual plagiarism (Pecorari, 2008) second; and (b) ability to extend the ideas being practiced to other research writing situations, fostering development. Research-based writing strategies and goals for scholarly writing challenge international students' conditioning as learners, thinkers, and academic writers. International graduate students need to know what to attend to in L2 academic and disciplinary writing with (a) declarative knowledge of facts, (b) conditional knowledge of context, and (c) procedural knowledge of how to produce a work product. At the very least, international graduate students need timely and formative feedback from engaged faculty in the academic and disciplinary writing situation that help them develop as learners.

Professional development for international graduate students in a U.S. professional school setting requires knowledge of person, task(s), and strategies. Professional development for their teachers and professors requires the same kinds of knowledge. Transformation for both (students and teachers) requires on-going professional development in changing contexts, beyond personal development for career advancement. If the proper role of educational research is to understand and elucidate, the proper role of higher-level educational institutions is to use this research to promote ethical teaching and responsible assessment of international graduate student writers traversing cultural, linguistic, disciplinary, and academic borders.

10 Coda Chapter: Transformation in a Nutshell

10.1 In the author's own words

The purpose of the research-based pedagogy in this book is for international EFL/ESL students and visiting scholars, such as those in the U.S. Fulbright and Humphrey Fellowship programs, know how to write better from a linguistic, intercultural literacy, and disciplinary perspective. The secondary purpose is to help them produce a graduate-level research paper or publishable article in English. In a second language English for Academic Purposes (EAP) course such as mine, the "how" may be more important than the "what" – the operational term being engagement. Intention for writing and attention to process drive change, defined as learning. Awareness of the pre-writing, drafting, and revising processes for discipline-specific academic audiences advances international students' knowledge of written language use in various communicative contexts with attention to accurate, appropriate, and meaningful use of vocabulary, syntax, and rhetorical structures. It means transforming previously learned (unconscious) patterns and habits into new (conscious) patterns of thought and behavior in each stage of writing. This transformation process, unique to each learner, is complex, dynamic, non-linear, and writer-specific. Systematic use of the literacy and language skills in the strategic competence context of this book supports learning and development for all academic writers: international and domestic, graduate and undergraduate, native and non-native English writers.

Four competences interact to produce good writing: grammatical, sociolinguistic, discoursal, and strategic. Writers may develop some of these competences more than others. My research focuses on developing strategic competence because it is an efficient, effective means for international graduate students to overcome limitations in their language proficiency and to stretch their ability to write well. This competence is critical for the ESP/EAP classroom because it helps EFL learners transform to ESL users using interactive (spoken and written) feedback to improve text being composed in real time. Research findings in this book show that developing strategic competence advances academic literacy for the international EFL/ESL student participants. Writing one's research involves transformation of students' state of knowledge. Development entails helping learners know themselves cross-culturally and linguistically by tapping into their background knowledge and experience with new knowledge of scholarly writing processes and strategies for increased writing competence.

In addition to student writer ability, this research has led me to think about my own strategic behavior for competence in teaching L2 academic legal writers and to consider content professors' role in assessing student learning through writing. Academic writing is a learned skill, not a commodity international students either have or do not have when they seek to advance their education in English-medium institutions and professional schools. It assumes knowledge on the part of all educators but not all international students. Content professors, in addition to writing teachers, must pay attention to academic writer development because neglecting the student as writer is neglecting the student as learner. All teachers and professors can be aware of content, process, and product: that is, (a) what students learn and how they access information for academic writing, (b) how they make sense of and come to understand disciplinary content, and (c) how they share what they have learned in a research paper or journal article. These fundamental components of the learning process are interactive. They require presence and collaboration among writing teachers and content professors. Learning to write well in the first or second language (L2) is difficult and does not require a native-speaker target. Explicit instruction and use of strategies help developing writers perform authentically, with power and authority required by professional, technical, bureaucratic, and social institutions.

The academic writer intervention associated with my research highlights certain characteristics of the three main approaches to composition pedagogy in the U.S.: that is, the product-, process-, and post-process approaches. From the product view, L2 academic writing instruction focuses on comparative patterns and ways of organizing text that include typical formats for research papers, memos, or reports; organization of information into paragraphs; and correct sentence structure and vocabulary. From the process view, the L2 academic writer is creator of original ideas, with the research paper representing student learning and content knowledge. Understanding how successful learners in this research discover ideas, express them in writing, and revise emergent texts helps other students develop as writers. To become good writers, international students need guided experiences with creating texts for various purposes and audiences including generating and sustaining clear, coherent, and convincing arguments in academic writing. From the post-process view, academic writing is also a social (transactional) process in professional, disciplinary context that entails mediation between the writer and his/her audience. Teachers and professors, therefore, need to create transactional support for learners to discover their own strengths and weaknesses as academic writers and as disciplinary thinkers. When writing instruction is reduced to a single method or set of formulas as in the narrow U.S. legal writing context, or when content is artificially separated from language use by professors who do not use a grading rubric, international students may be constrained by a focus on correct usage and grammar. Institutional editing of international students' doctoral work, furthermore, merely gives the appearance of good writing and pedagogy. From a transformation perspective, this practice may be considered educationally unethical. Instead, recursive practices such as extensive planning, peer- and teacher feedback at key stages, and informed revision and self-editing provide sound educational basis for student writer development.

In a learner-centered classroom, such as that described above, students discover how much they know, gain confidence in their self-expression and communication skills, and develop their critical and creative abilities. Teachers act as advisors, organizing the scholarly and disciplinary writing experience to help the student develop, not just the students' writing. The teacher's role is to assist developing writers express their own meanings in a safe, collaborative environment with minimal interference – without worry of plagiarizing. Students develop best as writers when they write something they care about and want to know more about through research. Helping them rise above their limitations opens the vertical dimension of depth and quality that requires their attention and ours as educators. By generating consciousness of their behavior patterns in writing, students can change them and come to see academic writing as a tool for disciplinary learning and means for clear expression that may transfer to other writing situations. As students become conscious participants in their own research writing processes, learner agency develops. They give each "step" or level of writing their full attention to achieve quality. Student writers gain power to create new knowledge from their own research, part of the transformative process in education.

In my work with international EFL/ESL graduate students and scholars, I try to help them shift attention from wanting to produce an excellent work product (instrumental motivation) in English to being an authentic researcher and competent writer (intrinsic motivation) as they draft their writing from research in stages. That is not to say that this shift happens for all student writers in all classes or that one kind of motivation is more powerful than another for learners to develop and achieve their goals. But there is no question that skilled writing is goal-directed and that goal-setting such as that provided by the research-based pedagogy in this book enhances student motivation and academic achievement. We know that to develop skill, writers need three things: motivation, knowledge of writing and language use, and advanced literacy strategies to put the new knowledge into action. These contribute to writer development on the novice-expert and language learning continua. International EFL/ESL scholarly writer research therefore crosses borders of academic and disciplinary learning and language use at the level of near-native language proficiency.

I conclude by saying that we can bring about a shift in EFL/ESL student-writer consciousness through our intention to help international graduate students write better. This book may be a transformational device for some people in education to initiate a renewed focus on developing the student writer as learner; for others, it may help recognize that we are already concerned with the development of the student writer and to intensify and accelerate the process. For international graduate students, though, this work is transformational because, in addition to new knowledge and scholarly writing skills that cross cultures of learning, it fosters ability to create knowledge from writing research rather than imitate what already exists. Empirical research confirms that the two sets of pedagogical tools in this book predict enhanced EFL/ESL scholarly writer performance. Application of these tools helps contribute to transformation in second and foreign language education and beyond.

References

Afflerbach, P. P., 1990. The influence of prior knowledge on expert readers' main idea construction strategies. Retrieved February 2010, from International Reading Web site: http://www.jstor.org/pss/747986

Agar, M. (1994). *Language shock: Understanding the culture of conversation.* New York: William Morrow and Company, Inc.

Alexander, P. A. (1997). Mapping the multidimensional nature of domain learning: The interplay of cognitive, motivational, and strategic forces. In M. L. Maehr & P. R. Pintrich (Eds.), *Advances in motivation and achievement* (Vol. 10, pp. 213–250). Greenwich, CT: JAI Press.

Alexander, P. A. (2003, August). *Expertise and academic development: A new perspective on a classic theme.* Keynote address presented at the 10th Biennial Conference of the European Association for Research on Learning and Instruction, Padua, Italy. Alexander Research Lab. Retrieved May 2006, from University of Maryland Web site: http://www.education.umd.edu/EDHD/faculty2/Alexander/ARL/projects.html

Alexander, P. A. (2003). The development of expertise: The journey from acclimation to proficiency. *Educational Researcher, 32*(8), 10–14.

Alexander, P. A. (2004). A model of domain learning: Reinterpreting expertise as a multidimensional, multistage process. In D. Y. Dai, & R. J. Sternberg (Eds.), *Motivation, emotion, and cognition: Integrative perspectives on intellectual functioning and development* (pp. 273–298). Mahwah, NJ: Lawrence Erlbaum Associates.

Alexander, P. A. (2006). Evolution of a learning theory: A case study. *Educational Psychologist, 41*(4), 257–264.

Alexander, P. A. (2006). *Psychology in learning and instruction.* Columbus, OH: Pearson Education, Inc.

Alexander, P. A., Graham, S., & Harris, K. R. (1998). A perspective on strategy research: Progress and prospects. *Educational Psychology Review, 10*(2), 129–154.

Anderson, J. R. (1996) ACT: A simple theory of complex cognition. *American Psychologist 51*(4), 355–365.

Anderson, Lorin W. & Krathwohl, David R. (2001). *A Taxonomy for Learning, Teaching and Assessing: a Revision of Bloom's Taxonomy.* New York. Longman Publishing.

Apple, M. W., Ganddin, L. A., & Hypolito, A. M. (2001). Paulo Freire 1921–97. In J. A. Palmer (Ed.), *Fifty modern thinkers on education: From Piaget to the present* (pp. 128–133). London and New York: Routledge.

Arnold, M. J. (1995). The lack of basic writing skills and its impact on the legal profession. *Capital University Law Review, 24,* 227: 228–255.

Bachman, L. F. (1990). *Fundamental considerations in language testing.* Oxford: Oxford University Press.

Bachman, L. F., & Palmer, A. S. (1996). Language testing in practice. Oxford: Oxford University Press.

Bain Butler, D. (2004). *Reading strategies for international law students.* Unpublished manuscript, University of Maryland at College Park.

Bain Butler, D., Zhou, Y., & Wei, M. (2013). When the culture of learning plays a role in academic English writing. In M. Bondi and C. Williams (Eds.), *ESP across cultures [Special issue]: Academic English across cultures: Vol. 10,* pp. 55–74.

Bandura, A. (1997). *Self-efficacy: The exercise of control.* New York: W. H. Freeman.

Bhatia, V. K. (1993). *Analyzing genre: Language in professional settings*. London: Longman.

Belcher, D. (1994). The apprenticeship approach to advanced academic literacy: Graduate students and their mentors. *English for Specific Purposes 13*(1), 23–34.

Bereiter, C. (1994). Constructivism, socioculturalism, and Popper's world 3. *Educational Researcher, 23*(7), pp. 21–23.

Bereiter, C. & Scardamalia, M. (1987). *The psychology of written composition*. Hillsdale, NJ: Erlbaum.

Berkenkotter, C., Huckin, T., & Ackerman, J. (1988). Conventions, conversations, and the writer: Case study of a student in a rhetoric Ph.D. program. *Research in the Teaching of English, 22*(1), 9–44.

Berkenkotter, C., Huckin, T. (1993). Rethinking genre from a sociocognitive perspective. *Written Communication 10*(4), 475–509.

Berkenkotter, C., & Huckin, T. (1995). *Genre knowledge in disciplinary communities*. Hillsdale: Lawrence Erlbaum.

Bhatia, V. K. (2002). A generic view of academic discourse. In J. Flowerdew (Ed.), *Academic Discourse* (pp. 21–39). London: Longman.

Bloch, J. (2012). *Plagiarism, intellectual property and the teaching of L2 writing*. Bristol, UK: Multilingual Matters.

Bourdieu, P. (2001). The forms of capital. In M. Granovetter & R. Swedberg (Eds.), *The sociology of economic life* (pp. 96–111). Boulder, Co: Westview Press.

Braine G. 2002. Academic literacy and the non-native speaker graduate student. *Journal of English for Academic Purposes* 1: 59–68. British Council/BBC (2014). Published on *Teaching English*. Retrieved March 22, 2014, from https://www.teachingenglish.org.uk/knowledge-database/language-usage

Byrnes, H. (2002). Toward academic-level foreign-language abilities. In B. L. Leaver & B. Shekhtman (Eds.), *Developing professional-level language proficiency* (pp. 34–58). Cambridge, UK: Cambridge University Press.

Byrnes, H. (2005). Content-based foreign language instruction. In C. Sanz, (Ed.), *Mind and context in adult second language acquisition: Methods, theory, and practice* (pp. 282–302). Washington, DC: Georgetown University Press.

Cahill, D. (2003). The myth of the 'turn' in contrastive rhetoric. *Written Communication. 20*(3), 170–194. Abstract obtained from *Linguistic Abstracts: Reading and Writing*, 2003, *19*, Abstract No. 03/R/111. http://www.uefap.com/writing/research/la_eg.htm

Callies, M. C. (2011, July 6). English for advanced learners: Linguists examine obstacles to native-like proficiency in foreign language acquisition. Message posted to news://www.sciencedaily.com/releases/2011/07/110706104650.htm

Canagarajah S. (2006). TESOL at 40: What are the issues? *TESOL Quarterly, 40*(1), 9–34.

Canagarajah, S. (2005a, July). Changing communicative needs, shifting pedagogical perspectives, revised assessment objectives. Paper presented at featured symposium on The Assessment of World Englishes, 14th World Congress of Applied Linguistics, Madison, WI.

Canagarajah, S. (2003). A somewhat legitimate and very peripheral participation. In C. Casanave & S. Vandrick (Eds.), *Writing for scholarly publications: Behind the scenes in language education* (pp. 197–210). Mahwah, NJ: Lawrence Erlbaum Associates, Publishers.

Canagarajah, S. (2002). Critical academic writing and multilingual students. Ann Arbor: MI: The University of Michigan Press.

Canagarajah, S. (2001). Addressing issues of power and difference in ESL academic writing. In J. Flowerdew & M. Peacock (Eds.), *Research perspectives on English for academic Purposes* (pp. 117–131). Cambridge, United Kingdom: Cambridge University Press.

Canale, M. (1983). From Communicative competence to communicative language pedagogy. In J. Richards and R. Schmidt (Eds.), *Language and communication*. London and New York: Longman.

Canale, M. & Swain, M. (1980). Theoretical bases of communicative approaches to second language teaching and testing. *Applied Linguistics 1*(1): 8–24.

Casanave, C. (1995). Local interactions: Constructing contexts for composing in a graduate sociology program. In D. Belcher and G. Braine (Eds.), *Academic writing in a second language: Essays on research and pedagogy* (pp. 83–110). Norwood: NJ: Ablex, 1995.

Casanave, C. (2004). *Controversies in second language writing: Dilemmas and decisions in research and instruction*. Ann Arbor: MI: The University of Michigan Press.

Casanave, C. and Vandrick, S. (Eds.). (2003). *Writing for scholarly publications: Behind the scenes in language education*. Mahwah, NJ: Lawrence Erlbaum Associates, Publishers.

Caudery, T. (2002) Teaching high-level writing skills in English at a Danish university. In B. L. Leaver & B. Shekhtman (Eds.), *Developing professional-level language proficiency* (pp. 177–196). Cambridge, UK: Cambridge University Press.

Celce-Murcia, M., Dörnyei, Z., & Thurrell, S. (1995). Communicative competence: A pedagogically motivated model with content specifications. *Issues in Applied Linguistics, 6*, 5–35.

Celce-Murcia, M. & Olshtain, E. (2005). Discourse-based approaches: A new framework for second language teaching and learning. In E. Hinkel (Ed.), *Handbook of research in second language teaching and learning* (pp. 729–739). Mahwah, NJ: Lawrence Erlbaum Associates.

Chalhoub-Deville, M. & Deville, C. (2005). A look back at and forward to what language testers measure. In E. Hinkel (Ed.), *Handbook of research in second language teaching and learning* (pp. 815–831). Mahwah, NJ: Lawrence Erlbaum Associates.

Chamot, A. U. (2004). Issues in language learning strategy research and teaching. *Electronic Journal of Foreign Language Teaching 1*(1), 12–25.

Chamot, A. U. (2009). *The CALLA handbook: Implementing the cognitive academic language learning approach*. White Plains, NY: Pearson Education.

Chamot, A. U. & O'Malley, J. M. (1994a). *The CALLA handbook: Implementing the cognitive academic language learning approach*. Reading, MA: Addison Wesley.

Chapelle, C., Grabe, W., & Berns, M. (1993). *Communicative language proficiency: definitions and implications for TOEFL 2000*. [ETS Internal Report.] Princeton, NJ: Educational testing Service.

Cherry, K. (2010). *What is Naturalistic Observation?* Retrieved April 16, 2010, from http://psychology.about.com/od/nindex/g/naturalistic.htm

Cherryholmes, C. H. (1992, August-September). Notes on pragmatism and scientific realism. *Educational Researcher, 14*, 13–17.

Coalition of Distinguished Language Centers (n.d.). *Home page*. Washington, D.C. Retrieved from the CDLC website December 6, 2008 http://www.distinguishedlanguagecenters.org/

Cohen, A. D. & Scott, K. (1996). A synthesis of approaches to assessing language learning strategies. In Rebecca L. Oxford (Ed.), *Language learning strategies around the world: Cross-cultural perspectives*. (Technical Report #13) (pp. 89–106). Honolulu: University of Hawai'i , Second Language Teaching and Curriculum Center.

Cohen, A. D., Oxford, R. L. & Chi, J. C. (n.d.) *Language strategy use survey.* Retrieved September 13, 2007 from http://carla.umn.edu/about/profiles/CohenPapers/Lg_Strat_Srvy.html

Cohen, A. D., & Macaro, E. (2008). *Language learner strategies: 30 years of research and practice.* Oxford: Oxford University Press.

Collier, V. (1995). Acquiring a second language for school. *Directions in Language & Education National Clearinghouse for Bilingual Education, 1*(4).

Collier, V. P. & Thomas, W. P. (1995). How quickly can immigrants become proficient in school English? *Journal of Educational Issues of Language Minority Students, 5,* 26–38. Alexandria, VA: Association for Supervision and Curriculum Development.

Colombi, M. C. & Schleppegrell, M. J. (2002). Theory and practice in the development of advanced literacy. In M. J. Schleppegrell and M. C. Colombi (Eds.), *Developing advanced literacy in first and second languages: Meaning and power* (pp. 1–20). Mahwah, NJ: Lawrence Erlbaum Associates, Publishers.

Commission on Behavioral and Social Sciences and Education National Research Council (2004). *How People Learn: Brain, Mind, Experience, and School.* Retrieved June 21, 2012 from www.csun.edu/~SB4310/How%20People%20Learn.pdf.

Conference on College Composition and Communication (last updated January 2001). *CCCC Statement on Second Language Writing and Writers.* Retrieved October 17, 2009, from http://www.ncte.org/cccc/resources/positions/secondlangwriting

Connor, U. (1996). *Contrastive rhetoric: Cross-cultural aspects of second-language writing.* Cambridge: Cambridge University Press.

Connor, U. & Kramer, M. (1995). Writing from sources: Case studies of graduate students in business management. In D. Belcher and G. Braine (Eds.), *Academic writing in a second language: Essays on research and pedagogy* (pp. 155–182). Norwood: NJ: Ablex, 1995.

Contento, L. (2009, June). *Tips for Teaching International Students about Plagiarism.* Paper presented at the Global Legal Skills IV Conference, Washington, DC.

Contento, L. (2011). Plagiarism: What Every Legal Writer Should Know. *Journal of the Russian Academy of Legal Sciences, 2,* 119–136.

Cook, V. (2012). The Native Speaker and the Second Language User. Plenary talk at FLTAL, Sarajevo, May 2012.

Cook, V. (2012). Some KEY issues for SLA RESEARCH. draft of paper in Luciana Pedrazzini, Andrea Nava (eds.) *Learning and Teaching English: Insights from Research,* Polimetrica Publisher, Italy.

Corder, S. P. (1974). *Error Analysis.* In J. P. B. Allen and S. Pit Corder (eds.) Techniques in Applied Linguistics, London: Oxford University Press, 122–154.

Coulson, D. M. (2009). Legal writing and disciplinary knowledge-building: A comparative study. *JALWD: Journal of the Association of Legal Writing Directors, 6,* 160–199.

Creswell, J. W. (1998). *Qualitative inquiry and research design: Choosing among five traditions.* Thousand Oaks, CA: Sage Publications.

Creswell, J. W. (2003). Research design: Qualitative, quantitative, and mixed methods approaches (2nd ed.). Thousand Oaks, CA: Sage Publications.

Creswell, J. W. & Plano Clark, V. L. (2007). *Designing and conducting mixed methods research.* Thousand Oaks, CA: Sage Publications.

Cumming, A. (1998). Theoretical perspectives on writing. *Annual Review of Applied Linguistics 18,* 61–78.

Cumming, A. (2001). The difficulty of standards, for example in L2 writing. In T. Silva & P. K. Matsuda (Eds.), *On second language writing* (pp. 209–229). Mahwah, NJ: Lawrence Erlbaum Associates, Publishers.

Cummins, J. (1979) Cognitive/academic language proficiency, linguistic interdependence, the optimum age question and some other matters. *Working Papers on Bilingualism, 19,* 121–129.

Cummins, J. (1979a). Linguistic interdependence and the educational development of bilingual children. *Review of Educational Research, 49,* 222–251.

Cummins, J. (1981). Age on arrival and immigrant second language learning in Canada. *Applied Linguistics, 2,* 132–149.

Cummins, J. (2000). *Language, power, and pedagogy: Bilingual children in the crossfire.* Clevedon, UK: Multilingual Matters.

Cummins, J. (2001). *Negotiating identities: Education for empowerment in a diverse society* (2nd ed.). Los Angeles, CA: California Association for Bilingual Education.

Cummins, J. (2003). BICS and CALP: Origins and rationale for the distinction. In C. B. Paulston & G. R. Tucker (Eds.), *Sociolinguistics: The essential readings* (pp. 322–328). London: Blackwell.

Cummins, J. (2005). A proposal for action: Strategies for recognizing heritage language competence as a learning resource within the mainstream classroom. *The Modern Language Journal, 89*(4), 585–592.

Cummins, J. (2009). Literacy and English-language learners: A shifting landscape for students, teachers, researchers, and policy makers. [Review of the condensed version of the much longer report titled *Developing literacy in second-language learners: Report of the national literacy panel on language-minority children and youth* (August & Shanahan, 2006)]. *Educational Researcher, 38*(5), 382–383.

Curry, M. J. & Lillis, T. (2004). Multilingual scholars and the imperative to publish in English: Negotiating interests, demands, and rewards. *TESOL Quarterly, 38*(4), 663–689.

Degueldre, C. & Lyman-Hager, M. A. (2005). Update on activities of the center for the advancement of distinguished language proficiency, including summer Arabic. In I. Dubinsky, & R. Robin (Eds.), *Teaching & learning to near-native levels of language proficiency 11: Proceedings of the fall 2004 annual conference of the coalition of distinguished language centers* (pp. 121–148). Salinas, CA: MSI Press.

Dole, J. A., Nokes, J. D., & Drits, D. (2008). Cognitive strategy instruction. From S. E. Israel & G. G. Duffy (Eds.), *Handbook of Research on Reading comprehension* (pp. 347–372). New York: Routledge.

Dörnyei, Z. (2003). *Questionnaires in second language research*: Construction, administration, and processing. Mahwah, NJ: Lawrence Erlbaum Associates, Publishers.

Durako, J. A., Stanchi, K. M., Edelman, D. P., Amdur, B. M., Brown, L. S., Connelly, R. L.(1997). From product to process: Evolution of a legal writing program. *University of Pittsburgh Law Review.*

Durst, R. K. (2006). Research in writing, postsecondary education, 1984–2003. *L1- Educational Studies in Language and Literature, 6* (2), 51–73.

Ebsworth, M. E. (2010). New books [Review of the book *Plagiarism, the internet and student learning*]. *Writing & Pedagogy, (2)*2, 321–324.

Ehrman, M. (2002). The learner at the superior-distinguished level. In B. L. Leaver & B. Shekhtman (Eds.), *Developing professional-level language proficiency* (245–259). Cambridge, UK: Cambridge University Press.

Ehrman, M. & Oxford, R. (1995). Cognition plus: Correlates of language learning success. *The Modern Language Journal, 79*(i), 67–89.

Ehrman, M. E., Leaver, B. L., & Oxford, R. L. (2003). A brief overview of individual differences in language learning. *Systems, 31(3):* 313–330

Ellis, R. (2006). Current issues in the teaching of grammar: An SLA perspective. *TESOL Quarterly,40*(1), 83–107.

Ellis, R. (2005). *Instructed second language acquisition: A literature review.* (Report to the Ministry of Education). Wellington, New Zealand: The University of Auckland, Auckland Uniservices Limited.

Engberg, J. (2009). Individual conceptual structure and legal experts' efficient communication. *International Journal for the Semiotics of Law, 22,* 223–243.

Fajans, E. & Falk, M. (2005). *Scholarly writing for law students: Seminar papers, law review notes and law review competition papers* (3rd ed.). St. Paul, MN: West Group.

Feak, C. B., & Reinhart, S. M. (1996). English for legal studies: An innovative program for students of law. Paper delivered at RELC Seminar, Singapore.

Feak, C. B., Reinhart, S. M., & Sinsheimer, A. (2000). A preliminary analysis of law review notes. *English for Specific Purposes 19,* 197–220.

Ferris, D. & Hedgcock, J. (2014). *Teaching L2 composition: Purpose, process, and practice.* New York: Routledge.

Flavell, J. H. (1979). Metacognition and cognition monitoring: a new era of cognitive developmental inquiry. *American Psychologist,* 34, 906–911.

Flower, L. & Hayes, J. (1981). A cognitive process theory of writing. *College Composition and Communication, 32,* 365–87.

Flowerdew, J. & Peacock, M. (2001). *Research perspectives on English for academic purposes.* Cambridge, UK: Cambridge University Press, 2001.

Fowler, H. R. & Aaron, J. E. (2001). *The Little, Brown handbook* (8th ed.). New York, NY: Addison-Wesley Educational Publishers Inc.

Fowler, J. F. (1995). *Improving survey questions: design and evaluation.* Thousand Oaks, CA: Sage Publications.

Fox, H. (1994). *Listening to the world: Cultural issues in academic writing.* Urbana, Il: National Council of Teachers of English.

Fox, J. (1989). *Inventory of writing strategies.* A checklist produced for the Writing Tutorial Service, Carleton University, Ottawa, Canada.

Francis, N. (2006). The development of secondary discourse ability and metalinguistic awareness in second language learners. *International Journal of Applied Linguistics, 16*(1), 37–60.

Galbraith, D., Ford, S., Walker, G., & Ford, J. (2005). The contribution of different components of working memory to knowledge transformation during writing. *L1- Educational Studies in Language and Literature,* (5), 113–145.

Gass, S. & Mackey, A. (2000). *Stimulated recall methodology in second language research.* Mahwah, NJ: Lawrence Erlbaum Associates, Publishers.

Gee, J. (2000a). The new literacy studies: From "socially situated" to the work of the social. In D. Barton, M. Hamilton, & R. Ivanic (Eds.), *Situated literacies: Reading and writing in context* (pp. 180–196). London: Routledge.

Glatthorn, A. A. (1998). *Writing the winning dissertation: A step-by-step guide.* Thousand Oaks, CA: Corwin press, Inc.

Goddard, C. (2010). Didactic aspects of legal English: Dynamics of course preparation. In M. Gotti and C. Williams (Eds.), *ESP across cultures [Special issue]: Legal English across cultures: Vol. 7*, 45–62.

Gordon, L. (2008). Writing and good language learners. In C. Griffiths (Ed.), *Lessons from good language learners* (pp. 244–255). Cambridge: Cambridge University Press.

Grabe, W. (2006). [Forward] In A. H. Cumming (Ed.), *Goals for academic writing: ESL students and their instructors.* (p. vii). Philadelphia, PA: John Benjamins.

Grabe, W. (2001). Notes toward a theory of second language writing. In T. Silva, P. K. Matsuda (Eds.), *On second language writing* (pp. 39–57). Mahwah, NJ: Lawrence Erlbaum Associates, Publishers.

Grabe, W. & Kaplan, R. (1996). *Theory & practice of writing.* Essex, UK: Addison Wesley Longman Limited.

Grabe, W. & Stoller, F. L. (1997). *Content-based instruction: research foundations.* Retrieved September 22, 2008, from the University of Minnesota, Reprinted on the CoBaLTT Web site with permission: http://www.carla.umn.edu/cobaltt/modules/principles/ grabe_stoller1997/READING1/foundation.htm

Graham, S. (2006). Strategy instruction and the teaching of writing. In C. A. MacArthur, S. raham, & J. Fitzgerald (Eds.), *Handbook of writing research* (pp. 187–207). New York, NY: The Guildford Press.

Greene, J. A. & Azevedo, R. (2007). A theoretical review of Winne and Hadwin's model of self-regulated learning: New perspectives and directions. *Review of Educational Research, 77*(3), 334–372.

Griffiths, C. (2008). *Lessons from good language learners.* Cambridge: Cambridge University Press.

Groom, N. & Littlemore, J. (2011). *Doing applied linguistics: A guide for students.* New York, NY: Routledge.

Gunderson, L., D'Silva, R. & Odo, D. (2014). *ESL (ELL) Literacy instruction: A guidebook to theory and practice* (3rd ed.). New York: Routledge.

Hacker, D. J., Dunklosky, J., & Graesser, A. C. (Eds.). (1998). *Metacognition in educational theory and practice.* Mahwah, NJ: Lawrence Erlbaum Associates.

Harris, S. (1992). Reaching out in legal education: Will EALP be there? *English for Specific Purposes, 11*(1), 19–32.

Hayes, J. & Flower, L. (1980). Identifying the organization of writing processes. In L. Gregg & E. Steinberg (Eds.), *Cognitive processes in writing* (pp. 3–30). Hillsdale, NJ: Erlbaum.

Hedgcock, J. (2005). Taking stock of research and pedagogy in L2 writing. In E. Hinkel (Ed.), *Handbook of research in second language teaching and learning* (pp. 597–613). Mahwah, NJ: Lawrence Erlbaum Associates.

Hergenhahn, B. R., & Olson, M. H. (2005). An introduction to theories of learning (7th ed.). Upper Saddle River, NJ: Pearson/Prentice Hall.

Hillocks, G. (2006). Two decades of research on teaching writing in the secondary schools in the U.S. *L1-Educational Studies in Language and Literature, 6*(2), 29–51.

Hinds, J. (1987). Reader versus writer responsibility: A new typology. In U. Connor and R. B. Kaplan (eds.), *Writing across languages: analysis of L2 text.* Reading, MA: Addison-Wesley.

Hinkel, E. (2011b). What research on second language writing tells us and what it doesn't. In E. Hinkel (Ed.), *Handbook of research in second language writing and learning* (Vol. 11, pp. 523–536). New York, NY: Routledge.

Hinkel, E. (2006). Current perspectives on teaching the four skills. *TESOL Quarterly, 40*(1), 109–131.

Hinkel, E. (2005). Analyses of second language text and what can be learned from them. In E. Hinkel (Ed.), *Handbook of research in second language teaching and learning* (pp. 615–628). Mahwah, NJ: Lawrence Erlbaum Associates.

Hoffman, C. (2011). Using Discourse Analysis Methodology to Teach "Legal English." *International Journal of Law, Language, & Discourse, (1)*2, 1–19.

Holliday, A. (1999). Small cultures. *Applied Linguistics 20*(2), 237–264.

Hu, J. (2001). *The academic writing of Chinese graduate students in sciences and engineering: Processes and challenges.* Unpublished doctoral dissertation, University of British Columbia, Vancouver, British Columbia, Canada.

Hu, J. (2006). Discovering emerging research in a qualitative study of ESL academic writing. *The Qualitative Report, (14)*4, 629–665.

Hyland, K. (2002). Genre: language, context and literacy. In M. McGroaty (Ed.), *Annual Review of Applied Linguistics, 22,* 113–35.

Hyland, K. (2003). *Second language writing.* New York, NY: Cambridge University Press.

Hyland, K. (2005). Digging up texts and transcripts: Confessions of a discourse analyst. In P. K. Matsuda & T. Silva (Eds.), *Second language writing research: Perspectives on the process of knowledge construction* (pp. 177–188). Mahwah, NJ: Lawrence Erlbaum Associates.

Hyland, K. (2006). *English for academic purposes: An advanced resource book.* New York, NY: Routledge.

Hymes, D. H. (1971). *On communicative competence.* Philadelphia, PA: University of Pennsylvania Press.

Hymes, D. H. (1972). *On communicative competence.* In J. Pride and A. Holmes (Eds.), *Sociolinguistics.* Harmsworth and New York: Penguin, 269–93. Institute of International Education (2013). *English-taught master's programs in Europe: A 2013 update.* Retrieved November 10, 2013, from http://www.iie.org/Research-and-Publications/Publications-and-Reports/IIE-Bookstore/English-Language-Masters-Briefing-Paper-2013-Update

Interagency Language Roundtable (2007). *Interagency Language Roundtable Language Skill Level Descriptions: Writing.* Washington, D.C. Retrieved from the ILR website December 12, 2013, from http://www.govtilr.org/skills/ILRscale5.htm

Jandt, F. (2007). *An introduction to intercultural communication: Identities in a global Community* (5th ed.). Thousand Oakes, CA: Sage.

Jaser, A., Al-Khanji, R. R., & Leaver, B. L. (2005). A demographic analysis of Arabic-speaking students who achieve native-like levels in English-writing skills. *Journal for Distinguished Language Studies, 3,* 41–61.

Johnson, E. M. (2008). An investigation into pedagogical challenges facing international tertiary-level students in New Zealand. *Higher Education Research & Development, 27*(3), 231–243.

Kamler, B. & Thomson, P. (2008). The failure of dissertation advice books: Toward alternative pedagogies for doctoral writing. *Educational Researcher, 37*(8), 507–514.

Kieffer, M. J., Lesaux, N. K., Rivera, M. & Francis, D. J. (2009). Accommodations for English language learners taking large-scale assessments: A meta-analysis on effectiveness and validity. *Review of Educational Research, 79*(3), 1168–1201.

Kissam, P. (1990). *Journal of Legal Education, 40*(3), 339–349.

Kozulin, A. (1986). *Thought and language: Lev Vygotsky* (Rev. ed.). Cambridge, MA: The MIT Press.

Kramsch, C. (1993). *Context and culture in language teaching*. Oxford, UK: Oxford University Press.

Krashen, S. (2011). Academic proficiency (language and content) and the role of strategies. *TESOL Journal, (2)*4, 381–393.

Kucer, S. (2014). *Dimensions of literacy: A conceptual base for teaching reading and writing in school settings* (4th ed.). New York: Routledge.

Lassig, C. J., Lincoln, M. E., Dillon, L. H., Diezmann, C. M., Fox, J. L., & Neofa, Z. (2009). Writing together, learning together: The value and effectiveness of a research writing group for doctoral students. In *Proceedings of Australian Association For Research In Education 2009 International Education Research Conference*, AARE, Canberra. Retrieved January 13, 2013, from http://www.aare.edu.au/09pap/las091458.pdf

Leaver, B. L. (2005). Native-like writing skills in English. In I. Dubinsky & D. Bain Butler (Eds.), *Teaching and learning to near-native levels of language proficiency III: Proceedings of the fall 2005 annual conference of the coalition of distinguished language centers* (pp. 19–22). Salinas, CA: MSI Press.

Leaver, B. L., & Shekhtman, B. (2002). Principles and practices in teaching superior-level language skills: Not just more of the same. In B. L. Leaver & B. Shekhtman (Eds.), *Developing professional-level language proficiency* (3–33). Cambridge, UK: Cambridge University Press.

Lee, D. S., Hall, C. & Hurley, M. (1999). *American legal English: Using language in legal contexts* (instructor's manual). Ann Arbor, MI: The University of Michigan Press.

Lefrançois, P. (2005). How do university students solve linguistic problems? A description of the process leading to errors. *L1-Educational Studies in Language and Literature, (5)*, 417–432.

Lehman, B., Nduna, J., van der Geest, T., & Winberg, C. (2004). *A meta-analysis of the teaching of technical writing to students for whom English is not a first language* ($5,000.) Conference on College Composition and Communication, National Council of Teachers of English. Retrieved June 3, 2008 from http://www.ncte.org/cccc/awards/124060.htm

Leki, I. (1991). Twenty-five years of contrastive rhetoric: Text analysis and writing Pedagogies. *TESOL Quarterly 25*(1), 123–143.

Leki, I. (1995). Coping strategies of ESL students in writing tasks across the curriculum. *TESOL Quarterly, 19*(2), 235–260.

Leki, I., Cumming, A., & Silva, T. (2008). *A synthesis of research on second language writing in English*. New York and London: Routledge, Taylor & Francis Group.

Lillis, T. & Curry, M. J. (2010). *Academic writing in global context: The politics and practices of publishing in English*. New York: Routledge.

Lonka, K., Chow, A., Keskinen, J., Hakkarainen, K., Sandström, N., & Phyältö, K. (2014). How to measure PhD students' conceptions of academic writing? *Journal of Writing Research 5*(3), 245–269.

Manchón, R. M., Roca de Larios, J., & Murphy, L. (2007). A review of writing strategies: Focus on conceptualizations and impact of first language. In A. D. Cohen & E. Macaro (Eds.), *Language learner strategies* (pp. 229–250). Oxford: Oxford University Press.

Manchón, R. M., Murphy, L., & Roca de Larios, J. (2005). Using concurrent protocols to explore L2 writing processes: Methodological issues in the collection and analysis of data. In P. K. Matsuda & T. Silva (Eds.), *Second language writing research: Perspectives on the process of knowledge construction* (pp. 191–205). Mahwah, NJ: Lawrence Erlbaum Associates, Publishers.

Marshall, C. & Rossman, G. B. (1999). *Designing qualitative research*, 3rd. ed. Thousand Oaks, CA: Sage Publications.

Matsuda, P. K. (2006). Second-language writing in the twentieth century: A situated historical perspective. In P. K. Matsuda, M. Cox, J. Jordan, & C. Ortmeier-Hooper (Eds.), *Second-language writing in the composition classroom: A critical sourcebook* (pp. 14–30). Boston, MA: Bedford/St. Martin's.

Maxwell, J. A. (2005). *Qualitative research design: An interactive approach*. Thousand Oaks, CA: Sage Publications.

Maxwell, J. A. (2006). Literature reviews of, and for, educational research: A commentary on Boote and Beile's "Scholars Before Researchers". *Educational Researcher, 35*(9), 28–31.

McCrehan Parker, C. (1997). Writing throughout the curriculum: Why law schools need it and how to achieve it. *Nebraska Law Review.*

McCutchen, D. (2000). Knowledge, processing, and working memory: Implications for a theory of writing. *Educational Psychologist, 35*(1), 13–23. Lawrence Erlbaum Associates, Inc.

Moore Howard, R., Serviss, T. & Rodrigue, T. (2010). Writing from sources, writing from sentences. *Writing & Pedagogy, (2)*2, 177–192.

Morse, J. M., Barrett, M., Mayan, M., Olson, K., & Spiers, J. (2002). Verification strategies for establishing reliability and validity in qualitative research. *International Journal of Qualitative Methods 1* (2), Article 2. Retrieved July 7, 2009 from http://www.ualberta.ca/~ijqm/

Mosby's Medical Dictionary, 8th edition. ©2009, Elsevier.

Mu, C. & Carrington, S. (2007). An investigation of three Chinese students' English writing strategies [Electronic version]. *Teaching English as a Second or Foreign Language, 11*(1), 1–23.

Myles, J. (2002). Second language writing and research: The writing process and error analysis in student texts. *Teaching English as a second or foreign language, 6*(2), 1–20. Retrieved June 14, 2007 from TESL-EJ http://www-writing.berkeley.edu/TESL-EJ/ej22/toc.html

National Capital Language Resource Center. (2003). *Goal: Communicative competence.* Washington, D.C. National Capital Language Resource Center. Retrieved February 1, 2009 from the NCLRC website http://www.nclrc.org/essentials/goalsmethods/goal.htm

Negro, I. & Chanquoy, L. (2005). The effect of psycholinguistic research on the teaching of writing. *L1-Educational Studies in Language and Literature, 5*, 105–111.

Nisbett, R. E. (2003). *The geography of thought: How Asians and Westerners think differently … and why.* New York: The Free Press. Editions also in print for the U.K. and Commonwealth countries, China, Italy, Japan, Korea, Taiwan, and Turkey, and in preparation for Poland, Thailand and Vietnam.

Newell, A. & Simon, H. A. (1972). *Human Problem Solving.* Englewood Cliffs, NJ., (summary paper).

Newell, G. (2006). Writing to learn: how alternative theories of school writing account for student performance. In C. A. MacArthur, S. Graham, & J. Fitzgerald (Eds.), *Handbook of writing research* (pp. 235–247). New York, NY: The Guildford Press.

Nunan, D. (1992). *Research methods in language learning.* New York, NY: Cambridge University Press.

Oates, L. (1997). Beating the odds: Reading strategies of law students admitted through alternative admissions programs. *The Iowa Law Review 83,* 139–160.

Oates, L. & Enquist, A. (2005). *Just writing: Grammar, punctuation, and style for the legal writer* (2nd ed.). New York, NY: Aspen Publishers.

Oates, L. & Enquist, A. (2009). *Just writing: Grammar, punctuation, and style for the legal writer* (Rev. ed.). New York, NY: Aspen Publishers.

Oxford, R. L. (1990). *Language learning strategies: What every teacher should know.* Boston, MA: Heinle.

Oxford, R. L. (1996). *Language learning strategies: Cross-cultural perspectives.* Manoa: University of Hawaii Press.

Oxford, R. L. (2002). Sources in variation in language learning. In R. Kaplan (Ed.), *Oxford Handbook of Applied Linguistics* (pp. 245–252). Oxford, UK: Oxford University Press.

Oxford, R. L. (2008). Learning Strategy Instruction as a Gateway. Unpublished manuscript, *University of Maryland at College Park.*

Oxford, R. L. (2011). *Teaching and researching language learning strategies.* London: Pearson Longman.

Oxford, R. L. & Allen, S. (1994, March). *Maryland Professors of Reading, SoMIRAC.* Pecorari, D. (2008). *Academic writing and plagiarism: A linguistic analysis.* London: Continuum

Pennington, M. (2010). Plagiarism in the academy: Toward a proactive pedagogy. *Writing & Pedagogy, (2)*2, 147–159.

Polio, C. (2012). How to research second language writing. In A. Mackey & S. M. Gass (Eds.), *Research methods in second language acquisition: A practical guide* (pp. 139–157). West Sussex, UK: Wiley-Blackwell.

Pray, L. & Jiménez, R. T. (2009a). Developing literacy in second-language learners. [Review of the recently published compilation of research titled *Developing literacy in second-language learners: Report of the national literacy panel on language-minority children and youth* (August & Shanahan, 2006)]. *Educational Researcher, 38*(5), 380–381.

Pray, L. & Jiménez, R. T. (2009b). A response to "Literacy and English-language learners: A shifting landscape for students, teachers, researchers, and policy makers" by Jim Cummins. *Educational Researcher, 38*(5), 384–385.

Prior, P. (1991). Contextualizing writing and response in a graduate seminar. *Written Communication,* 8, 267–310.

Prior, P. (1995). Redefining the task: An ethnographic examination of writing response in six graduate seminars. In D. Belcher and G. Braine (Eds.), *Academic writing in a second language: Essays on research and pedagogy* (pp. 47–82). Norwood, NJ: Ablex, 1995.

Pritchard, R. J. & Honeycutt, R. (2006). The process approach to writing instruction: Examining its effectiveness. In C. A. MacArthur, S. Graham, & J. Fitzgerald (Eds.), *Handbook of writing research* (pp. 275–290). New York, NY: The Guildford Press.

Raimes, A. (1987). Language proficiency, writing ability, and composing strategies: A study of ESL college student writers. *Language Learning 37*(3), 439–468.

Raimes, A. (1991a). Out of the woods: Emerging traditions in the teaching of writing. *TESOL Quarterly 25*(3), 407–430.

Raimes, A. (1992). *Exploring through writing: A process approach to ESL composition* (2nd ed.). New York: St. Martin's Press.

Ramsfield, J. (1997). Is 'logic' culturally based? A contrastive, international approach to the U.S. law classroom. *Journal of Legal Education, 47*, 157–204.

Ramsfield, J. (2005). *Culture to culture: A guide to U.S. legal writing.* Durham, NC: Carolina Academic Press.

Redden, E. (2008, June 5). English for graduate students [Electronic Version]. *Inside Higher Education.* Retrieved from http://www.insidehighered.com/news/2008/06/05/english

Riazi, A. (1995). *Socialization into academic writing in a second language: A social- cognitive analysis of test production and learning among Iranian graduate students of education.* Unpublished doctoral dissertation, University of Toronto, Toronto, Ontario, Canada.

Riazi, A. (1997). Acquiring disciplinary literacy: A social-cognitive analysis of text production and learning among Iranian graduate students of education. *Journal of Second Language Writing 6*(2), 105–37.

Sanz, C. (2005). Adult SLA: The interaction between external and internal factors. In C. Sanz, (Ed.), *Mind and context in adult second language acquisition: Methods, theory, and practice* (pp. 3–20). Washington, DC: Georgetown University Press.

Scardamalia, M., & Bereiter, C. (1991). Literate expertise. In K. A. Ericsson & J. Smith (Eds.), *Toward a general theory of expertise. Prospects and limits* (pp. 172–194). Cambridge, MA: Cambridge University Press.

Schram, T. H. (2003). *Conceptualizing qualitative inquiry: Mindwork for fieldwork in education and the social sciences.* Upper Saddle River, NJ: Pearson Education.

Schultz, K. (2006). Qualitative research in writing. In C. A. MacArthur, S. Graham, & J. Fitzgerald (Eds.), *Handbook of writing research* (pp. 357–373). New York, NY: The Guildford Press.

Segev-Miller, R. (2004). Writing from sources: the effect of explicit instruction on college students' processes and products. *L1–Educational Studies in Language and Literature, 4*(1), 5–33.

Shank, G. D. (2002). *Qualitative research: A personal skills approach.* Upper Saddle River, NJ: Pearson Education.

Shor, I. (1999). What is Critical Literacy? *Journal of Pedagogy, Pluralism & Practice, 4*(1). Retrieved April 29, 2006, from http://www.lesley.edu/journals/jppp/4/index.html

Silva, T. (1993). Toward an understanding of the distinct nature of L2 writing: The ESL research and its implications. *TESOL Quarterly 27*(4), 657–677.

Silva, T. (1992). L1 vs. L2 writing: ESL graduate students' perceptions. *TESL Canada Journal*, 10, 27–47.

Silva, T. (1990). Second language composition instruction: Developments, issues, and directions in ESL. In B. Kroll (Ed.), Second language writing: Research insights for the classroom (pp. 11–23). Cambridge: Cambridge University Press.

Silva, T., Thomas, S., Park, H., & Zhang, C. (2013). Scholarship on L2 writing in 2013: The year in review [Electronic Version]. *TESOL INTERNATIONAL SLW News Report.* Retrieved September 24, 2014, from http://newsmanager.commpartners.com/tesolslwis/issues/2014-09-24/6.html

Silva, T., Lin, M., & Thomas, S. (2012). Scholarship on L2 writing in 2012: The year in review [Electronic Version]. *TESOL INTERNATIONAL SLW News Report.* Retrieved October 16, 2013, from http://newsmanager.commpartners.com/tesolslwis/issues/2013-10-07/9.html

Silva, T., Pelaez-Morales, C., McMartin-Miller, C. & Lin, M. (2011). Scholarship on L2 writing in 2011: The year in review [Electronic Version]. *TESOL INTERNATIONAL SLW News Report.* Retrieved October 17, 2013, from http://newsmanager.commpartners.com/tesolslwis/issues/2012-11-20/3.html

Silva, T., McMartin-Miller, C., Jayne, V., & Pelaez-Morales, C. (2010). Scholarship on L2 writing in 2010: The year in review [Electronic Version]. *TESOL INTERNATIONAL SLW News Report.* Retrieved November 11, 2013, from http://newsmanager.commpartners.com/tesolslwis/issues/2011-11-30/9.html

Silver, C. (2006). Internationalizing U.S. legal education: A report on the education of transnational lawyers. *Cardozo Journal of International and Comparative Law, 14,* 143–175.

Silver, C. (2001). "Lawyers on Foreign Ground," in Mark Janis and Salli Schwarz, eds., Careers in International Law(ABA 2001), pp. 1–21

Sitko, B. (1998). Knowing how to write: Metacognition and writing instruction. In D. J. Hacker, J. Dunlosky, & A. C. Graesser (Eds.), *Metacognition in educational theory and practice* (pp. 93–115). Mahwah, NJ: Lawrence Erlbaum Associates.

Skehan, P. (1998). *A cognitive approach to language learning.* Oxford: Oxford University Press.

Smagorinsky, P. (2006). Writing in school contexts. *L1-Educational Studies in Language and Literature, 6*(2), 1–6.

Solano-Flores, G. (2008). Who is given what language by who, when, and where? The need for probabilistic views of language in the testing of English language learners. *Educational Researcher, 37*(4), pp. 189–199).

Spanbauer, J. (2007). Lost in translation in the law school classroom: Assessing required coursework in LL.M. programs for international students. *International Journal of Legal Information, Vol. 35, No. 3.* Retrieved January 16, 2008, from Social Science Research Network Web site: http://ssrn.com/abstract=1024262

Spatt, B. (1999). *Writing from sources* (5th ed.). Boston, MA: Bedford/St. Martin's.

Sperling. C. & Shapcott, S. (2012). Fixing students' fixed mindsets: Paving the way for meaningful assessment. *The Journal of the Legal Writing Institute, 18,* 39–84.

Spolsky, B. (Ed.). (1978). *Approaches to language testing.* Arlington, VA.: Center for Applied Linguistics.

Strauss, A. & Corbin, J. (1990). Basics of qualitative research: Grounded theory procedures and techniques. Newbury Park, CA: Sage.

Strycharski, A. (2005). Method: Surveys and statistical data. In M. Marshall (Ed.), *Composing inquiry: Projects and methods for investigation and writing* (pp. 43–68). Old Tappan, NJ: Pearson Custom Publishing.

Stryker, S. B. & Leaver, B. L. (1997a). Content-based instruction: From theory to practice. In Stephen B. Stryker and Betty Lou Leaver (Eds.), *Content-based instruction: Models and Methods* (pp. 282–309). Washington, DC: Georgetown University Press.

Sudman, S., Bradburn, N., & Schwarz, N. (1996). *Thinking about answers: The application of cognitive processes to survey methodology.* San Francisco, CA: Jossey-Bass Publishers.

Swain, M. (2005). The output hypothesis: Theory and research. In E. Hinkel (Ed.), *Handbook of research in second language teaching and learning* (pp. 471–481). Mahwah, NJ: Lawrence Erlbaum Associates.

Swales, J. (1990b). *Genre analysis: English in academic and research settings.* New York: Cambridge University Press.

Swales, J. M. & Feak, C. B. (2000). *English in today's research world: A writing guide.* Ann Arbor, MI: The University of Michigan Press.

Swan, M. (2007). Grammar, meaning and pragmatics: Sorting out the muddle. *Teaching English as a Second Language Electronic Journal, Vol. 11, No. 2.* Retrieved June 1, 2009, from *TESL-EJ*: http://tesl-ej.org/ej42/a4.html

Thomas, W. P. & Collier, V. P. (1999). Accelerated schooling for English language learners. *Educational Leadership, 56/7,* 46–49.

Torrance, M. & Galbraith, D. (2006). The processing demands of writing. In C. A. MacArthur, S. Graham, & J. Fitzgerald (Eds.), *Handbook of writing research* (pp. 67–80). New York, NY: The Guildford Press.

University of Denver, Sturm College of Law. (2009, May 15). *Assessment demystified, demonstrated, and deployed: Driving curriculum reform at your law school.* Retrieved May 15, 2009, from http://law.du.edu/documents/assessment-conference/AssessmentConferenceRFP.pdf

Volokh, E. (2007). *Academic legal writing: Law review articles, student notes, and seminar papers* (3rd ed.). New York: Foundation Press.

Vygotsky, L. (1978). *Mind in society: Development of higher psychological processes.* Cambridge, MA: Harvard University Press.

Vygotsky, L. (1986). *Thought and language.* Cambridge, MA: The MIT Press.

Wenden, A. L. (1991). *Learner strategies for learner-autonomy: Planning and implementing learner training for language learners.* Englewood Cliffs, NJ: Prentice Hall.

Wenger, E., & Lave, J. (1991). *Situated Learning: Legitimate peripheral participation.* Cambridge: Cambridge University Press.

Williams, J. D. (2014). *Preparing to teach writing: Research, theory, and practice.* New York: Routledge.

Wojcik, M. (2001). *Introduction to legal English: An introduction to legal terminology, reasoning, and writing in plain English.* Washington, DC: international Law Institute.

Wojcik, M. & Edelman, D. (1997). Overcoming challenges in the global classroom: Teaching legal research and writing to international law students and law graduates. *The Journal of the Legal Writing Institute, 3,* 127–142.

Woodward-Kron, R. (2007). Negotiating meanings and scaffolding learning: writing support for non-English speaking background postgraduate students *Higher Education Research & Development, 26*(3), 253–268.

Wydick, R. (2005b). *Plain English for lawyers: Teacher's Manual* (5th ed.). Durham, NC: Carolina Academic Press.

Wydick, R. (1998). *Plain English for lawyers* (4th ed.). Durham, NC: Carolina Academic Press.

Zhang, C. (2013). Effect of instruction on ESL students' synthesis writing. *Journal of Second Language Writing, 22,* 51–67.

Zhou, Y. (2010). *The lived experiences of L2 Chinese graduate students in American higher education: A phenomenological narrative inquiry.* Unpublished dissertation, University of Missouri-Kansas City.

Key Definitions

1. CALP: Acronym coined by Cummins (1979) that means cognitive academic language proficiency. It refers to skills in formal academic language learning (contrasted with informal social language learning). These include skills in listening, speaking, reading, and writing about content-area material in academic situations where students are expected to use English as a tool for learning (Cummins, 1981, 2000, 2001, 2003). Problems arise in law school context, for example, when professors and administrators assume that students are proficient in second language (L2) academic writing when they demonstrate good social English orally or have met university requirements for TOEFL, the test of English as a foreign language.

2. CALP SKILLS: Defined in this study as academic language skills for processing L2 academic English and L2 legal English relevant to content knowledge (Kieffer, Lesaux, Rivera, & Francis, 2009). CALP skills in this study are central to the legal research writing task: that is, analyzing, paraphrasing, summarizing, and synthesizing from printed legal sources. The term incorporates higher-order thinking, L2 legal and L2 academic language use, and L2 research writing at the level of professional (or higher) writing proficiency.

3. COMPOSING: Combining of structural sentence units into a unique, cohesive, and coherent language structure, as in academic writing, for (a) telling and retelling what is already known to the writer (e.g., narratives and descriptions), or (b) transforming (e.g., expository and argumentative/persuasive texts) through which an information-transfer problem is solved, both for the writer and for his or her intended audience (Grabe & Kaplan, 1996; Bereiter & Scardamalia, 1987).

4. CONDITIONAL KNOWLEDGE: "A form of metaknowledge that involves knowing which strategies are most useful for which purposes and when to employ them. Goes beyond strategy knowledge." (Oxford, 2011, p. 279)

5. DECLARATIVE KNOWLEDGE: "In cognitive information processing, 'declarable' (speakable, identifiable) knowledge that is *not* automatic or outside of consciousness. Consists of *semantic knowledge* (facts, concepts, names, dates, rules) and *episodic knowledge* (based on memory of an event). A learning strategy can be a form of declarative knowledge if the learner can readily talk about it. Learners mentally organize and represent declarative knowledge as schemata. Such knowledge is easily lost if not practiced or used." (Oxford, 2011, p. 281)

6. DISCOURSE: Language produced as an act of communication. This language use implies the constraints and choices which operate on writers/speakers in particular contexts and reflects their purposes, intentions, ideas, and relationships with readers/ hearers (Hyland, 2006).

7. DISCOURSE COMMUNITY: A term, according to Swales (1990b)[1], that has its roots in the sociolinguistic concept of "speech community": that is, a community that shares similar norms of speech (written and oral) and cultural concepts.

8. DRAFTING: "The stage of the writing process when ideas are expressed in connected sentences and paragraphs" (Fowler & Aaron, 2001, p. 951).

9. EAP: Acronym for English for Academic Purposes: for example, scholarly legal writing which is intentional, reasoned, and oriented to problem-solving in a second, third, or forth academic language.

10. EDITING: "A distinct step in revising a written work, focusing on clarity, tone, and correctness. Compare *revising*" (Fowler & Aaron, 2001, p. 951).

11. EFL: Acronym for English as a foreign language. A foreign language is typically a subject studied at school or university rather than a communication tool.

12. ESL: Acronym for English as a second language. A second language is a means of communication learned in a community where the language serves daily social and communicative functions for the majority of people in that community. This term can be pejorative in professional school context because of its association with remedial learning or remediation.

13. ESP: Acronym for English for Specific Purposes: for example, legal English that crosses cultures and educational systems.

14. GENRE: Broadly, a way of using discourse. The term usually refers to a set of texts that share the same socially recognized purpose and which, as a result, often share similar rhetorical and structural elements to achieve this purpose (Hyland, 2006). Explicitly teaching genre conventions helps student attain some level of participation in the academic legal discourse community (Feak et al., 2000).

15. KNOWLEDGE-TELLING: Based on Bereiter and Scardamalia (1987), a less-skilled process approach to writing that is more concerned with generating content than planning and revising (Hyland, 2003).

16. KNOWLEDGE-TRANSFORMING: Based on Bereiter and Scardamalia (1987), a more-skilled process approach to writing that includes problem-solving, analysis, reflection, and goal-setting "to actively rework thoughts to change both...text and ideas" (Hyland, 2003, p. 12).

17. L1: Acronym for a person's first or native language.

18. L2: This acronym has been used to refer to any additional language (second, third, fourth, or higher) learned beyond the L1, whether this occurs in a *foreign language context*, in which English is not the medium of daily communication, or a *second language context*, in which the language being learned is the commonly spoken language (Oxford, 2007, p. 2).

19. L2 WRITERS: Acronym for individuals who are literate in their first language(s) and who learn to write an additional language.

---

1 Swales (1990b) was among the first to study the initiation and socialization processes that international graduate students go through to become literate professionals in their discourse communities. Other relevant L2 case study research includes Prior (1995), Belcher (1994), and Casanave (1995).

20. LEARNING STRATEGIES: Broad, goal-directed, self-regulated actions that learners chose from among alternatives and employ, with some degree of consciousness, for their own purposes (for example, to improve L2 learning, complete L2 tasks, and/or take greater responsibility for and control over learning) in specific sociocultural settings (Oxford, 2011).

21. LITERACY: Ability to encode and decode discourse, not just the ability to manipulate grammatical rules and vocabulary: in other words, the essence of academic education (Grabe & Kaplan, 1996).

22. NATIVE SPEAKER: Traditionally, a person who has proficiency in and intuition about a language by virtue of having acquired a language in infancy. Now very much a challenged and contested term owing to widely varying positions of bilingualism (Hyland, 2006) and the idea of the L2 legal writer as social actor, as in the European Economic Community (EEC).

23. PRE-WRITING: (developing, planning) "The stage of the writing process when one finds a topic, explores ideas, gathers information, focuses on a central theme, and organizes material" (Fowler & Aaron, 2001, p. 950).

24. PROCEDURAL KNOWLEDGE: "In cognitive-information processing, habitual or automatic knowledge that is outside consciousness" (Oxford, 2011, p. 294). This kind of knowledge is related to the "*hows* of understanding" efficient and effective task performance (Alexander, 2006, p. 76).

25. PROCESS APPROACH: A teaching approach to writing which emphasizes the development of good practices by stressing that writing is done in stages of planning, drafting, revising and editing which are recursive, interactive, and potentially simultaneous (Hyland, 2006). "The process orientation also implies a strong concern for the learner's strategies for gaining language skills" (Oxford, 1990, p. 5).

26. REVISING: "The stage of the writing process in which one considers and improves the meaning and underlying structure of a draft" (Fowler & Aaron, 2001, p. 963).

27. STRATEGIC COMPETENCE: Generally, the way in which a writer, when faced with a communicative problem, improvises his or her way to a solution using a "variety of communicative strategies" appropriately (Hyland, 2003, p. 32). Specifically, knowing how to (a) recognize and meet discourse community expectations, (b) work around gaps in one's knowledge of the academic or disciplinary language, (c) consider the academic language in the disciplinary context (adapted from the NCLRC 2003/Grice), and (d) consider the interplay between the social and cognitive dimensions of writing (Manchón et al., 2007) to show both communicative competence and domain learning in scholarly writing.

28. STRATEGIES INSTRUCTION: The teaching of strategies in at least three different ways: TYPE 1, Blind (embedded); TYPE 2, Awareness-only; TYPE 3 Explicit (Oxford, 2011).

29. WRITING STRATEGIES: Actions or activities consciously chosen by learners from among language, literacy, and culture alternatives for the purpose of regulating their own writing in a specific sociocultural setting (adapted from Griffiths, 2008 and Oxford, 2011).

30. WRITING SKILLS: Actions that learners may use unconsciously to improve their writing that are acquired or learned, as opposed to abilities which L2 learners may think innate.

Appendix A: Academic English Writing Questionnaire ©

Native academic language_____Country of origin _____Code name/number___

Academic English Writing Questionnaire

The purpose of this survey is find out what YOU think about academic English writing for graduate school. <u>There are no right or wrong answers</u>. So, please answer the questions based on what you really think. Your answers will be kept confidential and will not affect anyone's opinion of you.

Directions

In this questionnaire, you will find statements describing academic writers and the process of writing an academic English assignment or paper. Indicate HOW WELL EACH STATEMENT DESCRIBES YOU by writing a number beside each statement according to the following scale:

> **1 –** I strongly **disagree**
> **2 –** I disagree
> **3 –** I neither agree nor disagree
> **4 –** I agree
> **5 –** I strongly **agree**

___ 1. Different cultures and disciplines have different kinds of texts and writing styles.

___ 2. Standards for what is considered good academic writing are established by culture.

___ 3. Writing well in my native language is very important in my native academic culture.

___ 4. Academic writing in my native culture is *knowledge telling* or stating knowledge.

___ 5. Academic writing in my native culture is *knowledge transforming* or deepening the level of understanding to include analysis, synthesis, and evaluation of research.

___ 6. Revising is a very important stage of writing in my native academic culture.

___ 7. Academic writers in my native culture need a controlling idea for writing.

___ 8. Academic writers in my native culture borrow other writers' ideas randomly because knowledge is the common property of human beings, not personal intellectual property.

___ 9. Academic writers in my native culture let readers infer the meaning of their writing rather than express their meaning directly or explicitly.

___ 10. Good academic writers in my native culture refer to authoritative sources in their writing.

___ 11. Good academic writing in my native culture means working hard for clear meaning.

___ 12. Academic writing in any culture is a socialization process because to do it well, one must learn from others.

___ 13. Academic writing in English involves a different process from writing in my native academic language.

___ 14. Effective and efficient academic writing in English involves conscious use of strategies.

___ 15. Academic writing in English is a complex process because it involves learning from source text as well as communicating what I learned to a highly educated reader.

___ 16. I have been taught how to write using authority from printed (and electronic) sources.

___ 17. I always consider my purpose, audience, and level of formality for writing.

___ 18. As I write in English, I concentrate on both the content and on the language.

___ 19. I prefer to concentrate on the content first, before concentrating on my language use.

___ 20. My sentences are not too long or complex so they can be immediately understood.

___ 21. When I revise, I pay attention to how ideas are connected in my sentences, in my paragraphs, and in the sections of my writing assignment or paper.

___ 22. I like to have criteria for assessing the quality of my writing in stages: that is, pre- writing, drafting, and revising.

___ 23. I like to follow my original plans without revising them.

___ 24. When I do not understand an academic writing assignment, I ask the professor for clarification.

___ 25. Sometimes I ask my classmates to clarify the writing task for me.

___ 26. I generate ideas by thinking about what I have written and by making associations.

___ 27. I refine my ideas by interacting with people at different stages of my writing.

___ 28. I improve my English academic writing by speaking about my work to others.

___ 29. I re-use language from source text in English academic writing.

___ 30. My first draft is usually close to my final one.

___ 31. I correct language-related issues only after revising my ideas.

___ 32. When revising a paper, I leave it for several days to have an objective perspective of my own writing.

___ 33. When revising, I examine each idea again and see how it is developed within each paragraph or paragraph block (section).

___ 34. I consider various ways of organizing ideas, depending on my purpose, such as comparison and contrast, cause-effect, problem and solution, pros and cons.

___ 35. I paraphrase information in English by putting source material into my own words.

___ 36. I summarize information in English simply by reducing source text.

___ 37. I summarize information in English complexly by selecting and reorganizing source text.

___ 38. I synthesize information in English by combining and connecting source text.

___ 39. I analyze information in English by reflecting and breaking down source text into its parts

___ 40. I write to state knowledge in English by listing, repeating, or paraphrasing source text.

___ 41. I write to understand, remember, summarize simply, or extend notes in English to myself.

___ 42. I write to learn, problem-solve, summarize complexly, or synthesize information in English.

___ 43. I write to critique, persuade, or interpret evidence selectively and appropriately in English.

___ 44. Writing well in English is important for my studies in graduate school.

___ 45. Writing well in English is important for my career or profession.

___ 46. I am like an *architect* when I write in English because I plan, draft, and then edit my own work.

___ 47. I am like a *laborer* when I write in English because I slowly build and correct my language as I write.

___ 48. I am like an *artist* when I write in English because I re-work and revise my writing as I go along rather than follow a strict plan or outline.

49. Another word or comparison that describes me as an academic writer is:

_____

_____

50. Another word or comparison that describes the process of writing in academic English is:

_____

_____

Appendix B: Beliefs about Academic Writing and Instruction Questionnaire

Topic: Beliefs about academic writing and instruction (based on Casanave, 2004)

1. How do you characterize "improvement" in your academic (scholarly) legal writing?
(1) Read through these 10 improvements slowly, before writing anything.
(2) Then consider what you believe each improvement means for you, adding your own at the end.
(3) Finally, rank or order the improvements, from most important (1) to least important (10).

AREA	IMPORTANCE (#1 most → #10 least)
Increase in fluency	_____
Increase in grammatical accuracy	_____
Clearer expression of original thinking and voice	_____
More detail and depth of content	_____
More effective use of "expert" writing processes	_____
More effective use of "expert" writing strategies	_____
More confidence and motivation	_____
Increased knowledge of scholarly writing conventions	_____
Better ability to revise in response to law professor's feedback	_____
Increased ability to self-edit	_____
Other: _____	_____
_____	
Other: _____	_____
_____	
Other: _____	_____
_____	

2. Look at the following list of beliefs, then circle whether you agree or disagree with each one.

1) Graduate students benefit greatly from explicit instruction and feedback in research writing. *Agree   Disagree*

2) Graduate students' research writing improves primarily through a process of natural development that occurs as a result of practice over time. *Agree   Disagree*

3) English teachers should provide graduate students with the kinds of feedback they want even if there is little evidence that it leads to improved writing. *Agree   Disagree*

4) Graduate students can and should be taught particular writing processes and strategies. *Agree   Disagree*

5) Graduate students in law school should be taught the formal structures and conventions for scholarly (critical) writing through explicit instruction. *Agree   Disagree*

6) Graduate students' scholarly (critical) writing will improve if students become aware of the complex social-cultural nature of writing. *Agree   Disagree*

7) Graduate students' images of themselves as writers will improve if students become aware of the complex social-cultural nature of writing. *Agree   Disagree*

8) Graduate students' scholarly (critical) writing improves most from a pattern-governed, "keep-it-simple" approach, even if it does not reflect the complex realities of writing. *Agree   Disagree*

Please provide a personal comment or reflection:

_____

_____

_____

Appendix C: Research Writing/Grading Schedule

Note to international student writers

When you submit a research paper for writing course credit, each draft must contain your own assessment of your own work. Quality checklists for self-assessment are uploaded onto the course homepage for each stage of writing (pre-writing, drafting, and revising). Knowledge of criteria for assessment allows for reflection, revision, and transfer of learning to other research papers and writing situations. Setting deadlines for research and writing helps. You may use the schedule below.

RESEARCH WRITING/ GRADING SCHEDULE

If your working thesis is original and your research shows that the legal topic needs to be developed in some way, you are ready to set up a tentative schedule for research and writing with formative assessment (structured feedback) in 3 stages. Writing and revising for each stage is worth **30% (90% total)**, with 10% extra credit.

Reading and writing tasks:	Planned deadline
30% Stage 1: "Researching to learn"	
_____Researching completed	_____
_____Note-taking completed	_____
_____Drafting of outline completed	_____
_____Meeting with advisor, law professor for feedback	_____
_____Quality check: self evaluation/ teacher evaluation	_____checklist___
30% Stage 2: " Writing to learn"	
_____Drafting from legal sources completed	_____
_____Drafting with footnotes completed (mid-term)	_____
_____Quality check: self evaluation/ teacher evaluation	_____checklist___
30% Stage 3: " Writing to communicate"	
_____Revising from legal sources completed	_____
_____Revising with plain English writing strategies completed	_____

> **Key points** associated with revising:
> − semantic (sentence-to-sentence) cohesiveness
> − pragmatic (speaker-to-speaker) coherence

_____Revising to add authoritative citations completed	_____
_____Editing and proofreading completed	_____
_____Quality check: self evaluation/ teacher evaluation	_____checklist___
_____Submit research product for law course credit	_____

Appendix D: Strategic Competence Questionnaire (SCQ): 4 stages

STRATEGIC COMPETENCE FOR PROFESSIONAL PROFICIENCY IN SCHOLARLY SECOND LANGUAGE (L2) LEGAL WRITING
STAGE 1

Research topic/title: _____

Task Specific Pre-Writing Strategies

On the following pages, you will find statements describing conscious, goal directed actions legal research writers may take more than once while preparing to write a scholarly (academic) research paper. These actions, intentionally used to prepare for writing effectively and efficiently using L2 legal English, are called *pre-writing strategies*. Please read each statement carefully, then write the response (1, 2, 3) that BEST DESCRIBES YOU while you were preparing to write the first draft of your major analytical research paper, fall 2008. There are no right or wrong answers.

1. **Yes**, true of me
2. **No**, not true of me
3. Don't know

READING TO WRITE STRATEGIES

1. I used these legal reading strategies to find a topic, thesis, or claim for my major analytical research paper, fall 2008 *(all that apply)*

Conceptual

___I read for a purpose.
___I noted important details from the reading relevant to my topic.
___I summarized from the reading.
___I constructed notes from the reading.
___I annotated the reading with critical comment.
___I drew conclusions from the reading relevant to my thesis/claim.
___I "talked back to the text" by problem posing while reading.
___Other _____

> 1. **Yes,** true of me
> 2. **No,** not true of me
> 3. Don't know

Rhetorical

___I noted aspects of organizational structure for reading comprehension.
___I noted aspects of organizational structure for reuse in my writing.
___*Other* _____

Linguistic

___I noted key legal terms for reading comprehension.
___I noted key legal terms for reuse in my writing.
___I noted key English phrases for reading comprehension.
___I noted key phrases for reuse in my writing.
___I paraphrased in English for reading comprehension.
___I paraphrased in English for reuse in my writing.
___I translated from my first language (L1).
___I annotated in a language other than English.
___*Other* _____

2. I used these writing strategies for combining reading, note-taking, and thinking to discover what is important or true for me about my research topic, thesis, or claim for my major analytical paper, fall 2008 *(all that apply)*

___ I used texts or quotes from experts to stimulate thoughts and ideas.
___ I brainstormed or exchanged ideas with others about my research project.
___ I read other writers for modeling of style and organization.
___ I made a chart of persuasive legal sources.
___ I planned in my native language before beginning to write.
___ I made notes in my native language before beginning to write.
___ I made a preliminary outline or table of contents.
___ I started to write immediately, without a plan.
___ I made a timetable for when I would do my writing, allowing time for revising.
___ I found a quiet place where I could concentrate on my legal writing.

1. **Yes,** true of me 2. **No,** not true of me 3. Don't know

___ I made a list of vocabulary/legal terms/concepts I wanted to use before writing.

___ I considered general problems related to scholarly legal writing (e.g., audience, purpose, rhetorical structure, length of paper).

___ *Other* _____

READING TO LEARN

3. I used these cognitive academic language skills to prepare to write the first draft my major analytical paper, fall 2008 (*all that apply*)

___ I paraphrased information by putting source material (text) into my own words.

___ I summarized information simply by reducing source text.

___ I summarized information complexly by selecting and reorganizing source text.

___ I synthesized information by combining and connecting source text.

___ I analyzed information by reflecting and breaking down source text into its parts.

DEVELOPING PROFICIENCY

4. I used these legal writing activities to develop my ability to write an analytical paper, fall 2008 (*all that apply*)

___ writing articles for professional journals

___ editing (e.g., Human Rights) column/articles/books

___ writing papers for law school classes

___ preparing for a dissertation in my home country

___ writing memoranda and summary reports for *American Legal Institutions*

___ writing columns or scholarly articles for publishing or posting on the web

___ other (*please describe*) _____

> 1. **very** important
> 2. **somewhat** important
> 3. **not** important

LANGUAGE, COMPOSITION, AND KNOWLEDGE

5. These are my areas of concern in language and legal composition before writing my major analytical research paper in English, fall 2008 (*all that apply*)

___ organization
___ grammar
___ punctuation
___ meaning (content analysis)
___ legal style (ABC: accuracy, brevity, and conciseness)
___ social-cultural appropriateness for the U.S. law school educated reader
___ formal vs. informal English language (register)
___ references and citations to scholarly legal works
___ stages of legal writing (e.g., write to learn before writing to communicate)
___ *other* _____

6. These are my areas of concern in writing knowledge before writing my major analytical research paper in English, fall 2008 (*all that apply*)

___ *Knowing more about American law school conventions*
___ *Knowing more about how to write in English from L2 legal sources*
___ *Knowing more about the English language and the basic linguistic system*
___ *Knowing more about research writing as a process for effective legal writing*
___ *Knowing more about the kinds (genres) of legal writing*
___ *Knowing more about the assessment criteria for scholarly legal writing*
___ *Knowing more about my academic world as material for L2 law classroom discussion.*
___ *other* _____

IDENTIFYING MY USE OF LANGUAGE

7.a I used a language other than English in this (pre-writing) stage for reading, note-taking, or thinking (*check one*).

___ 1. **Yes,** true of me
___ 2. **No,** not true of me
___ 3. Don't know

7.b **If yes,** please give details.

_____
_____
_____
_____

DEVELOPING AS A LEGAL WRITER

8. Please describe how the strategies you used in this (pre-writing) stage are helping you develop competency as an L2 legal writer.

_____
_____
_____
_____

9. Please describe how preparing to write a research paper in U.S. law school context is similar to or different from preparing to write a research paper in your home university or law school.

_____
_____
_____
_____

Thank you for participating in this study.

STRATEGIC COMPETENCE FOR PROFESSIONAL PROFICIENCY
IN SCHOLARLY SECOND LANGUAGE (L2) LEGAL WRITING
STAGE 2

Research topic/title: _____

Task Specific Drafting Strategies

On the following pages, you will find statements describing conscious, goal directed actions legal research writers may take more than once while drafting a scholarly (academic) research paper. These actions, intentionally used for drafting effectively and efficiently using L2 legal English, are called *drafting strategies*. Please read each statement carefully, then write the response (1, 2, 3) that BEST DESCRIBES YOU while drafting your major analytical research paper, fall 2008. There are no right or wrong answers.

> 1. **Yes,** true of me
> 2. **No,** not true of me
> 3. Don't know

DRAFTING STRATEGIES

1. I used these strategies for getting words and concepts down effectively on paper while drafting my major analytical paper, fall 2008 (*all that apply*).

___ I focused on what authority is predominant to begin writing.
___ I summarized information from persuasive legal sources to begin writing.
___ I synthesized information from persuasive legal sources to begin writing.
___ I paraphrased from legal sources to begin writing (knowledge telling strategy).
___ I used my knowledge of audience and purpose for writing to guide my drafts.
___ I focused on the Background section to get started.
___ I focused on the Discussion (Analysis) section to get started.
___ I re-read legal texts that served as rhetorical models.
___ I reordered information from legal source texts to use in my drafts.
___ I conferenced with the instructor/professor to refine and clarify my ideas.
___ I collaborated with classmates to refine and clarify my ideas.
___ I considered various ways of organizing ideas related to my purpose.

> 1. **Yes,** true of me
> 2. **No,** not true of me
> 3. Don't know

___ When I could not think of the correct expression to write, I usually found a different way to express the idea (e.g., I used a synonym or described the idea).

___ I monitored my text for errors while I wrote.

___ I reviewed what I had already written before generating additional content.

___ I rejected irrelevant substantive content while I wrote.

___ I postponed editing my English until I finalized the content (analysis).

___ I wrote two drafts.

___ I wrote three or more drafts.

___ I changed my organization as needed.

___ I reassessed or changed my purpose as needed.

___ I changed my ideas or made my ideas clearer as I wrote more drafts.

___ I used a bilingual legal dictionary.

___ I used an American legal English dictionary.

___ I wrote run-on sentences in English to get important ideas down before revising.

___ I used both English and my native language to avoid interrupting my thinking.

___ I wrote in English, leaving gaps for missing English words.

___ *Other* _____

WRITING TO LEARN

2. I used these cognitive academic language skills for effectively drafting my major analytical paper, fall 2008 (*all that apply*)

___ I paraphrased information by putting source material (text) into my own words.

___ I summarized information simply by reducing source text.

___ I summarized information complexly by selecting and reorganizing source text.

___ I synthesized information by combining and connecting source text.

___ I analyzed information by reflecting and breaking down source text into its parts.

___ *other* _____

> 1. **Yes,** true of me
> 2. **No,** not true of me
> 3. Don't know

IDENTIFYING MY PURPOSE AND LEVELS OF COMPOSING

3. I used these broad levels of writing purpose for effectively drafting my major analytical paper, fall 2008 (*number all that apply*).

___ I wrote to state knowledge by listing, repeating, or paraphrasing source text.

___ I wrote to understand, remember, summarize simply, or extend notes to myself.

___ I wrote to learn, problem-solve, summarize complexly, or synthesize source text information.

___ I wrote to critique, persuade, or interpret evidence selectively and appropriately.

___ *other* _____

_____

IDENTIFYING MY USE OF LANGUAGE

4. a I used a language other than English in this (drafting) stage for writing my paper (*check one*).

___ 1. **Yes,** true of me
___ 2. **No,** not true of me
___ 3. Don't know

4. b **If yes,** please give details.

_____
_____
_____
_____

DEVELOPING AS A LEGAL WRITER

5. Please describe how the strategies you used in this (drafting) stage are helping you develop competency as an L2 legal writer.

_____

_____

_____

_____

6. Please describe how drafting a research paper in U.S. law school context is similar to or different from drafting a research paper in your home university or law school.

_____

_____

_____

_____

> *Thank you for participating in this study.*

STRATEGIC COMPETENCE FOR PROFESSIONAL PROFICIENCY
IN SCHOLARLY SECOND LANGUAGE (L2) LEGAL WRITING
STAGE 3.a

Research topic/title: _____

Task Specific Revising Strategies

On the following pages, you will find statements describing conscious, goal directed actions legal research writers may take more than once while revising a
scholarly (academic) research paper. These actions, intentionally used for revising effectively and efficiently using L2 legal English, are called *revising strategies*.
Please read each statement carefully, then write the response (1, 2, 3) that BEST
DESCRIBES YOU while revising your major analytical research paper, fall 2008.
There are no right or wrong answers.

> 1. **Yes**, true of me
> 2. **No**, not true of me
> 3. Don't know

REVISING STRATEGIES

1. I used these strategies to decide what should be changed, deleted, added, or
retained while revising my major analytical paper, fall 2008 (*all that apply*).

___ I read critically and reflected on my own written drafts.
___ I reused self-created materials such as notes or outlines to help me revise.
___ I used summary as I revised.
___ I used paraphrase as I revised.
___ I used synthesis as I revised.
___ I re-ordered my writing as I revised.
___ I made legal content revisions.
___ I made lexical/vocabulary revisions.
___ I made linguistic/grammar revisions.
___ I asked myself if I repeated key words and phrases for cohesion and empha-
    sis.
___ I asked myself if I included the right level of detail.
___ I asked myself if my purpose is clear.
___ I asked myself if my message is clear.

1. **Yes,** true of me
2. **No,** not true of me
3. Don't know

___ I asked myself if I addressed the needs of my reader.

___ I got feedback from peers (about what stood out for them) to assess how effectively I communicated my message.

___ I got feedback from my writing instructor to assess how effectively I communicated my message.

___ I got expert writing feedback from my instructor to build or re-construct my analysis.

___ I got expert legal opinion of my analysis from my content law professor.

___ I asked myself if there was a large and a small organization to what I had written.

___ I asked myself if I used headings, subheadings, and logical connectors effectively.

___ I revised my paper at least once to improve the language and the content (analysis).

___ I revised my paper to ensure sentence to sentence (semantic) cohesiveness.

___ I revised my paper to ensure speaker to speaker (pragmatic) coherence.

___ I added critical comment after quotations that end paragraphs.

___ I used (or re-used) reference materials when revising.

___ I discussed my text with a knowledgeable writer or instructor who put the text in his/her own words, and then I compared the paraphrase to my original version.

___ I changed material.

___ I added material.

___ I deleted material.

___ I compared my writing to a model when revising.

___ I revised the analytical Discussion section before the Introduction and Conclusion.

___ I reflected on my content learning when revising.

___ *Other* _____

> 1. **Yes,** true of me
> 2. **No,** not true of me
> 3. Don't know

EDITING STRATEGIES

Editing is part of the revising process that involves polishing and checking for conventions rather than for content in stage 3 of the writing process.

2. I used these strategies to edit effectively before submitting my major analytical paper, fall 2008 (*all that apply*).

___ I asked myself whether my paper was an example of good legal writing.
___ I proofread my legal writing at least once for form (*e.g.*, paragraph structure).
___ I proofread my legal writing for sentence structure (syntax).
___ I proofread my legal writing for proper word choice (diction).
___ I proofread my legal writing for punctuation.
___ I proofread my legal writing for capitalization.
___ I proofread my legal writing for spelling (e.g., Microsoft Word "Tools").
___ I proofread my legal writing for appearance (e.g., spacing, indentation).
___ for citation.
___ I engaged in peer review with fellow classmates– non-native speakers included.
___ I considered legal English style techniques (below) to enhance clarity and readability in my legal writing.
___ *Other* _____

GRAMMAR STRATEGIES

Editing in second language (L2) legal English also involves the use of *plain English writing* strategies (that is, grammar strategies for clear, accurate expression of ideas in English).

3. I used these grammar strategies to communicate effectively in writing before submitting my major analytical paper, fall 2008 (*check all that apply*).

___ I checked to see whether I used short and medium-length sentences.
___ I checked whether my sentences contained concrete subjects and active verbs.

> 1. **Yes,** true of me
> 2. **No,** not true of me
> 3. Don't know

___ I tried to avoid nominalizations (the practice of changing verbs to nouns)

___ I made one point per sentence, preferring simple and complex sentence structures to compound sentence structures.

___ I made sentences affirmative, not negative.

___ I preferred active voice to passive voice with some exceptions.

___ I used parallel structures in sentences containing multiple elements.

___ I used clear and logical lists with grammatically parallel elements.

___ I used familiar words instead of flowery language or ornate words.

___ I used consistent wording/phrasing without changing words for variety (e.g. "The defendant *proposes* ... This *proposal* is ...").

___ I kept subjects + verbs/verbs + objects undivided, without interrupting phrases

___ I used accurate and adequate punctuation as "road signs" in my legal writing.

___ I used precise transitions to convey exact connections.

___ I used consistent parallel word signals such as *first* and *second*.

___ I provided structural clues and repeated key structure words to improve readability (e.g., *that*).

___ I used simple past tense for events that already occurred.

___ I used quotations only when necessary.

___ I avoided long, multi-clause sentences ("headnote" legal style).

___ *Other* _____

WRITING TO COMMUNICATE

4. I used these cognitive academic language skills for effectively revising and editing my major analytical paper, fall 2008 (*all that apply*).

___ I paraphrased information by putting source material (text) into my own words.

___ I summarized information simply by reducing source text.

___ I summarized information complexly by selecting and reorganizing source text.

___ I synthesized information by combining and connecting source text.

> 1. **Yes,** true of me
> 2. **No,** not true of me
> 3. Don't know

____ I analyzed information by reflecting and breaking down source text into its parts.

____ *other* _____

IDENTIFYING MY PURPOSE AND LEVELS OF COMPOSING

5. I used these broad levels of writing purpose for effectively revising my major analytical paper, fall 2008 *(all that apply)*.

____ I wrote to state knowledge by listing, repeating, or paraphrasing source text.

____ I wrote to understand, remember, summarize simply, or extend notes to myself.

____ I wrote to learn, problem-solve, summarize complexly, or synthesize information.

____ I wrote to critique, persuade, or interpret evidence selectively and appropriately.

____ *other* _____

KNOWLEDGE TRANSFORMING

6. Revising (stage 3) was <u>the most effective stage</u> for transitioning my writing from *knowledge telling* (stating knowledge) to *knowledge transforming* (deepening my level of understanding to include analysis, synthesis, evaluation of research) *(check one)*.

____ 1. **Yes,** true of me
____ 2. **No,** not true of me
____ 3. Don't know

7. This particular stage 3 strategy helped me <u>the most</u> to deepen my thinking in English while revising my major analytical paper, fall 2008 *(check one)*.

____ using analysis to generate original content
____ integrating propositions (e.g., statements/assertions) for conciseness

---

1. **Yes,** true of me
2. **No,** not true of me
3. Don't know

___ integrating propositions (e.g., statements/assertions) for comprehensiveness
___ using revising routines for accuracy in thought and expression
___ using editing routines for clarity in thought and expression
___ using plain English writing strategies for accuracy, brevity, and clarity
___ *Other* _____

_____

8. This particular strategy group helped deepen my thinking in English <u>the most</u> while revising my major analytical paper, fall 2008 (*check one*).

___ *Conceptual transforming* (for refining my working thesis)
___ *Rhetorical transforming* (for binding my overall structure *e.g.,* problem-solution)
___ *Linguistic transforming* (for getting away from the language of my source texts)

9. This particular *linguistic transforming* strategy helped me <u>the most</u> to transform text information while revising, giving me authorship of my major analytical paper, fall 2008 (*check one).*

___ I used lexical repetition by repeating key legal terms and phrases.
___ I used source texts or quotations to support my own text.
___ I paraphrased (by stating knowledge–not composing).
___ I summarized (composed by selecting and reorganizing).
___ I synthesized (composed by combining and connecting).

IDENTIFYING MY USE OF LANGUAGE

10.a I used a language other than English in this (revising) stage for writing my paper (*check one*).

___ 1. **Yes,** true of me
___ 2. **No,** not true of me
___ 3. Don't know

10.b **If yes,** please give details[below].

_____

_____

_____

_____

DEVELOPING AS A LEGAL WRITER

11. Please describe how the strategies you used in this (revising) stage are helping you develop competency as an L2 legal writer.

_____

_____

_____

_____

12. Please describe how revising a research paper in U.S. law school context is similar to or different from revising a research paper in your home university or law school.

_____

_____

_____

_____

Thank you for participating in this study.

STRATEGIC COMPETENCE FOR PROFESSIONAL PROFICIENCY
IN SCHOLARLY SECOND LANGUAGE (L2) LEGAL WRITING
STAGE 3.b

Title: _____

Legal Writing Proficiency and Strategies Instruction

Much legal writing is expository writing that analyzes a topic, explains factual information, supports a subject, or presents an idea. You often do one or all when writing a legal memo, substantive email, or scholarly article. In legal writing within the U.S. law school context, you have been concerned with effectiveness rather than pure literary form. Please read each statement carefully, then *check* or write the response (1, 2, 3) that BEST DESCRIBES YOU NOW (a) after revising your major analytical research paper, fall 2008 and (b) after completing a semester of the *Advanced English for Legal Research Writer's* course. There are no right or wrong answers.

CAN DO CHECKLIST OF DEFINING ABILITIES

1. *Check* everything you can do now in legal (expository) writing:

Level 3 (General Professional Proficiency)

- *I can write effectively in most informal written exchanges on social topics.* _____
- *I can write effectively in most formal written exchanges on professional topics.* _____
- *I can write reports, summaries, and short research papers on current events with reasonable ease.* _____
- *I can write reports, summaries, and short research papers on particular areas of interest or on special fields with reasonable ease.* _____
- *I can control structure, spelling, and general vocabulary to convey my message accurately, clearly, and concisely (even if my style may be obviously foreign).* _____
- *I can write without the kind of errors that may interfere with reader comprehension* _____
- *I can generally control my punctuation in legal writing.* _____

- *I can employ a variety of language structures in legal writing.* _____
- *I can write with only a few sporadic (scattered) errors in basic structures.* _____
- *I can write with only occasional errors in the <u>high-frequency complex structures</u> (e.g., articles, prepositions, past perfect/progressive tenses, past/perfect modals.* _____
- *I make more errors in the <u>low-frequency complex structures</u> (e.g., passive voice, gerunds /infinitives, conditional/future perfect/and compound tenses such as past perfect progressive, etc.) when I write.* _____
- *I can consistently control compound and complex structures in legal writing.* _____
- *I can make the relationship of ideas consistently clear in legal writing.* _____

Level 4 (Advanced Professional Proficiency)

- *I can use English to write accurately in both formal and informal styles pertinent to my professional school needs.* _____
- *I can write with relatively few grammatical errors in English, including those in <u>low- frequency complex structures</u> (above)* _____
- *I can consistently tailor my legal writing to suit my readers' (audience) needs.* _____
- *I can express subtleties and nuances (shades of meaning) in legal writing.* _____
- *I can write clearly, consistently, and explicitly in legal memos and other analytical papers.* _____
- *I can employ a variety of rhetorical patterns to convey meaning in legal writing.* _____
- *I can use a wide variety of cohesive devices such as ellipsis (...), parallelisms, and subordinate clauses in a variety of ways.* _____
- *I can write on all topics normally pertinent to professional school needs.* _____
- *I can write on all topics normally pertinent to social issues of a general nature.* _____

Level 5 (Functionally Native Proficiency)

- *I can write with proficiency equal to that of a law school educated native speaker.* ____
- *I can write legal English documents without nonnative errors of structure, spelling, style, or vocabulary.* _____
- *I can write and edit both formal and informal professional correspondence.* _____
- *I can write and edit official reports, documents, and professional articles.* _____
- *I can edit writing for special legal purposes such as scholarly writing.* _____
- *I can write clearly, explicitly, informatively, **and** persuasively in one document.* _____
- *To enhance clarity and readability, I can employ a wide range of stylistic devices known as plain English writing strategies (e.g., keeping the subject and verb undivided and focused on your point; using precise transitions to convey exact connections).* _____

STRATEGIES INSTRUCTION

1. **Very** important
2. **Somewhat** important
3. **Not** important

2. *Check* how important direct (explicit) writing strategies instruction was for you to develop an *efficient writing process*, fall 2008 research paper *(all that apply)*.

___ direct instruction was important at *early* stages (e.g., pre-writing – drafting)
___ direct instruction was important at *later* stages (e.g., drafting – revising)
___ direct instruction was important at *all* stages (e.g., pre-writing, drafting, revising)

3. *Check* how important direct (explicit) writing strategies instruction was for you to develop an *effective writing product*, fall 2008 research paper *(all that apply)*

___ direct instruction was important at *early* levels (e.g., conceptual – rhetorical)
___ direct instruction was important at *later* levels (e.g., rhetorical – linguistic)
___ direct instruction was important at *all* levels (e.g. conceptual, rhetorical, linguistic)

1. **Very** important
2. **Somewhat** important
3. **Not** important

4. *Check* how important direct (explicit) writing feedback was for you as a second language (L2) legal writer to complete your fall 2008 research paper *(all that apply)*.

___ legal English writing teacher interactive/corrective feedback were important
___ peer native-English speaker (non-teacher) correction/explanation were important
___ peer non-native English speaker (class-mate) correction/explanation were important
___ content law professor interactive/substantive feedback were important (if available)

5. *Identify* additional kinds of writing tools or support you might need to survive/thrive as a legitimate participant in your scholarly legal discourse[1] community.

Please be specific.

_____

_____

---

1 The word "discourse" in this context means English language produced as an act of communication (Hyland, 2006).

Appendix E: Interview Protocol (IP)

INTERVIEW PROTOCOL (IP)

Purpose: Triangulation and exploration of student perceptions, meanings, and interpretations of strategic competence in scholarly legal writing

Project title: *Strategic competence for professional proficiency in scholarly second language (L2) legal writing: A mixed methods study*

Brief description of the project: The *research purpose* is to disclose dynamic factors that contribute to strategic competence for professional proficiency (or higher) in scholarly L2 legal writing.

Time recorded interview begins:_____**ends:** _____

Date: _____

Place: law school

Interviewer: Donna Bain Butler

Interviewee: _____

Position of interviewee: Advanced English, Master of Laws (LL.M.) student

Two questions will be asked after student fills out questionnaire for each stage of writing (stages 1, 2, 3.a, 4). The first is a closed-ended question that asks student about effective writing strategies (using the strategic competence questionnaire to stimulate recall). The second is an open-ended question that probes student's response to # 1:

1. Thank you for filling out the questionnaire. Can you please tell me which strategies helped you the most for

Stage	#	*Check*
preparing to write?	1	
drafting?	2	
revising?	3a	
proficiency/instruction	3b	below
rewriting for publication?	4	

2. That's interesting...Can you tell me more? *(researcher probes)*

Two questions will also be asked after student completes questionnaire section 3b:

1. Let's review your perceptions of writing strategies instruction (*questionnaire*). I'd like you to tell me more about your experience learning scholarly legal writing.

2. Now let's look at the proficiency checklist. How do you think you have been building proficiency or expertise in legal writing over time, since taking my course?

Appendix F: Quality Assessment Tools (SQAT/TQAT): 4 stages

STUDENT'S QUALITY ASSESSMENT TOOL (SQAT) STAGE 1

PRE-DRAFTING CHECKLIST FOR STUDENTS

Check what you have done to prepare for writing your first draft in L2 English:

_____ 1. I have started with what I already know and think.

_____ 2. I have defined a suitable topic that is interesting and authentic to my experience.

_____ 3. I have explained why this topic is important (at this time, to this audience).

_____ 4. I have identified my purpose for legal research writing (based on Ramsfield, 2005)
   • To synthesize a body of law not yet pulled together
   • To criticize or support a recent opinion
   • To expand a field of knowledge by offering a new direction for a specific area of law
   • To dismiss another article by criticizing a theory or argument made by another scholar
   • To foreshadow or predict developments in the law
   • To suggest changes in the status quo of the law
   • To make sense out of a confusing array of issues
   • To propose a plan of action on a legal issue

_____ 5. I have narrowed my legal topic (e.g., by brainstorming within context or with my professor).

_____ 6. I have formulated research question(s) to reflect what I think about my legal topic.

_____ 7. I have a point of view or opinion on the topic; I know what I want to say about the topic; or I know how I see or think about the topic.

_____ 8. I have identified the type of research paper I want to write (e.g., an *analytical* paper that explores or fleshes out an unresolved legal topic or a *persuasive* paper that takes a stand on a legal issue and uses evidence to back-up my stance).

_____ 9. I have formulated a **working thesis**.

___ 10. I have found primary and secondary sources to support my working the-sis.

___ 11. I have read through all my sources.

___ 12. I have evaluated my sources.

___ 13. I have taken notes in English on my sources (e.g., annotated, research journal).

___ 14. I have made a working bibliography of my sources.

___ 15. I have organized my legal research into a **working outline**.

___ 16. I have decided on my approach (e.g., descriptive, analytical, compara-tive, critical)

___ 17. I feel prepared to write draft #1 (that is, to synthesize and integrate my legal sources into an essay format for a "paper").

TEACHER'S QUALITY ASSESSMENT (TQAT) STAGE 1

PRE-DRAFTING EXTERNAL CONTROL FOR TEACHER-RESEARCHER

Check what student has done to prepare for writing the first draft in L2 English: that is,

___ 1. started with what (s)he already knows and thinks.

___ 2. defined a suitable topic that is interesting and authentic to student's ex-perience.

___ 3. explained why this topic is important (at this time, to this audience).

___ 4. identified the purpose for legal research writing (based on Ramsfield, 2005)

- To synthesize a body of law not yet pulled together
- To criticize or support a recent opinion
- To expand a field of knowledge by offering a new direction for a specific area of law
- To dismiss another article by criticizing a theory or argument made by another scholar
- To foreshadow or predict developments in the law
- To suggest changes in the status quo of the law
- To make sense out of a confusing array of issues
- To propose a plan of action on a legal issue

___ 5. narrowed his/her legal topic (e.g., by brainstorming within context or with law professor).

_____ 6. formulated research question(s) to reflect what student thinks about legal topic.

_____ 7. stated a point of view or opinion on the topic; knows what (s)he wants to say about the topic; or knows how (s)he sees or thinks about the topic.

_____ 8. identified the type of research paper (s)he wants to write (e.g., an *analytical* paper that explores or fleshes out an unresolved legal topic or a *persuasive* paper that takes a stand on a legal issue and uses evidence to back-up the student's stance).

_____ 9. formulated a **working thesis**.

_____ 10. found primary and secondary sources to support his/her working thesis.

_____ 11. read through all his/her sources.

_____ 12. evaluated those sources.

_____ 13. taken notes in English on the sources (e.g., annotated, research journal).

_____ 14. made a working bibliography of the sources.

_____ 15. organized the legal research into a **working outline**.

_____ 16. decided on an approach (e.g., descriptive, analytical, comparative, critical)

_____ 17. seems prepared to write draft #1 (that is, to synthesize and integrate legal sources into an essay format for a "paper").

Student's code name: _____   Appendix F   Date: _____

STUDENT'S QUALITY ASSESSMENT TOOL (SQAT) STAGE 2

*OUTLINE → DRAFTING CHECKLIST FOR SEMINAR PAPERS AND LAW REVIEW ARTICLES

Topic: _____*Full bibliography attached: YES___NO___*

Introduction (This section prepares your reader for purpose of your paper. Can be written in full only after the research draft is complete.)

___ 1.   I have introduced and noted why topic is important.
___ 2.   I have briefly summarized necessary background information.
___ 3.   I have stated my thesis: an original and supportable proposition about the subject; problem+solution; "one new point, one new insight, one new way of looking at piece of law"
___ 4.   I have conveyed my organization of the paper.

Background (This section prepares your reader for analysis with historical issues and context for why topic is important. You can write this part first but you must revise after Discussion section is complete.)

___ 1.   I have described the genesis (origin) of the subject.
___ 2.   I have described the changes that have occurred during its development.
___ 3.   I have explained the reasons for the changes.
___ 4.   I have described where things are now. (You may also want to indicate the reasons for further change- focus/paper)

Comment is an analysis of controversy-law vs. Casenote that focuses on judicial opinion: 1. Include the relevant facts. 2. Include the procedural history. 3. Include the court's holding and reasoning at each level, as well as the reasoning of dissenting or concurring opinions (based on Fajans & Falk, 2000).

FOCAL POINT

Analytical Discussion: (This section gives your original analysis of the subject matter; may consist of both a critique of existing approaches and a proposed solution. Re-introduces thesis or focus; provides brief background summary; provides analysis with support in each paragraph, for each issue, in each sub-section.)

Large-scale organization

____ A.   I have discussed the major issues.

____ B.   I have separated issues and sub-issues (with Headings and Sub-headings).

____ C.   I have ordered issues logically (e.g. A-1, A-2/ B-1, B-2, B-3/ C-1, C-2).

Small-scale organization

____ 1.   I have introduced and concluded on each issue.

____ 2.   I have presented my argument and rebutted opposing arguments.

____ 3.   I have very clear organizational paradigms (patterns) where appropriate (e.g., problem-solution – most common, cause and effect, comparative pattern.)

Conclusion

____ 1.   I have restated my thesis without being obviously redundant.

____ 2.   I have summarized the major points I want my legal reader to remember, to reflect upon.

____ 3.   I have made some recommendations if appropriate.

TEACHER'S QUALITY ASSESSMENT TOOL (TQAT) STAGE 2

*OUTLINE→DRAFTING EXTERNAL CONTROL MEASURE FOR SCHOLARLY LEGAL WRITING

Topic: _____*Full bibliography attached: YES___NO___*

Introduction (This section prepares reader for purpose of your paper. Can be written in full only after the research draft is complete.)

____ 1.   Student has introduced and noted why topic is important.

____ 2.   Student has briefly summarized necessary background information.

____ 3.   Student has stated thesis: an original and supportable proposition about the subject; problem+ solution; "one new point, one new insight, one new way of looking at piece of law" R. Delgado.

____ 4.   Student has conveyed organization of the paper.

Background (This section prepares reader for analysis with historical issues and context for why topic is important. Can write this part first but must revise after Discussion section is complete.)

___ 1. Student has described the genesis (origin) of the subject.

___ 2. Student has described the changes that have occurred during its development.

___ 3. Student has explained the reasons for the changes.

___ 4. Student has described where things are now. (May also want to indicate the reasons for further change-focus/paper)

Statement of the Case (<u>casenote</u>: focuses on one judicial opinion vs. <u>comment</u>: analysis of controversy-law):
1. Include the relevant facts. 2. Include the procedural history. 3. Include the court's holding and reasoning at each level, as well as the reasoning of dissenting or concurring opinions (based on Fajans & Falk, 2000)

FOCAL POINT

Analytical Discussion: (This section gives original analysis of the subject matter; may consist of both a critique of existing approaches and a proposed solution. Re-introduces thesis or focus; provides brief background summary; provides analysis with support in each paragraph, for each issue, in each sub-section.)

Large-scale organization

___ A. Student has discussed the major issues.

___ B. Student has separated issues and sub-issues (with Headings/Sub-headings).

___ C. Student has ordered issues logically (e.g. A-1, A-2/ B-1, B-2, B-3/ C-1, C-2).

Small-scale organization

___ 1. Student has introduced and concluded on each issue.

___ 2. Student has presented argument and rebutted opposing arguments.

___ 3. Student has very clear organizational paradigms (patterns) where appropriate (e.g., problem-solution – most common, cause and effect, comparative pattern.)

Conclusion

___ 1. Student has restated thesis without being obviously redundant.

___ 2. Student has summarized the major points for legal reader to remember, to reflect.

___ 3. Student has made some recommendations if appropriate.

*Note: A good outline asserts student's ideas, usually in full (if unpolished) sentences

Student's code name: _____   Appendix F   Date: _____

STUDENT'S QUALITY ASSESSMENT TOOL (SQAT) STAGE 3.a

FOR STUDENTS TO END REVISING PROCESS (based on Ramsfield, 2005)

Title: _____

1. Audience   **Check**
Does paper include all information needed by your specific audience?   _____
Does paper account for your readers' background knowledge?   _____

2. Purpose
Is your overall purpose evident throughout the paper?   _____
Does it relate directly to a precise and explicit thesis statement or claim? _____
Is your paper original, analytical, and creative–not just descriptive?   _____
Is the purpose explained early enough to satisfy the reader?   _____
Is your point of view made clear in the Introduction?   _____
Do you say if it is primarily persuasive or informative or something else? _____

3. Content
Is thesis statement supported by enough research to be useful to reader? _____
Have all legal materials been accurately synthesized?   _____
Do all parts of the paper support the thesis?   _____
Has extraneous or unhelpful material been deleted?   _____
Are all relevant views on topic presented accurately?   _____
Do footnotes function properly? e.g., Do they do one of the following: _____
- cite authority for all unoriginal propositions;
- expand on one authority by offering other, related sources where appropriate;
- add detail, explanation, or definitions needed by the uninitiated reader;
- add detail for the reader using the paper as a scholarly tool; or
- give the text of a statute, regulation, quote, or specific source being discussed?

4. Organization
A. Does the structure flow from the substance?   _____
    i. Are the parts of the whole congruent with some logical rationale?
       e.g.,   _____
       • parts used in previous cases,

- parts used in a statute,
- parts used in other legal documents,
- parts of an overall process, or
- different causes of one effect?

ii.   Is the paper's organization consistent and unified throughout the document?   _____

iii.   Is each section internally logical?   _____
- Do paragraphs within each section connect to each other?
- Is each paragraph logically structured, whether deductively, inductively, or some other pattern?
- Are sentences organized logically, e.g., less important ideas are subordinated, main ideas are in independent clauses, and PARALLEL STRUCTURE are used to present like ideas?

B. Is the structure obvious to any reader?   _____
- Will any reader, at any point, not understand the writer?
- Does the Introduction present a roadmap or blueprint for the paper?
- Is each section's relationship to the thesis statement or claim clearly reflected by its order in the organization?
- Is the paper written in layers, using headings, footnotes, or paragraph blocks so that the reader can easily identify each part's role in the whole?

5. Clarity
Will the reader, at any point, not misunderstand the content?   _____
Is the phrasing clear?   _____
- Is word choice precise?
- Is plain English used, but jargon and legalese omitted?
- Do the subject-verb clauses carry your message, remind the reader of the thesis?

Is the text readable?   _____
- Is there only one main point per sentence?
- Are topic sentences generally the first sentences of the paragraphs?
- Are subjects and verbs close together?
- Is passive voice avoided unless needed?
- Are nominalizations minimized or avoided?

Does phrasing emphasize key points?   _____
- Are key points made in positions of emphasis?
- Is repetition used effectively where appropriate?
- Does parallel structure reveal parallel ideas?
- Do short sentences make emphatic points or catch the reader's attention?

Do all wording changes flow together to create an eloquent whole?   _____
- Do all emphatic techniques reinforce the content, rather than distract from it?
- Are any phrases or techniques overused, drawing attention to the phrase itself?
- Is emphasis focused on key points, not overused as a technique?

6. Mechanics
Is English grammar correct?   _____
Is punctuation correct?   _____
Are citations correct?   _____
Have you proofread for wrong or overused words?   _____

TEACHER'S QUALITY ASSESSMENT TOOL (TQAT) STAGE 3.a

TEACHER'S EXTERNAL CONTROL MEASURE OF REVISING PROCESS
(based on Ramsfield, 2005)

Title: _____

1. Audience **Check**
Does paper include all information needed by your specific audience?   _____
Does paper account for your readers' background knowledge?   _____

2. Purpose
Is the overall purpose evident throughout the paper?   _____
Does it relate directly to a precise and explicit thesis statement or claim? _____
Is paper original, analytical, and creative—not just descriptive?   _____
Is the purpose explained early enough to satisfy the reader?   _____
Is the point of view made clear in the Introduction?   _____
Do you say if it is primarily persuasive or informative or something else? _____

3. <u>Content</u>
Is thesis statement supported by enough research to be useful to reader? _____
Have all legal materials been accurately synthesized? _____
Do all parts of the paper support the thesis? _____
Has extraneous or unhelpful material been deleted? _____
Are all relevant views on topic presented accurately? _____
Do <u>footnotes</u> function properly? e.g., Do they do one of the following: _____
- cite authority for all unoriginal propositions;
- expand on one authority by offering other, related sources where appropriate;
- add detail, explanation, or definitions needed by the uninitiated reader;
- add detail for the reader using the paper as a scholarly tool; or
- give the text of a statute, regulation, quote, or specific source being discussed?

4. <u>Organization</u>
A. Does the structure flow from the substance? _____
  i. Are the parts of the whole congruent with some logical rationale? e.g., _____
     - parts used in previous cases,
     - parts used in a statute,
     - parts used in other legal documents,
     - parts of an overall process, or
     - different causes of one effect?
  ii. Is the paper's organization consistent and unified throughout the document? _____
  iii. Is each section internally logical? _____
     - Do paragraphs within each section connect to each other?
     - Is each paragraph logically structured, whether deductively, inductively, or some other pattern?
     - Are sentences organized logically, e.g., less important ideas are subordinated, main ideas are in independent clauses, and PARALLEL STRUCTURE are used to present like ideas?
B. Is the structure obvious to any reader? _____
  - Will any reader, at any point, not understand the writer?
  - Does the Introduction present a roadmap or blueprint for the paper?

- Is each section's relationship to the thesis statement or claim clearly reflected by its order in the organization?
- Is the paper written in layers, using headings, footnotes, or paragraph blocks so that the reader can easily identify each part's role in the whole?

5. Clarity
Will the reader, at any point, not misunderstand the content?   _____
Is the phrasing clear?   _____
- Is word choice precise?
- Is plain English used, but jargon and legalese omitted?
- Do the subject-verb clauses carry your message, remind the reader of the thesis?

Is the text readable?   _____
- Is there only one main point per sentence?
- Are topic sentences generally the first sentences of the paragraphs?
- Are subjects and verbs close together?
- Is passive voice avoided unless needed?
- Are nominalizations minimized or avoided?

Does phrasing emphasize key points?   _____
- Are key points made in positions of emphasis?
- Is repetition used effectively where appropriate?
- Does parallel structure reveal parallel ideas?
- Do short sentences make emphatic points or catch the reader's attention?

Do all wording changes flow together to create an eloquent whole?   _____
- Do all emphatic techniques reinforce the content, rather than distract from it?
- Are any phrases or techniques overused, drawing attention to the phrase itself?
- Is emphasis focused on key points, not overused as a technique?

6. Mechanics
Is English grammar correct?   _____
Is punctuation correct?   _____
Are citations correct?   _____
Have you proofread for wrong or overused words?   _____

Student's code name: _____ Appendix F   Date: _____

STUDENT'S QUALITY ASSESSMENT TOOL (SQAT) STAGE 3.b

STUDENT'S SELF-REPORT ON PROFICIENCY AND INSTRUCTION

Title: _____

1. **Yes, very much** improved
2. **Yes, somewhat** improved
3. **No,** not improved
4. Don't know

Check how you may have improved as a scholarly legal writer, spring/fall, 2008 *(all that apply)*.

Area of Writing	Improvement
Increase in fluency	_____
Increase in grammatical accuracy	_____
Clearer expression of original thinking	_____
Clearer expression of critical voice	_____
More detail	_____
More depth of legal content	_____
More efficient legal writing process	_____
More effective legal writing product	_____
More effective use of writing strategies	_____
Increase in confidence	_____
Increase in motivation	_____
Increase in knowledge of scholarly writing conventions	_____
Better ability to revise in response to feedback	_____
Increase in ability to self-edit	_____
Stronger professional identity	_____

Other _____

_____

_____

Student Comment:

_____

_____

TEACHER'S QUALITY ASSESSMENT TOOL (TQAT) STAGE 3.b

TEACHER OBSERVATION ON PROFICIENCY AND INSTRUCTION

Title: _____

1. **Yes, very much** improved
2. **Yes, somewhat** improved
3. **No,** not improved
4. Don't know

Check how you may have improved as a scholarly legal writer spring/fall, 2008 *(all that apply).*

Area of Writing	Improvement
Increase in fluency	_____
Increase in grammatical accuracy	_____
Clearer expression of original thinking	_____
Clearer expression of critical voice	_____
More detail	_____
More depth of legal content	_____
More efficient legal writing process	_____
More effective legal writing product	_____
More effective use of writing strategies	_____
Increase in confidence	_____
Increase in motivation	_____
Increase in knowledge of scholarly writing conventions	_____
Better ability to revise in response to feedback	_____
Increase in ability to self-edit	_____
Stronger professional identity	_____
Other _____	

Student's code name: _____   Appendix F   Date: _____

STUDENT'S QUALITY ASSESSMENT TOOL (SQAT) STAGE 4

CHECKLIST FOR WHAT MAKES A PAPER PUBLISHABLE

Title: _____

Assessment criteria for scholarly second language (L2) legal writing

My paper is	Yes	No	Somewhat
Original			
Comprehensive			
Correct in language use			
Correct in wording			
Clear			
Readable			
Logical in large-scale organization – major issues, sub-issues			
Logical in small-scale organization – individual issues			
Concise – according to law journal specifications			
Socially/culturally appropriate – with extensive use of footnotes			

Additional comment:

_____

_____

_____

_____

<u>TEACHER'S QUALITY ASSESSMENT TOOL (TQAT) STAGE 4</u>

CHECKLIST FOR WHAT MAKES A PAPER PUBLISHABLE

Title: _____

Assessment criteria for scholarly second language (L2) legal writing

Student's paper is	Yes	No	Somewhat
Original			
Comprehensive			
Correct in language use			
Correct in wording			
Clear			
Readable			
Logical in large-scale organization – major issues, sub-issues			
Logical in small-scale organization – individual issues			
Concise – according to law journal specifications			
Socially/culturally appropriate – with extensive use of footnotes			

Additional comment:

_____
_____
_____
_____

Appendix G: The Process of Scholarly Writing ©

THE PROCESS OF SCHOLARLY WRITING					
WRITER-CENTERED → READER-CENTERED					
STAGE	PREWRITING: READING, NOTETAKING & THINKING			WRITING AS LEARNING		WRITING AS COMMUNICATION
PURPOSE	1 FINDING A TOPIC	2 NARROWING THE TOPIC	3 CREATING A THESIS	4 GETTING STARTED	5 WRITING DRAFTS	6 REVISING AND POLISHING

This figure was reprinted with permission from the source publication, *Scholarly Writing for Law Students* (Fajans & Falk, 2005).

Linear Model: Useful for Novices

Appendix H: Strategies Checklist: Self-Editing for Clarity ©

SELF-EDITING STRATEGIES CHECKLIST

The following checklist will help academic writers communicate clearly in writing before submitting a paper for evaluation or a journal article to an editor for review (*check one*).

> 1. **Yes,** true of me
> 2. **No,** not true of me
> 3. Don't know

____ I checked to see whether I used short and medium-length sentences.

____ I checked whether my sentences contained concrete subjects and active verbs.

____ I tried to avoid nominalizations (the practice of changing base verbs to nouns)

____ I made one point per sentence, preferring simple and complex sentence structures to compound sentence structures.

____ I made sentences affirmative, not negative.

____ I preferred active voice to passive voice with some exceptions.

____ I used parallel structures in sentences containing multiple elements.

____ I used clear and logical lists with grammatically parallel elements.

____ I used familiar words instead of flowery language or ornate words.

____ I used consistent wording/phrasing without changing words for variety

____ I preferred nouns to pronouns as in the example above.

____ I kept subjects + verbs/verbs + objects undivided, without interrupting phrases.

____ I used accurate and adequate punctuation as "road signs" in my academic writing.

____ I used precise transitions to convey exact connections.

____ I used consistent parallel word signals such as *first* and *second*.

____ I provided structural clues and repeated key structure words to improve readability (e.g., *that*).

____ I used quotations only when necessary.

____ I avoided long, multi-clause sentences that obscure meaning.

Appendix I: Strategies for Academic English Writers: 3 stages

STRATEGIES FOR ACADEMIC ENGLISH WRITERS
STAGE 1 Pre-Drafting
Thinking, Planning, Organizing

Research topic/Working title: _____

Pre-Writing Strategies

On the following pages, you will find statements describing <u>conscious, goal directed actions successful research writers may take more than once while preparing to write an academic (scholarly) paper</u>. These actions, intentionally used to prepare for writing effectively and efficiently in second language (L2) academic English, are called *pre-writing strategies*. Please read each statement carefully, then write the response (1, 2, 3) that BEST DESCRIBES YOU now, while preparing to write the first draft of your research paper. Reflect on your choices.

1. **Yes,** true of me
2. **No,** not true of me
3. Don't know

1. I use these research-based strategies to find a topic, thesis, or claim for my research paper. These are all deeper-level actions that help develop thinking and generate new ideas for a research paper (*all that apply*).

Conceptual
____ I read for a purpose.
____ I summarize from the reading.
____ I annotate the reading with critical comment.
____ I draw conclusions from the reading relevant to my thesis/claim.
____ I "talk back to the text" by problem posing while reading.

Linguistic
____ I note key terms for reuse in my writing.
____ I note key English phrases for reading comprehension.
____ I paraphrase in English for reading comprehension.
____ I paraphrase in English (with citation) for reuse in my writing.

> 1. **Yes,** true of me
> 2. **No,** not true of me
> 3. Don't know

2. I use these research-based strategies for combining reading, note-taking, and thinking to discover what is important or true for me about my research topic, thesis, or claim for my paper (*all that apply*).

____ I use texts or quotes from experts to stimulate thoughts and ideas.
____ I brainstorm and exchange ideas with others about my research project.
____ I read other writers for modeling of style and organization.
____ I make a preliminary outline or table of contents.
____ I have a quiet place where I can concentrate on my legal research and scholarly writing.

Note: Consider these in addition to general problems related to scholarly (academic) or disciplinary writing such as audience, purpose, and length of paper.

3. I use these academic language skills to prepare to write the first draft my research paper (*all that apply*).

____ I analyze information by reflecting and breaking down source text into its parts.
____ I summarize information simply by reducing source text.
____ I summarize information complexly by selecting and reorganizing source text.
____ I paraphrase information by putting source text into my own words.
____ I synthesize information by combining and connecting source text.

DEVELOPING AS A WRITER

Consider how preparing to write a graduate-level research paper in second language (L2) academic English is similar or different from preparing to write in your first (L1) academic language. In other words, what do you want to remember to do the next time you write a research paper or article in English?

_____
_____
_____
_____

STRATEGIES FOR ACADEMIC ENGLISH WRITERS
STAGE 2 Drafting

Working title: _____

Task Specific Drafting Strategies

On the following pages, you will find statements describing <u>conscious, goal directed actions successful research writers may take more than once while drafting write an academic (scholarly) paper</u>. These actions, intentionally used for drafting effectively and efficiently using L2 academic English, are called *drafting strategies*. Please read each statement carefully, then write the response (1, 2, 3) that BEST DESCRIBES YOU while drafting your major analytical research paper. Reflect on your choices.

> 1. **Yes**, true of me
> 2. **No**, not true of me
> 3. Don't know

DRAFTING STRATEGIES

1. I use these research-based strategies for getting words and concepts down effectively on paper while drafting my academic paper (*all that apply*).

____ I summarized information from (primary or secondary) sources to begin writing.

____ I paraphrased or quoted sources to begin writing (knowledge telling strategy).

____ I re-read disciplinary texts such as journal articles that served as rhetorical models.

____ I reordered information from source texts to use in my draft.

____ I conferenced with a professor or peers to refine and clarify my ideas.

____ I postponed editing my English writing until I finalized the content (analysis).

____ I wrote long, run-on sentences in English to get important ideas down before revising.

____ I used both English and my native language to avoid interrupting my thinking.

____ I wrote for a planned amount of time (for example, 2–4 hours).

Other _____

_____

> 1. **Yes,** true of me
> 2. **No,** not true of me
> 3. Don't know

WRITING TO LEARN

2. I use these academic language skills for effectively drafting my paper (*all that apply*).

___ I paraphrased information by putting source material (text) into my own words.

___ I summarized information simply by reducing source text.

___ I summarized information complexly by selecting and reorganizing source text.

___ I synthesized information by combining and connecting source text.

___ I analyzed information by reflecting and breaking down source text into its parts.

___ *other* _____

IDENTIFYING MY PURPOSE AND LEVELS OF COMPOSING

3. I use these broad levels of writing purpose for effectively drafting my paper (*all that apply*).

___ I wrote to state knowledge by listing, repeating, or paraphrasing source text.

___ I wrote to understand, remember, summarize simply, or extend notes to myself.

___ I wrote to learn, problem-solve, summarize complexly, or synthesize source text information.

___ I wrote to critique, persuade, or interpret evidence selectively and appropriately.

___ *other*_____

STRATEGIES FOR ACADEMIC ENGLISH WRITERS
STAGE 3 Revising

Final title: _____

Task Specific Revising Strategies

On the following pages, you will find statements describing <u>conscious, goal directed actions successful research writers may take more than once while revising write an academic (scholarly) paper</u>. These actions, intentionally used for revising effectively and efficiently using L2 academic English, are called *revising strategies*. Please read each statement carefully, then write the response (1, 2, 3) that BEST DESCRIBES YOU while revising your final draft. There are no right or wrong answers.

> 1. **Yes**, true of me
> 2. **No**, not true of me
> 3. Don't know

REVISING STRATEGIES

1. I use these research-based strategies to decide what should be changed, deleted, added, or retained while revising my final draft before submitting for review and assessment (*all that apply*).

___ I read critically and reflected on my own written drafts.

___ I asked myself if I repeated key words and phrases for cohesion and emphasis.

___ I asked myself if my purpose is clear.

___ I asked myself if my message is clear.

___ I got feedback from my writing instructor to assess how effectively I communicated my message.

___ I got expert writing feedback from my instructor to build or re-construct my analysis.

___ I asked myself if I used headings, subheadings, and logical connectors effectively.

___ I added critical comment after quotations that end paragraphs.

___ *other* _____

REFLECTING ON KNOWLEDGE TRANSFORMING

Revising (stage 3) is an effective strategy for transitioning my academic writing from *knowledge telling* (stating knowledge) to *knowledge transforming* (deepening my level of understanding to include analysis, synthesis, evaluation of research).

___ 1. **Yes,** true of me
___ 2. **No,** not true of me
___ 3. Don't know

PLAIN LANGUAGE GRAMMAR STRATEGIES

Editing is part of the revising process that involves use of plain language techniques to enhance clarity and readability. These are deeper-level writing strategies for clear, accurate expression of ideas in academic English.

1. **Yes,** true of me
2. **No,** not true of me
3. Don't know

2. I use these research-based grammar strategies to communicate effectively in writing before submitting my final draft for review and assessment (*all that apply*).

___ I made one point per sentence, preferring simple and complex sentence structures to compound sentence structures.
___ I avoided long, multi-clause sentences that obscure meaning.
___ I tried to avoid nominalizations (the practice of changing verbs to nouns).
___ I kept subjects + verbs/verbs + objects undivided, without interrupting phrases.
___ I used familiar words instead of flowery language or ornate words.
___ I used consistent wording/phrasing without changing words for variety
___ I used accurate and adequate punctuation as "road signs" in my legal writing.
___ I used consistent parallel word signals such as *first* and *second*.
___ *other*

> 1. **Yes,** true of me
> 2. **No,** not true of me
> 3. Don't know

EDITING STRATEGIES

In addition to self-editing for clarity, editing involves polishing and checking for conventions

3. I use these research-based strategies to edit with a "purpose in mind" before submitting my final draft for review and assessment (*all that apply*).

___ I asked myself whether my paper was an example of good academic writing.
___ I proofread my academic writing for sentence structure (syntax).
___ I proofread my academic writing for proper word choice (diction).
___ I proofread my academic writing for punctuation.
___ I proofread my academic writing for spelling (*e.g.,* Microsoft Word "Tools").
___ I proofread my writing for citation to authority.
___ *other* _____

WRITING TO COMMUNICATE

4. I use these research-based academic language skills for effectively revising and editing my final draft (*all that apply*).

___ I paraphrased information by putting source material into my own words.
___ I summarized information simply by reducing source or draft text.
___ I summarized information complexly by selecting and reorganizing my draft text.
___ I synthesized information by combining and connecting my draft text.
___ I analyzed information by reflecting and breaking down source/draft text into its parts.
___ *other* _____

Please address any questions or concerns you may have with the writing teacher.

Appendix J: Checklists of Goals for Academic English Writers: 3 Stages

PRE-DRAFTING CHECKLIST (STAGE 1)
GOALS FOR ACADEMIC ENGLISH WRITERS

Check only what you have done to prepare for writing the first draft of your research paper or article. Then copy and paste this self-assessment checklist to your conceptual outline, making any necessary revisions. Finally, submit to teacher for feedback and review. *Note: A conceptual outline is different from a skeletal outline or Table of Contents. It uses full sentences, with a Problem Statement, Purpose Statement, and Thesis Statement (that states your topic and what you think about that topic) OR, it is uses a Research Question (that your paper proposes to answer if the topic is new to you). It also includes a Working Bibliography.*

_____ 1. I have started with what I already know and think.

_____ 2. I have defined a suitable topic that is interesting and authentic to my experience.

_____ 3. I have explained why this topic is important (at this time, to this audience).

_____ 4. I have identified my purpose for research and writing.

_____ 5. I have narrowed my research topic (e.g., by brainstorming with my professor).

_____ 6. I have formulated a research question to reflect what I think about my research topic/**OR**

_____ 7. I have formulated a working thesis by stating my point of view or opinion on the topic.

_____ 8. I have identified the type of research paper I want to write (e.g., an *analytical* paper that explores or fleshes out an unresolved topic, or a *persuasive* paper that takes a stand on issue and uses evidence to back-up my stance).

_____ 9. I have found (primary and secondary) sources to support my working thesis.

_____ 10. I have read through all my sources.

_____ 11. I have evaluated all my sources.

_____ 12. I have taken notes in English or another language citing my sources.

_____ 13. I have made a working bibliography of my (primary and secondary) sources.

_____ 14. I have organized my legal research into a conceptual outline (defined above).

_____ 15. I have decided on my approach (e.g., descriptive, analytical, comparative, critical).

_____ 16. I feel prepared to write my first draft (that is, to synthesize and integrate my sources into an essay format for a "paper").

DRAFTING CHECKLIST (STAGE 2)
GOALS FOR ACADEMIC ENGLISH WRITERS

Check only what you have done to prepare your first draft in English; not all sections may apply. Then copy and paste this self-assessment to your draft, make any necessary revisions, and submit to teacher for feedback and review.

Introduction (This section prepares your reader for purpose of your paper. Can be written in full only after the research draft is complete.)

___ 1. I have introduced and noted why topic is important.

___ 2. I have briefly summarized necessary background information.

___ 3. I have stated my thesis (i.e., an original and supportable proposition about the subject; Problem + Solution; one new point, one new insight, or one new way of looking at issue)

___ 4. I have conveyed my organization of the paper.

Background (This section prepares your reader for analysis with historical issues and context for why the topic is important. You can write this part first but revise after Discussion section is complete.)

___ 1. I have described the genesis (origin) of the subject.

___ 2. I have described the changes that have occurred during its development.

___ 3. I have explained the reasons for the changes.

___ 4. I have described where things are now. (You may also want to indicate the reasons for further change- focus/paper.)

FOCAL POINT

Analytical Discussion: (This section gives your original analysis of the subject matter; may consist of both a critique of existing approaches and a proposed solution. Re-introduces thesis or focus; provides brief background summary; provides analysis with support in each paragraph, for each issue, in each sub-section.)

Large-scale organization
___ A. I have discussed the major issues.
___ B. I have separated issues and sub-issues (with Headings and Sub-headings).
___ C. I have ordered issues logically (e.g. A-1, A-2/ B-1, B-2, B-3/ C-1, C-2).

Small-scale organization
___ 1. I have introduced and concluded on each issue.
___ 2. I have presented my argument and rebutted opposing arguments.
___ 3. I have very clear organizational paradigms (patterns) where appropriate (e.g., problem-solution; comparative pattern.)

Conclusion
___ 1. I have restated my thesis without being obviously redundant.
___ 2. I have summarized the major points I want my reader to remember or reflect upon.
___ 3. I have made some recommendations if appropriate.

REVISING & EDITING CHECKLIST (STAGE 3)
GOALS FOR ACADEMIC ENGLISH WRITERS

Title: _____

1. Audience   **Check**
Does paper include all information needed by your specific audience?   _____
Does paper account for your readers' background knowledge?   _____

2. Purpose
Is your overall purpose evident throughout the paper?   _____
Does it relate directly to a precise and explicit thesis statement or claim? _____
Is paper original, analytical, and creative – not just descriptive?   _____
Is the purpose explained early enough to satisfy the reader?   _____
Is your point of view made clear in the Introduction?   _____
Do you say if it is primarily persuasive or informative or something else? _____

3. Content
Is thesis statement supported by enough research to be useful to reader? _____
Have all legal materials been accurately synthesized?   _____
Do all parts of the paper support the thesis?   _____
Has extraneous or unhelpful material been deleted?   _____
Are all relevant views on topic presented accurately?   _____
Do footnotes function properly? e.g., Do they do one of the following: _____
- cite authority for all unoriginal propositions;
- expand on one authority by offering other, related sources where appropriate;
- add detail, explanation, or definitions needed by the uninitiated reader;
- add detail for the reader using the paper as a scholarly tool; or
- give the text of specific source being discussed?

4. Organization
A. Does the structure flow from the substance?   _____
    i. Are the parts of the whole congruent with some logical rationale? _____
    ii. Is the paper's organization consistent and unified throughout? _____
    iii. Is each section internally logical?   _____
       • Do paragraphs within each section connect to each other?

- Is each paragraph logically structured, whether deductively, inductively, or some other pattern?

Are sentences organized logically, e.g., less important ideas are sub-ordinated, main ideas are in independent clauses, and PARALLEL STRUCTURE are used to present like ideas? _____

B. Is the structure obvious to any reader? _____
- Will any reader, at any point, not understand the writer?
- Does the Introduction present a roadmap or blueprint for the paper?
- Is each section's relationship to the thesis statement or claim clearly reflected by its order in the organization?
- Is the paper written in layers, using headings, footnotes, or paragraph blocks so that the reader can easily identify each part's role in the whole?

EDITING FOR CLARITY & CORRECTNESS

5. Clarity

Will the reader, at any point, not misunderstand the content? _____

Is the phrasing clear? _____
- Is word choice precise?
- Is plain English used, but jargon and legalese omitted?
- Do the subject-verb clauses carry your message, remind the reader of the thesis?

Is the text readable? _____
- Is there only one main point per sentence?
- Are topic sentences generally the first sentences of the paragraphs?
- Are subjects and verbs close together?
- Is passive voice avoided unless needed?
- Are nominalizations minimized or avoided?

Does phrasing emphasize key points? _____
- Are key points made in positions of emphasis?
- Is repetition used effectively where appropriate?
- Does parallel structure reveal parallel ideas?
- Do short sentences make emphatic points or catch the reader's attention?

Do all wording changes flow together to create an eloquent whole?   _____
- Do all emphatic techniques reinforce the content, rather than distract from it?
- Are any phrases or techniques overused, drawing attention to the phrase itself?
- Is emphasis focused on key points, not overused as a technique?

6. Mechanics
Is English grammar correct?   _____
Is punctuation correct?   _____
Are citations correct?   _____
Have you proofread for wrong or overused words?   _____

Appendix K: Syllabus with Formative Assessment

Academic English Writing Syllabus

Course Description and Overview

Academic English writing is vital for the academic and professional success of international students and visiting scholars. Many have difficulty expressing thoughts in writing even with good analytical skills. Many may not know how to use printed/published sources appropriately and thus be threatened with charges of plagiarism: a multi-faceted issue linked to language use and cross-cultural literacy. The study of literacy and language demonstrates that knowledge construction in writing and language learning are both developmental processes that are socioculturally grounded rather than one set of universal cognitive skills that transfer.

This professional development course is designed for international graduate students who have learned English in a second language (ESL) or foreign language (EFL) context or who use English as their first academic language. Face-to-face classroom methods are combined with computer mediated activities to promote learner outcomes associated with academically valued writing that requires composing skills which transform information or transform the language itself.

Course Objectives

Students will (a) construct new knowledge through research and writing from multilingual sources, (b) develop cross-cultural understandings about scholarship, and (c) develop skills for professional proficiency in writing while preparing a research paper for graduate school or an article for publication.

Student Learning Outcomes

This course facilitates the graduate student shift from writer-centered learning (with a focus on content) to reader-centered communication (with a focus on form and meaning). This shift implies a move from knowledge telling to knowledge transforming (Bereiter & Scardamalia, 1987): that is, from simply stating knowledge from source text to communicating a deeper level of understanding that includes analysis, synthesis, and evaluation of research.

Based on Bloom's Taxonomy of higher order thinking, students will:
- schedule deadlines for research and for writing;
- define research problem, purpose, and thesis/research question;
- use a working outline and annotated bibliography if teacher acts as academic advisor;
- assemble a working draft from primary and secondary sources using citation;
- revise each draft after receiving teacher feedback;
- evaluate each draft and stage of writing (pre-writing, drafting, revising) with course tools;
- demonstrate critical thinking and complex reasoning;
- support analytical thinking clearly, concisely, and accurately (objective, scientific style);
- use plain language techniques to communicate complex ideas;
- analyze and use grammar as an element of style and meaning;
- discuss syntax (structure) and language use knowledgeably;
- employ declarative (conscious) knowledge of discourse strategies;
- operate with a critical, independent voice as a scholarly writer in disciplinary context; and
- develop the confidence necessary to assume a professional identity in English.

Pedagogical Approach

A dialogic model of teaching and learning (Vygotsky, 1978) takes place in which the learner interacts with the teacher and peers at recursive stages of writing to produce quality text that meets cultural and disciplinary standards. Students interact with their own text and reflect on their research and writing processes with evidence-based course tools that are valid and reliable:
- *Strategies for Academic English Writers*©: pre-writing, drafting, revising (3 stages)
- *Checklists of Goals for Academic English Writers*©: pre-writing, drafting, revising

Course Structure

The course operates at two levels for each stage of writing (pre-writing, drafting, and revising). The first level deals with writers' *processes* (strategies and skills), and the second level deals with *goals for production* that advance proficiency (competence): that is, planning (metacognitive) competence, rhetorical (genre) competence, and communication (high communicative precision) competence.

Student-centered agendas feature oral presentations with PowerPoint technology followed by question and answer (Q&A) dialogic sessions.

Class agendas follow a process approach to writing, with student self-assessment, teacher evaluation and feedback at each stage, based on the following (7 week, intensive) themes:

1. Understanding and Articulating EFL/ESL Academic English Writer Needs
2. Rhetorical Preferences and Style: Academic Writing Across Cultures
3. Focusing on Problem, Purpose, Thesis Statement/ Research Question(s)
4. Presenting a Professional Outline, *stage I* (oral, written)
5. Drafting/Patch Writing with Citations: Writer as Learner
6. Presenting Large-Scale Organization, *stage 2* (oral, written)
7. Making the switch from Writer- to Reader- Centered Drafting, *stage 3* (written)

Class Schedule

Depending on motivation and need, students can progress at their own pace. Assignments are due when agreed upon by teacher and student.

Course Requirements

Two general rules are to be observed throughout. First, the three sets of assignments (outline, draft, and revised draft) should be carried out with great specificity as indicated by the teacher. Second, students should not decide for themselves that there are some writing situations to which planning, goals for revising, and strategies for self-reflection do not apply. This may interfere with the learning process and transfer of learning. The writing tasks and course tools meet the conditions necessary for transfer. The overall aim is to improve written language use and to extend the ideas being practiced to other professional writing situations with advanced knowledge of purpose, audience, register, and academic English discourse.

Evaluation

All students must complete 1 questionnaire and 1 self-assessment checklist for each stage of writing: pre-writing, drafting, and revising (30% each). The strategies questionnaires assist you with your research writing *processes*, and the goals checklists help you self-evaluate your research *product* at each stage to improve quality.

Grading and Formative Assessment

90% Stage 1, Stage 2, and Stage 3 writing task assignments and revisions
10% Extra credit e.g., guided revisions, presentations of research and discourse-based grammar

Academic Integrity

Note to professors
When students submit a paper prepared in this course to a professor for academic credit, that paper is the student's own best work. Students are taught how to edit and revise their own writing: a requirement for professional proficiency and disciplinary literacy. In this course, students learn to control their own language "conceptually, culturally, coherently, and cohesively" (Gambhir, CDLC 2005). At no time does the writing teacher revise or edit students' work. When reviewing student papers, she does so according to ethical standards by reading and assessing parts of a paper at different times for form and content, then probing for meaning in planned, individual consultations so students know how to revise.

Note to international graduate student writers
When you submit a research paper to your writing teacher, each draft must contain your assessment of your own work using the quality checklists provided for each stage of writing (pre-writing, drafting, and revising). Knowledge of criteria for assessment allows for reflection, revision, and transfer of learning to other research papers and professional writing situations. A guideline for setting deadlines will also be provided.

Index

Authors are not listed in this subject index. Readers requiring a complete list of cited authors and works should consult the References section.